LION MAN

LION MAN

The Autobiography

IAN McGEECHAN

SIMON &
SCHUSTER

London · New York · Sydney · Toronto

A CBS COMPANY

First published in Great Britain by Simon & Schuster UK Ltd, 2009
A CBS COMPANY

1 3 5 7 9 10 8 6 4 2

Simon & Schuster UK Ltd
1st Floor
222 Gray's Inn Road
London
WC1X 8HB

www.simonandschuster.co.uk

Simon & Schuster Australia
Sydney

All photos © Colorsport
Statistics supplied by John Griffiths

A CIP catalogue for this book is available
from the British Library.

ISBN: 978-1-84737-602-2 (Hardback)
ISBN: 978-1-84737-603-9 (Trade Paperback)

Typeset by M Rules
Printed in the UK by CPI Mackays, Chatham ME5 8TD

To Judy, Rob and Heather.
Rugby has often been as big a part
of their lives as of mine

Contents

1

Phokeng

30 May 2009. Royal Bafokeng Sports Palace, Phokeng, near Rustenberg, 150 kilometres north-west of Johannesburg, South Africa. 3 p.m.

The Bafokeng people (Bafokeng translates as 'People of the Dew') have their own customs and their own king. In the ground beneath their feet lie the world's most extensive deposits of platinum and near the Sports Palace you can see winding gear employed in the platinum mines. They are shrouded in white, almost as if they are ghostly coal mines.

The Sports Palace surprises you at first. It looms up out of nothing, on the high veldt, built with the profits from platinum, and will host matches in the 2010 football World Cup.

Naas Olivier, the fly-half for the Royal XV, kicks off, long to the deep left-hand corner. The tour has begun. It is more than 120 years since a British Isles team first toured in the Southern Hemisphere, and eighty-five years since the team was first referred to as the 'Lions'.

Michael Blair, the scrum-half from Scotland, wearing the red jersey, white shorts and blue and green socks of the Lions, calls for the ball and, as it falls towards him, he prepares to initiate the first play of what one observer has fittingly called 'the Last Great Sporting Adventure'.

2

Langdale Pikes

Alfred Wainwright, fell walker, author and lover of the Lake District, wrote of Langdale Pikes, in the heart of the Lakes: 'Such beauty. Once seen, never forgotten.' He continued: 'They give a remarkable impression of remoteness.'

Wainwright did not mention anything about the Pikes giving a remarkable impression of anxiety, but that is what I was feeling. It was August 1988 and I was walking through Langdale Valley, below the Pikes, with Tara, the red setter. The family – my wife Judy and our children, Robert and Heather – was holidaying in a favourite campsite in the valley. Shortly before the holiday, and completely out of the blue, I had been offered, and had accepted, the post of head coach of the 1989 British and Irish Lions party, which would tour Australia in the Southern Hemisphere winter of 1989.

At the time, I had already been appointed head coach of Scotland, although I had not yet begun my tenure. My first game in charge, against Australia at Murrayfield that autumn, was still months away. I had enjoyed several seasons with Scotland as assistant coach to Derrick Grant, the wise Borderer and a man I admired as much as anyone I have met in the game.

Derrick Grant was a fine mentor in more ways than one. A great student of Scottish history, he was particularly well read on the subject of the reivers, the cattle and sheep raiders who operated in the Scottish Borders during the Middle Ages. He explained how the outnumbered Scots, lacking resources and weaponry for stand-up confrontation, were extremely clever in where they chose to fight, how they kept the high ground, and how they learned, with speed, precision and cunning, to harry and offset superior forces with their raiding. I found all this wonderfully analogous to rugby.

The Scotland appointment was a thrilling new stage of a long journey which began when I started to coach Headingley, the club based in Leeds, the city in which I was born in October 1946. I played for Headingley from 1964 to 1979 and I took up the coaching reins as soon as I retired from playing for them. They were my only club, and I won all my thirty-two Scotland caps as a Headingley player.

People ask me if coaching was in my blood. Probably. I suppose I was never the sort of player who simply switched off after a game and forgot the rugby. I loved to think about how individual players and teams could have performed better, loved to talk through technical matters with the doyens of Headingley, such as Bernard White, my first coach at Headingley, who had a vast store of knowledge and experience. Whatever coaching groups I have been part of, one of the great delights has been the conversations, the sharing of ideas, the boot room of rugby life.

The prospect of becoming national coach at Murrayfield was such an exciting one for me that I did not allow it to be overshadowed by the usual day-to-day anxieties of life in that era of rugby union. How, for instance, under the pervading amateur ethos of the game, could I ever do justice to such a massive challenge in Scotland, fulfil all my obligations as a teacher at Fir Tree Middle School, in Leeds, and continue to make ends meet for Judy and our children? I suppose I felt that the post represented a peak of my career. I was nearly forty-two.

Some time during that period in 1988 I took a telephone call from Clive Rowlands, a West Walian, a former captain of Wales, a future president of the Welsh Rugby Union, and a man who, because he had captained Wales in all the Tests he had played in, was known as 'Top Cat'.

It is said that Clive was responsible for changing a rugby law all on his own. He had been captain and scrum-half of Wales in a match against Scotland at Murrayfield in 1963 in which there were 111 line-outs – it seems amazing how they managed to fit them all in. Wales dominated the line-outs and just about every time they won the ball Rowlands kicked it back into touch. It must have made for a grim spectacle, and not long after that the International Rugby Board (IRB) brought in the Australian dispensation law, meaning that you could no longer kick directly into touch from outside the 25-yard line.

Rowlands had the broadest Welsh accent imaginable, to which he added an extra rasp. 'I want you to be head coach of the 1989 Lions,' he said down the telephone. 'If you are up for it, I don't want to look any further.' No interview, nothing. He said he liked what I had done with the Scotland backs. I accepted. Goodbye.

There on Langdale Pikes it suddenly hit me. 'Hell. What am I doing? Why me? What have I taken on?' I realised the calibre of the distinguished players who would be under me, and wondered how I would deal with them. It was a quiet moment in the Lakes, but one filled with uncertainty matched by excitement.

Naturally, I knew about the concept of the Lions: how wonderful, singular, epic, different, elevated, vivid and tough they were. I had toured with the brilliant 1974 Lions to South Africa, which many regard as the greatest in history, and also the 1977 tour of New Zealand, which many regard as the gloomiest. 'A Lions tour is a cross between a medieval crusade and a Sunday School outing,' wrote one observer. It was just that, even if the modern-day professional Lions experience is far less of a jaunt and infinitely more serious.

Until you have actually been selected as a Lion, you never believe you will make it. It is something magical, something up

there in the clouds. The 1974 Five Nations tournament had
ended with Scotland playing France on Saturday afternoon and
on the Sunday I flew home to Leeds. I picked up a newspaper on
the plane. The article I read was setting out predictions for the
Lions selection, due to be made any day. It printed photographs
of thirty players, the newspaper's choice. One of them was me. I
looked at the photograph, and the word 'Lion'. I was being talked
about in a party which would include Scotland's Willie John
McBride and Ian McLauchlan, and two supreme Welshmen,
Gareth Edwards and J. P. R. Williams. I was going to be part of a
group like that? A few days later, the letter came through the door.
It was true. I was.

I knew how unique the Lions were. Players from four nations
who had just spent three months knocking the living daylights out
of each other in the home internationals, who were divided by
national flags and anthems and fervent national passions (and who
would be reverting to the same as soon as the Lions tour was over)
would come together to blend, with the coaches, into an entity.
Sometimes, as I knew from 1974 and 1977, that blend would be
the equivalent of the forging of iron; sometimes, the blend did not
quite work.

The aim was to win a Test series played in one of the three great
rugby nations in the Southern Hemisphere – South Africa, New
Zealand or Australia – in which it was also essential to absorb the
culture, the differences, the problems and the harsh attitudes in
each country. In fact, unless you took the whole culture on board,
you could not win a Test series.

The Lions do not exist until the players meet for the tour; they
have never existed before as a squad – even though there is usually
a hard core which has made a previous Lions tour. But that would
have been at least three years, and a lifetime, before, and to a different country with different challenges. The team, as I once said,
had no character, no identity and no meaning until it assembled.

And when the tour is over, the party disintegrates. It's over.
Perhaps twenty years after the trip those particular Lions may call

a reunion but in the form in which it did battle that squad is gone. There is one chance only for that group, on one tour, for a few short months, and it can become a matter of some devastation if they do not take that chance.

I also knew how ferociously difficult it was. Our 1974 tour to South Africa was in many ways a shining exception. History shows that the overwhelming majority of Lions teams lost because of the strengths and passions of the host nations, the alien environments and a thousand and one other problems the coach has to attend to. I learned that everything – absolutely everything – has to go right. And more than that. On Lions tours, everything has to be the same – the same principles and key tasks must apply, the rhythm of it all must be the same. And yet, on every new tour, everything is always completely different.

And so, walking in the Lake District that August day I might have felt slightly worse had I known what was to happen next. In my first match as Scotland coach that autumn, against Bob Dwyer and an Australian team some of us would meet a year hence as Lions, we lost 32–13. More than lost. We were hammered.

I would have been utterly incredulous had I known that I would not only become the only man ever to coach more than one Lions party, but that I would coach four Lions tours, each of them epics of a different kind, and be part of the coaching group on another; incredulous if I had known then that Lions rugby would become part of my soul, and take up so much of my working life – even if the basis of my enjoyment and my whole coaching philosophy was nothing more complicated than a love of working on the training field in a tracksuit, with a group of outstanding players.

Judy, my wife, and I are inveterate walkers in the Lakes; we have all of Wainwright's books, and we have carefully marked them with the dates on which we followed his various walks. In some of the less hectic years we have done two a year. Twenty years on from August 1988, almost to the day, when I was a tiny figure in a landscape in the Langdale Valley, I heard that I had been appointed head coach for the 2009 British and Irish Lions tour of South Africa.

This promised to be the most difficult Lions tour yet. South Africa's leading players were speaking openly that their entire focus was on the Lions series; that it was all they had thought about since winning the World Cup in Paris in 2007 and, indeed, it had occupied the thoughts of many since the Lions had beaten them in a stunning Test series in 1997, my favourite of all my tours as head coach.

The degree of interest in the 2009 tour from the public in the four nations was stunning. There was a time when people saw the Lions as something from the amateur era that could not survive in the professional. It seems to me that they are now far bigger than ever. The *Sunday Times* ran a round-table chat with some famous rugby figures about possible Lions selections, and the online version of it received more than 700,000 hits.

Walking the dogs in 2009 and contemplating this latest challenge, I was aware that some things had not changed in twenty years. Tara had gone but had been replaced by Rosie and Toby, but the honour, the challenge, the excitement and the degree of difficulty for the Lions were still awe-inspiring.

3

Govan

South to Southampton, north to Scotland

One day in 1937, my father, Bob McGeechan, and his father set out from their home in Braid Street, Govan, not far from the docks and shipyards in Glasgow, in a motorcycle and sidecar. That machine always loomed large in so many old family stories. It was used extensively for family trips, most notably to aid in the escape from the harsh surroundings of the city up to Loch Lomond. Dad was one of nine, and so I always imagined that sidecar crammed with children, some of them maybe even hanging off the sides. My grandmother had died after giving birth to twins, the eighth and ninth offspring, and so my father and his two eldest sisters, Jean and Elizabeth, took over the mantle of caring for the family.

On this occasion they were travelling way south, on a trip of well over five hundred miles and decades before motorways, to Southampton. Dad had joined the Argyll and Sutherland Highlanders and was embarking at Southampton for Palestine. His father, my grandfather, took him and his kit all the way to the South Coast to see him off. He was only seventeen. The last time Dad saw his father he was waving at Southampton docks as the boat set sail. He died before Dad came home.

We were a services family. Both my grandfather and my father had attended Queen Victoria School in Dunblane, a famous army school. It was a tradition for the eldest son in any generation of McGeechans to join the military. Dad was the second son but Alan, the eldest, had an eye defect and so it was the second brother who followed the line.

In a sense, I suppose I broke with tradition by opting for a career in teaching and then as a professional rugby coach, though my nephew, Phil McGeechan, has maintained the family tradition. He is an officer in the Royal Marines and was recently decorated for service in Afghanistan, as a forward radio operator, right at the front line.

Dad was still in Palestine when war broke out and he was moved straight on to some of the main theatres of war – serving in Africa, the Middle East and Crete. He was also a bandsman, an accomplished clarinetist. After the war he used to play in a band at home in Leeds.

He served chiefly in the medical corps, as a stretcher-bearer at the fronts during the fighting. At first, he had a charmed existence. On one occasion, he was standing near the bows of a ship with some fellow soldiers and, for some reason, moved to the stern. The ship came under fire, a shell landed where he had been standing and the soldiers he had been talking to were killed. Later during the war, in the North African desert, he was in a convoy of lorries which came under attack from a fighter plane. They all dived out, took cover on both sides of the road, and a school friend with whom he had shared a great deal of his army experiences was hit by a bullet and killed, on the opposite side of the road.

But Dad's luck finally ran out. The Argylls took a heavy pounding on Crete and in 1943 they were attacked by a dive-bomber as they sailed off the coast of the island. A bomb landed near the bows and the blast went right through the ship. Dad was in a corridor and it enveloped him. He sustained severe burns. He was invalided home, and sent to a special burns unit far away from his family home in Glasgow. That unit was in Leeds, Yorkshire.

Figuratively speaking, Dad never left Leeds. While convalescing, he met Hilda Shearer, from Morley, just outside Leeds. She was an athlete and ballet dancer, a fervent sports fan and as staunch a Yorkshirewoman as Dad was a Scot. People wonder why they never returned to Scotland to live. Judy, my wife, always feels that it was my mother's wish which tended to hold sway in the marriage, though perhaps Govan, a rough place in those days, was not the best prospect for a young Yorkshire lady.

Dad recovered well from his burns, so well that eventually he was reposted. My parents were married in 1944, then Dad left for the Middle East and was there when the war ended. I was born in Leeds two years after they married. In the early 1950s, still serving, he was called up again – I can remember him leaving with his kit, bound for the Argylls' staging camp in Stirling and then for Korea. I remember, too, how dismayed we all were, especially Mum, that he was going off to war again.

But in the end he did not have to go, I believe because he had done so many years' active service, and he was deemed therefore to have done his stint. It was another narrow escape, because many of his unit were killed in Korea.

Bob McGeechan won boxing titles in the army. He was only five foot six and obviously pugnacious in the ring, but outside it he was the kindest, mildest, most decent, least demonstrative and most supportive man imaginable. There were so many examples of this. By my late teens, I was playing rugby for Headingley, then one of the top clubs in the north of England. I was just a lad from the local secondary modern school. Headingley drew most of its players from the major northern public schools, such as Leeds Grammar, Sedburgh and Ampleforth College.

Dad would come along to watch every game I played in, and would make his own way there and back on public transport. He never stayed on after the game, never came to the clubhouse. He was too self-effacing. But before every match, in those pre-decimalisation days, he would always slip a £5 note into my pocket so that I could stand a round of drinks and would not be embarrassed. Later, I found out that this amounted to a quarter of his weekly salary as an engineer. My mother told me that he would walk absolutely miles to and from work to save the money to be able to give it to me. I discovered that after he had died.

The first time I was chosen to play for Yorkshire Colts was in 1965; it was away down in Coventry, against Warwickshire. I played at fly-half. Both Mum and Dad came and it was the first time Dad had seen me play properly. They travelled down on the bus – a major expedition in those days – and they went back on the bus, too. When I arrived home, Dad told me how well I had done. 'I didn't realise you were as good as that,' he said.

Yet even in times of hardship, when Dad might have been anxious for Neil, my younger brother, and me to bring in something to help with the household finances, he would always put our happiness first. By the age of twenty I had made a name for myself with Headingley. Wakefield Trinity were the biggest name in rugby league at the time and the great Neil Fox, one of the true Wakefield icons, had seen me play at Headingley. One day, he and some colleagues came to our house, a bungalow in Holly Avenue, in suburban Leeds.

They did not actually open a suitcase containing bundles of banknotes – as legend has it that rugby league scouts used to do when trying to recruit young Welsh players in their own front rooms – but they wanted me to join Wakefield Trinity, and whatever they were offering was going to be more than I would earn in years in my chosen career as a teacher. They had a row of figures – this, they said, is the signing-on fee, this is the match fee, this is what you get if you win. Mr Fox and his colleagues left, and we all agreed that we'd think about it.

After they had gone and the door was shut behind them, Dad took me aside. 'Look,' he said. 'What are you going to enjoy playing most? Forget about the money. What are you going to be happiest doing?'

'If I am honest,' I can remember answering, 'I think I want to stay in rugby union.'

'Well, that's fine,' Dad said. 'We don't have to talk about anything else.' And that was that. He could have been forgiven for pushing me strongly towards the Wakefield Trinity contract and the money. But he did not.

Importantly at that time, as well as playing rugby I was also very keen on cricket. Occasionally, because cricket had a certain ambience, and because the players were a nice bunch of lads, Dad would stay and have a drink after coming to watch me play. After the game, whether it had been home or away, we'd all find a pub and have a few drinks. When he came along and was chatting with the lads and myself it was probably the happiest I ever saw him.

Dad died in 1969, at forty-eight, only three months after Judy and I were married. He was a smoker and he died of lung cancer. He must have been in pain at our wedding but never complained. A modest man, that was not his way. It is only when you examine the wedding photographs closely that you realise he was not at all well at the time.

I had just started teaching in September 1968. I had been picked for Yorkshire the weekend he died but I pulled out of the game because I knew he wasn't going to last very long. I sat with him all the Saturday night and he died on the Sunday morning. Emotionally I was all over the place for a long time and it is true that Dad's influence on me is still pervasive to this day. Judy was incredibly supportive, but to die at only forty-eight still seems to me ridiculously young.

Dad's death still resonated three years later, in the autumn of 1972, when I won my first cap for Scotland against the All Blacks at Murrayfield. As I was walking on the pitch before the game, taking in the atmosphere and the weather conditions at that most nervous of times, I was approached by the pipe major, who was about to lead the band in the pre-match entertainment.

Judy was up in the stands. She had already read in the match programme that the band at Murrayfield that day was from the Queen Victoria School, Dunblane. The pipe major asked after my dad. He told me that he had been brought up with Dad, and had fought with him and that he regarded him as a terrific man, and said how close their friendship had been.

Emotionally, it hit me with tremendous force. I had to tell him that Dad had died. Nothing that happened in the game against the All Blacks could have been quite so emotional, and it hardly needs saying that I regard the fact that he never saw me play for Scotland, let alone the Lions, as a source of the deepest sadness, although that day I felt that Dad was with me.

Considering that I was born and bred in Yorkshire, was Yorkshire by residence, accent, possibly even by temperament; considering that my mother was from Yorkshire, that I married a Yorkshire girl and my earliest sporting ambition was to play cricket for Yorkshire and was to live most of my life in the White Rose county, it might seem odd that I was at Murrayfield playing for Scotland in the first place.

My antecedents were Scottish, of course. All my father's brothers and sisters still lived in Scotland and we used to go up to Glasgow to visit the family. But apart from two short spells in Edinburgh, neither of which was entirely happy for various reasons, I have never spent a significant amount of time north of the border.

In the late 1960s I was offered a trial for England by Mickey Steele-Bodger, then the chairman of England selectors. I turned it down, though it seems that I may not have mentioned that to Judy at the time.

The Scottishness came as a shock to Judy. Just after we were married, I took a group of children down to Twickenham to watch an England–Scotland match. Scotland won, 16–15, a very rare win at what the English like to call Headquarters. I was absolutely thrilled. Judy was bewildered by my reaction. She told an interviewer recently: 'He was so pleased because Scotland had won. I was just gobsmacked. I said: "Why are you so pleased? England lost!" That was the first time I really knew how pro-Scottish he was, and I had known him then for a long time. He had never made anything obvious of it. Ian's Dad didn't have a broad

Glaswegian accent either, he'd lost most of it during the years he had spent in Yorkshire. He just had a slight twang you'd notice when you met him first.' Judy gradually came to terms with the fact that she had married a latent Scot.

Looking at my Scotland caps and my apparent affiliation to things Scottish, people have always assumed that my father must have insisted on me opting for Scotland. It is not true. Dad was never one to impose anything on anyone and he did not like overt Scottish nationalism. He disliked the story Denis Law used to tell, with relish, that he was deliberately out on the golf course the day England won the World Cup in 1966.

If Scotland were playing England in any kind of sporting contest, he would support Scotland, but otherwise he would support England, especially at football, which he loved. He was delighted when they won the 1966 World Cup. He used to take me to watch Leeds United and sit me on a railing at the old Elland Road ground, in the days when you could still wander round to different parts of the stadium. I worshipped the great John Charles.

'Look,' Dad would say, 'I fought a war alongside these people. I went through a lot with English people and I admire them. I am not going to show hostility to them now.' I could never say that a latent hostility towards the English did not surface in me later, but I think the fact that I opted for Scotland, have always felt Scottish and maintained the bond came not from what my father said so much as what he was, how he conducted himself, and also from my high regard for him.

Yet it would also be ridiculous even to try to pretend that Yorkshire has not rubbed off on me. As I say, it has given me a home, an accent, a start in life and rugby, a wife. People seem to object to accusations that Yorkshire people have certain traits, especially that they can be direct, perhaps a little dour and stubborn. Unfair? Of course not. Judy and I always feel that we Yorkies are most things we are cracked up to be, for good or ill, and that bloody-mindedness seems to flow through the veins.

Among the defining arenas of Yorkshire sporting life are the county's cricket leagues. As I have said, my ambition, as a good Yorkshireman, was to play cricket for the county, and I came so close that I remember being harangued by one particular angry England international in the nets for not bowling him the ball exactly where he wanted it.

In my later teens I used to play for Hunslet Nelson, a great old club with origins going back to 1810, who played in the Central Yorkshire League. Hunslet is very much the other side of the tracks in Leeds; Judy used to say that she never realised that part of the city even existed, although she frequently risked it and ventured over to watch me play.

Given the grim surroundings, Hunslet Nelson played in what can only be described as a small oasis. There was a big bank of hoardings and, at the end of the hoardings, a small door. Once you opened the door, you dropped down, entirely unsuspectingly, into a cricket ground you would hardly know was there. It was a haven, a fantastic place.

One season we were top of the league and our opposition were Whitehall Printers, who were second. This was cricket of the hard school. If we avoided defeat, we won the league. If we lost to Whitehall, they won it. A draw for us was the absolute minimum.

Whitehall Printers batted first and scored around 160, but our reply was a disaster. When I went in, at number eight, we were 48–6, with John Webster and myself, aged seventeen, at the crease. There were fully thirty-eight overs remaining, standing between us and the title.

We had a conference in the middle and decided that we were not going to get the runs. We would play for the draw that was lurking in the very far distance. John took one end and I took the other, and we set out our stall to block our way to the title. You can imagine the banter and the verbals, with the fielders clustered round the bat. It was cut-throat stuff. Apparently you could hear the sledging on the boundary.

We batted out the full thirty-eight overs, for a grand total of four runs. The bowler delivering the last over was so annoyed that he rolled the last ball underarm along the wicket. We did not lose another wicket and we won the league. I am sure that it was the Yorkshire trait in me rising. 'Bugger it. I am not going to lose, and to hell with entertainment.'

Boring batting? Or sheer Yorkshire bloody-mindedness? As we celebrated our league title, I didn't stop to worry about which it was. On reflection, perhaps I have taken nationality and pride in Scotland from my dad, and then other important traits from my immediate environment.

I was born in Kirkstall, a Leeds suburb, and my brother Neil was born two years later. At the age of four, I started at Kirkstall Road School. My career at that school was a brief one. My mother had dropped me off first thing but I simply did not like the look of the place. I walked two miles home. My mother, answering the door, found me standing there. She could not believe it. In my mind's eye I can still recall details of that two-mile walk.

The nearest school to home was actually only a few hundred yards away, but it had been full when my mother had applied. But after the Long Walk Home, she tried again. She told them that she was worried that I'd be running away all the time from Kirkstall Road. They relented, and let me in. This time I decided to stay.

Mum was in one sense born too early. She loved sport: she'd watch everything she could and she adored the Olympics. She would play cricket with us on the beach at Bridlington and regarded Scarborough as too up market to visit. Frankly, these days of Sky Sports and their blanket coverage would have been made for her. I never realised how much she followed what Neil and I did until she died in 1994 at seventy-four, and we found reams and reams of cuttings about us. She kept anything and everything I had given her, menus from dinners, mementos, everything.

Unlike Dad, she did see me play for Scotland at Murrayfield. She would often stay at home looking after Robert and Heather, our children, when I was away playing but she did come up now and then, thank goodness, and she also saw me taking Scotland coaching sessions later on. She came down and watched my last game for Headingley in 1980.

Mum was quite conservative and she loved her routines. She washed on a Monday, it was fish on a Friday, and so on. She was very methodical. She would also be ready two hours before we remotely needed to go anywhere, and that is probably why I became a last-minute man, in reaction to Mum.

She was also a great maker of lists. On Saturdays, she would have her lists ready – one for the grocer, one for the baker, and so on. From around the age of five, I would take the lists and bring back the shopping. On the Saturday morning that Judy and I were married Mum gave me the list as usual, I went to do the shopping, came home and put on my suit and went to the church. Routines . . .

After primary school, I went to West Park, a mixed secondary school. Eventually, the school became too big and they split up the boys and girls; the girls kept West Park and the boys went to Moor Grange, a new school they had just built. I did my O levels there but because it was a secondary modern there was no sixth form and they didn't do A levels, so I moved on again, to Allerton Grange, a big new school in an era when comprehensive schools had become all the rage.

It would be wrong to pretend that certain circumstances in my childhood were not advantageous. During the period when we didn't have our own house, we lived with my aunt, who had a sweet shop. What could be better? There was also the Abbey cinema next to us, and on Fridays I was taken there and left on my own. The cinema people would look after me, and at the end of the show they'd take me by the hand and lead me home. I used to lap up all kinds of films.

We were also the first family in the area to have a television. It was a Sobell, which Mum and Dad bought so that they could watch the Coronation in 1953. There was one channel – BBC. Not BBC1, just BBC. The occasion of the year in many households of that era, the great family viewing day, was the FA Cup Final, and I can remember our front room being crowded with people who came to watch it. There would be twelve or thirteen in there, crammed round this tiny television set, and me sitting at the front.

From there, I watched Stanley Mortensen score a hat-trick for Blackpool against Bolton in the 'Matthews Final' of 1953 and I can remember watching three years later as Bert Trautmann, the former German paratrooper who played in goal for Manchester City, made saves in a 3–1 win over Birmingham. Only later was it discovered that he had broken his neck during the game. When he went up to get his medal his head was at a strange angle.

There was nothing structured about my early sporting career. I had the classic street-games background, battling all day at various sports, often with brother Neil as opposition. There was no specialisation: you would just play whatever sport or game was appropriate, in whatever version, with however many numbers there were around, on whatever surface or space was available, in whatever season. What could be better?

These days we parcel up youngsters far too soon; we send them to mini rugby or to other specific sports at the age of six. When I became director of rugby for the Scottish Rugby Union decades later, in 1999, my affection for street sports (and their like), and my belief that children should simply take part in a wide range of activities for far longer and specialise only much later, led me to urge a move away from specialisation and back towards some of the old practices.

When I used to play in the street, the opportunities for practising ball skills, for sharpening reactions, were endless. Dad used to take me to the park near Kirkstall Abbey for football and cricket, just for pick-up games. There was a stable at the back of our house which we were allowed to use as a store, and being a stable it had a double door – I would open the top half and spend ages kicking a ball through it, to see how many times consecutively I could hit the target. I would also bowl for hours against a lamppost, entirely on my own.

We even used to play football and cricket on the cobbles. Imagine the reactions you needed for that. Even in the playground at West Park High School, where we were not allowed to play ball games, we used to play touch and pass with a training shoe stuffed with socks. I used to play tennis for hours, hitting the ball against the wall. Youngsters miss out on such delights nowadays.

I was very small as a child. At the age of eleven I was four foot six and weighed only four stone six; even when I started playing for Headingley first team, I was only just over ten and a half stone. I have a photograph of me taken after I had won the Leeds Schools triple jump title, with a leap of thirty-eight feet four and a half inches. In it, I seem to be surrounded by giant, muscle-bound lads. Judy says that my mother told her I used to eat hardly anything at all, and that my staple diet was bread and jam.

And I used to run everywhere. And I mean, run. If I missed the bus to school I'd run the entire journey without a second thought. It was probably between two or three miles from home to school. If I missed the bus coming home, I would just run back.

Later, football and cricket began to dominate my life. As well as going to watch Leeds United with Dad, when I was in my teens youngsters were allowed in for free to the final session of play at Headingley cricket ground, even for Test matches. I saw Freddie Trueman and Brian Statham, county players for Yorkshire and Lancashire respectively, opening the bowling for England and it fanned a massive affection for cricket. I found out years afterwards that Judy was among those who came in for the last session, too.

By the late 1960s we had moved to a council flat in Tinshill, an upmarket part of Leeds. We had a bigger television then, too. One day I watched a rugby match, between Scotland and England. I was very taken by a player called, appropriately enough, Ken Scotland, a full-back, an attacker who seemed to stand out in the game. So did the warm tones of the Scottish commentator, whose name was Bill McLaren.

Cricket remained my number one sport for a long time and I developed into a good swing bowler, left arm around the wicket.

One of the major influences on me was Ken Dalby, a maths teacher whom I first came across at West Park and then he went to Moor Grange at around the same time as I did. He was also the manager of Leeds rugby league club, and he had taken Leeds to Wembley for the Challenge Cup Final in 1957, when they beat Barrow. Leeds were a great team to support at that time, with the great Lewis Jones in the side.

Ken was a very nice man, and it's true to say he was ubiquitous. He was a really keen cricketer and he'd place a florin (in pre-decimalisation days a two-shilling coin) on one of the three stumps and would tell me to knock it off. That meant that most of my practice was aimed at one stump. He had also written books on cricket at Headingley and he knew Bill Bowes, the fast bowler who had played in the Bodyline series in Australia in 1932–33, and, in the second Test, had bowled Donald Bradman for a duck with a slower ball when the Don had been expecting a bouncer.

Because I had been successful as a teenage cricketer, Bowes came to watch me play. He approached me afterwards and offered me snippets of advice. Eventually he brought me into the Yorkshire set-up – I proudly played for Yorkshire Schools for the first time in 1964 and then for Yorkshire Federation from 1965 onwards.

The swing I had was natural: given good conditions, I could bend the ball a mile. I could start it three feet outside off stump and hit the wicket. And even though I was never really fast, the batsmen never seemed to get hold of me. In some games for Hunslet Nelson, in the forty-five-over competition, I would bowl twenty-three overs in succession from one end, unchanged, and hardly be out of breath.

When I got to the Yorkshire nets, they tried to get me to bowl the ball that swung the other way, from leg to off to the right-hander instead of the one that swung into him. But I could never quite master that one, and for a while the fact that I was trying messed up my action.

In those days I played alongside Richard Lumb, Barrie Leadbeater and Geoff Cope, all of whom went on to have long careers with Yorkshire, and we were often called up to bowl to Geoff Boycott in the nets because people like Fred Trueman and others refused to. The traditional language in the Yorkshire dressing room at the time was comprised of a torrent of effing and blinding but to spend time with the master batsman was good for me.

Boycott was incredibly particular. He'd say: 'Right. The next three balls I want six inches outside my off stump, just short of a length.'

'Right, now bowl me three yorkers.'

'Now I want three on my leg stump.' If you were off line, he would shout: 'Bowl it where I effing tell you!'

On occasions, I played with the great man for Yorkshire Owls. The Owls were a mixture of county cricketers and league players who always played away, mainly in Lincolnshire and East Yorkshire, and, because we were such a good side, we always batted first to prolong the game and probably to suit Boycott as well. I remember playing one game and finding Boycott with his ear glued to the radio to find out if he had been selected for a Test match at Headingley. We thought him a miserable sod, though. He used to open the bowling, open the batting and he'd even keep wicket sometimes as well.

Furthermore, I also once admitted in a newspaper article that Brian Close, the gritty and belligerent Yorkshire and England cricketer, had been my inspiration. 'It was a great time to be involved with Yorkshire cricket and I believe that the lessons I learned there had a profound effect on the rest of my career,' I wrote. 'At that time, I had two great heroes, both players who had immense skill, but also people who worked at getting the best out of themselves. As a role model, Gary Sobers was the closest to the sort of player I wanted to be, a left-arm over-the-wicket bowler, somebody who could swing the ball, cut it, spin it, whatever he wanted to do. And he could bat as well. But it was as a left-arm bowler that he really struck a chord.'

I was also rubbing shoulders with Brian Close. Again, he was a magnificent sportsman, obviously a superb bat, either left-handed or right, but he could bowl, too, swinging or cutting the ball, and he was a scratch golfer. Actually, I played more with Boycott, but he was a more difficult person to get along with . . . he was too single-minded. Playing in a Sunday League match, forty-five overs a side, he would go out and bat for forty of them. Nothing mattered other than his own practice. But what he shared with a lot of the Yorkshire team of the time was a superb work ethic.

What somebody like Close had to add to that was a total dedication to winning. He made a point of putting himself in dangerous spots just to psych out the opposition. I remember him fielding at short leg, the ball hitting him on the head, splitting it open. With blood pouring from the wound, all he could think about was calling 'Catch it' to the wicketkeeper.

Remember, we are talking about days before all the padding modern cricketers wear. He would stand up to the fastest bowling with no more protection than a box and never let them see him flinch. He would sometimes come off covered in bruises, battered black and blue, but the bowlers never saw him give way. That is how important winning was.

For a young player, that and the Yorkshire humour were two great toughening-up experiences. If you can face a good fast bowler with the opposition wicketkeeper talking to you – 'Dodgy wicket this, can't say, might keep low, might rear off a length and take your head off' and so on as he runs in – you can face just about anything. So of course it toughened me up.

The kind of meticulous attention to detail, the tough mental approach, the knowledge that it is all about winning, all lessons that the likes of Close taught me, stayed with me throughout my rugby career.

I was small for a first-class rugby player, even in those days, and tiny by today's standards. I knew that if I didn't stand up for myself people would be after me all game. So when I tackled I would try everything legal to injure the other player. I never broke the rules, but if I could have broken a rib hitting somebody with my shoulder, I would have done. I knew from my cricketing experiences that if you let them see a weakness, they will be after it until it breaks you.

Later, it was the attention to detail that helped. It may have also been something of the schoolmaster in me, but when I started coaching I developed my own system of notational analysis. I would do it live during the game and afterwards could use it to tell the players what they needed to work on, what their opponent tended to do in given positions. It all helped to give me an edge when it mattered. Good habits never leave you, and those Yorkshire cricketers, at a time when Yorkshire cricket provided the core of the England team, had a strong influence that is still with me to this day.

Yet there are so many happy memories of cricket at Yorkshire, at Hunslet Nelson and, later, for Horsforth – tough games in tough towns and villages but on lovely grounds, often in the curiously named Heavy Woollen League, named after the area. When I retired from playing rugby at thirty-three, I was tempted to take up cricket again. However, I'd been away all that time, often for months on end, and when I announced that as I'd finished rugby I was thinking about restarting cricket, I didn't find Judy in total agreement.

My brother Neil stayed on the football route. I may have won most of the street games because I was a couple of years older, but he was to grow four inches taller than me. He had trials with Scunthorpe as a goalkeeper, and they were very keen to sign him. However, he had already become successful as a knitwear buyer, and would later travel around the world for his work. So he opted to play semi-professional for Guiseley, in the Yorkshire League, so that he could fit his career in alongside the sport. He recently bought the knitwear arm of the company he worked for, and is now running his own knitwear firm.

But watching Ken Scotland and Scotland on television must have struck some kind of chord with me. I was attracted to rugby and, initially, to rugby league. The clubs used to organise school leagues and they'd give you good kit. Even then, before the days of branding, this was a key factor. Kirkstall St Stephens, my primary school, played in blue jerseys with three yellow swords on the front. We started by playing touch and pass in what was more of an indoor cellar than a gym, and it was always used for storage, so we'd be playing surrounded by furniture. I played in the U11s, from the age of nine, when I would have been tiny. I was intimidated by the bigger lads and I did not enjoy it at all.

Throughout later life my team was always smaller!

But by the following season I was playing with lads of my own age, and we were playing competitive, inter-league sport at the age of ten. I remember coming up against John Atkinson, who played for Iverson House and who went on to become a great rugby league winger. I was the scrum-half. At four foot six and four stone six pounds, the choices of position for me were not exactly limitless. I had also developed a really big sidestep, partly, I suppose, as a result of developing my reflexes on the cobbles and in street games, and partly because there were any number of much bigger lads who had to be avoided if I was to survive.

But I had learned to live on my wits, I had learned street skills. I had learned, too, that biggest is not always best.

At Allerton Grange School, in my upper-sixth years, they made five people prefects who were only in the fifth form. One of them was the highly attractive Judy Fish. As she said: 'I was Miss Goody Two Shoes. I was quite clever, I never did anything wrong at school. So they made me a prefect. Ian and I used to notice each other when we were on duty together.

'I wasn't really a sporting person, I had scored for a cricket club for a while, but as a family our big thing was walking. In the school holidays, Mum would do a picnic and we'd go off somewhere. We'd go to Bolton Abbey, near Skipton, out in the Dales, or we'd catch a bus somewhere and walk from there.

'One day my friend suggested we went to badminton. Ian used to go to the class, too. It was my friend who wanted to go more than me. She said: "Come on. It'll be a laugh."' They came, and it was.

Judy's family were all born and bred in Leeds. Her grandmother was sixty-nine when Judy was born and Judy spent a fair bit of time with her. Theirs was a musical family and a piano was a fixture in their lives. When she was three, Judy sat down and played a nursery rhyme, she started piano lessons when she was five and played at school assembly when she was eight.

Judy's mum and dad, Irene and Tom, were both big Yorkshire characters. Judy was very close to her mum, who followed us down to Northampton when I was coaching there, and died at eighty-six. She was very funny but also a devoted churchgoer, a Methodist. As kids, Judy and I both went to church, separately, as Methodists. Judy used to go three times on Sunday because her mum was a Sunday School teacher. You can see a lot of her mum in Judy, especially her Yorkshire straightforwardness and honesty.

Judy had to leave school at seventeen, just as she was starting her A levels. It was a simple matter of having to bring income into the household in a crisis, after a freakish accident struck down her father – literally. Leeds experienced some bad gales that year and he was struck by a coping stone which blew off the roof of a school as he was walking past. It was a million-to-one accident and the blow led to diabetes. It meant that he could no longer do his job. He was a travelling representative, and he loved it, but doctors could not stabilise his condition well enough for him to drive and he had to give up working.

Judy was one of the high-fliers at school. She was doing maths and accountancy when she was in the fifth form and I was in the upper sixth. Her results were phenomenal and she was going to go into accountancy full time. In those un-emancipated days, there seemed to be resistance to the idea that an accountant might be a woman. It was almost a closed shop. But they asked her to do some sample work and when she handed it in, they immediately put her on to the course. That's how good Judy was.

Then her father had his accident. She had to give up on her

dreams of a career and left school to earn some money for the family. She went into the civil service. 'I always regretted leaving school, and still do,' she says.

Judy's support and patience has also been remarkable. Latterly life for me as a professional coach has meant a certain amount of moving – between Northampton, Scotland, Leeds and Buckinghamshire. Much earlier in my career, I would set off for tours lasting months and months, often when the only real means of communication were letters that Judy would have to send to some box number in South Africa or New Zealand; and I seemed to develop the knack of setting out on one of these crusades just after we had moved house, leaving Judy to sort out various domestic disasters.

Rugby only went professional in the mid-1990s, and for years, especially while teaching at Fir Tree Middle School in the reign of a particular headmaster not well disposed to me, I used to lose up to a third of my salary because I had to coach Scotland, and even the Lions, in time off without pay. Judy had to take a range of jobs, some of which she disliked, to help make up the shortfall and to pay the mortgage.

In 2009, I changed tactics. When I was leaving for the 2009 Lions tour of South Africa, the house was in great shape. But Heather, our daughter, was getting married, to Charlie Beech, her fiancé and the Wasps prop. So I left Judy to help with wedding arrangements instead.

Judy and I recently celebrated our fortieth wedding anniversary. She has effectively put everything on the back burner for me, all the way through, from school and then through our early married years. At first, we used to foster children, some of them real problem kids. We had a tiny black baby for two years, until he was put up for adoption. He had to leave while I was away with the 1974 Lions in South Africa; we also fostered twins for a while, a brother and a sister. One of the children was a real problem, and the social workers told us that we had to pin the child to the bed to stop him creating havoc. Judy simply refused to do it; she took time with him and showed him some love, and he was transformed.

When I wasn't getting paid in the mid-1990s, Judy used to go out and work in the kitchens at student halls of residence. That was often the difference between us keeping or losing the house.

As I have mentioned, Judy was a tremendous pianist from an early age and her music teacher told her that she should take it further, perhaps go to college with a view to becoming a music teacher. Eventually, in 1987, when Heather was just over four, and reaching school age, and I had come back from a World Cup, she went to what is now Leeds Met University to do a BEd Honours in music and PE.

She taught at a school near us for a time but, once again, my career intervened. I had to move to Scotland to work for Scottish Life, during a brief period out of rugby and in industry, so Judy had to hand in her notice so that she could come to Scotland with me. Everything we've done she has made fit.

Judy has also been a fantastic sounding board for me. If any problems arise, outside or inside rugby, we have always talked things through. At Northampton, once the video analysis tapes of the previous day's game came in on a Sunday morning we used to watch the game together and she would ask, 'Why are you doing that?'

She got to the point where she'd say: 'Look, let me make a coffee; don't start until I've made a coffee. I want to see what happened.'

Judy has always created better, nicer atmospheres in boardrooms or clubhouses wherever we have been, because she's just so open about the rugby, but also about people and about gathering them in. The wife of one of the Wasps board members told her: 'You have changed the atmosphere in and around the board and the club in these past four years. It is much more relaxed. There is a really nice feeling here.'

The Yorkshire way is, famously and as I have intimated, to call a spade a spade, of course. The reason why I get on with people and with coaches like Shaun Edwards and Jim Telfer is the same reason why I am so close to Judy. If something is not right, just like Shaun and Jim she will just say it, straight out, but for all the right and honest reasons. And like Shaun and Jim, Judy is a good listener as well. Often, she has had to be.

She has been a bit more than just a support while I have been away. She has been 50 per cent of my thinking, and my best friend. Sometimes, I will turn down invitations because I would rather be with her.

After forty years, the feeling between us is, uncannily, the same as it was at the very beginning. Who says badminton is a waste of time?

Neither Robert nor Heather would ever say it's been a nine-to-five upbringing. There have been too many odd hours, long absences and house moves! I would also suggest that they realise how proud of them Judy and I have always been. Rob has travelled miles and miles with me, from the time when I started coaching Headingley. When we were having the team meeting, he would sit in the dressing room or on the physio's couch. Even before, as a three- or four-year-old, he would come to games with me and be scampering about the place.

When I became involved with Scotland, he used to travel everywhere in the car with me. He would come to every game I watched, almost with exception, whether I was driving up through the Borders to Scotland or taking the train down to London. He used to get very excited when we got ready on a Saturday morning. Say I was going to watch a game in the Borders, we would stop somewhere for morning coffee on the way up from Leeds, have some lunch, take in the game. Afterwards he would come into the clubhouse with me, then we'd stop for fish and chips in Newcastle.

So, from the age of three or four right through to eleven or twelve, I suppose, we travelled together. Then Heather hit the trail, too. She didn't do as much of the travelling then but got really involved in the games, particularly when I was coaching at

Northampton. And with Scotland. For both of them, their very first flight was to New Zealand, all twenty-six hours of it, to be there for the Second Test of the Scotland tour in 1990.

They are so used to travelling or to having to change plans at the last minute, so they rarely get fazed by things. They are very relaxed and easy. They don't get bothered because they have had so many different things thrown at them. Heather will talk to anybody. I think it's just because she's come across so many different people in so many different countries. Rob is a little more shy. He still likes his rugby but these days it's probably Heather on whom rugby has more of a grip.

Now, Rob is forging his own life in Sheffield with his girlfriend, though he still comes down for the big games. He is area manager for South Yorkshire for an electrical distribution company. He felt the pressure of the McGeechan name most at Royal High School, when we lived in Edinburgh. Everybody was expecting him to be a brilliant international player. We told him that rugby was an option, not a sacred duty, and that if he wasn't enjoying it he should stop, which he did. He has always loved football so I was quite happy when he went over to the round ball and he still plays five-a-side. He is also a successful DJ, good enough for bookings in Ibiza, which is the Mecca.

Heather has been delightful because, even when she got to sixteen or seventeen, when Dads become *persona non grata*, we always stayed close. She loves being part of the rugby and, indeed, it produced a husband for her. She and Charlie Beech, the promising Wasps prop who had such a good season in 2008–09, were married in August 2009. I made sure that when Judy was making all the arrangements I was away with the Lions. It must be said that to have a prop in the family is interesting, and Judy now gets a front row perspective. When she was at Northampton as an eight-year-old, she was always more interested in the props. It is still fantastic when we all get together and also that Judy and Heather made a flying visit to South Africa for the Second Test in Pretoria in July 2009. It was a shattering weekend all round in rugby terms, so not the best choice. But to have them there when I was feeling so low was brilliant and it was a good distraction on the Monday to be combing Johannesburg for a wedding ring for Heather. And to remember that the family would soon be gathering for the big day. And typically for a Yorkshireman with Scottish blood, and just a few miles of travel on the clock, we would be gathering in Marlow, Bucks. Just the latest port of call.

4

The Somme, and Headingley

Call to arms, and the greatest game

If Gareth Edwards is the greatest rugby player I have ever seen – and I have seen a few – the one I most admire is John Abbott King, who played for Headingley, Yorkshire and England. I never actually saw him play, not even on film, and I have never spoken to anyone who saw him play either.

King features in the annual *Yorkshire Rugby Football Union Commemoration Book 1914–19 and Official Handbook 1919–20.* The *YRFU Commemoration Book,* before or since, has probably never been the most compelling read or the biggest seller, but I have that particular edition, bound in red vellum, and it is incredible. I came across it in a favourite haunt, a second-hand bookshop. It is full of the usual material – lists of officers of the Union, minutes of meetings, historical articles, expenditure accounts, laws, rules, coverage of every Yorkshire club, reminders to uphold the sacred amateur code at all times. Dour reading for some, perhaps.

And yet I can never open that book, or even discuss it, without becoming very emotional. It gives the fixtures for all the member clubs of the Yorkshire RFU for season 1919–20. Some clubs are represented by a blank page. For Baildon, Batley and Leeds Rifles RFC, for example, it reads, 'owing to losses in the War, it will not be possible to run a team this year'. The College of the Resurrection RFC, incidentally, had a full fixture list.

The 1919–20 yearbook also bears the strapline 'Commemoration Book, 1914–19'. It is an absolutely magnificent tribute. The language is expressive, to say the least. The dedication reads: 'With sorrowful hearts but with a mighty pride, this book is reverently dedicated to all our Yorkshire players who played "The Great Game".' It further refers to 'the heroic splendour of our youth'.

Now, in the first decade of the twenty-first century, we have long since stopped referring to war and the war dead as 'playing a game', great or otherwise, but in those far-off Olympian days it was just part of the language, reflecting the straightforward courage of the time.

But there is no doubt about something else the book also mentions: 'The truly magnificent response of the rugby union men of Yorkshire' to the call to arms for the First World War. When war was declared, both the RFU at Twickenham and the Yorkshire RFU issued appeals to rugby men to join up, and they did so in extraordinary numbers. There were repeated requests that the services should establish the so-called Pals Regiments for rugby players only, so that members of teams would serve together.

Thank goodness such requests fell on deaf ears. When I was teaching in Leeds, we would often delve into the history of the city and how it grew. I used to take the kids round in a bus to different parts. I was interested in the Pals Regiments and found that a huge number of Leeds men joined a Pals Regiment from Woodhouse, a set of terraces stretching from the centre of Leeds up towards the university.

If you go through those streets you learn that almost none of the men came back from the war. They all enlisted together, they were all in the same Pals Regiment, all in the same battle. So many of them died together. That was why they stopped the Pals. If they were in the wrong place, they all got wiped out together. So when the letters came home, they were covering streets with hardly any survivors. Entire communities wiped out.

The most haunting part of the yearbook for 1919–20 is that for every club it lists separately all those who enlisted and served, all those who fell and the military honours they were awarded. The numbers in each category are staggering. And every Yorkshire rugby man who died gets a full-page picture to himself, giving his regiment and the theatre of war in which he met his fate: killed at the Somme; died at Bois-Grenier; died of wounds at Ypres; killed at Suvla Bay, Gallipoli.

The range of regiments, ranks and theatres of war is also remarkable. Of the Yorkshire team of 1913–14, faithfully listed in playing positions, every single player enlisted – some are marked as 'twice wounded', others as 'three times wounded'.

Headingley were then one of the biggest clubs in Yorkshire; they continued to be for decades afterwards. They were the only club for whom I ever played, they gave me a grounding in playing and coaching, one in which I was surrounded by wise rugby men and great friends, where we played a brand of rugby I loved, and around which, for a time, my social life was centred. But times change. Headingley were swallowed up in 1997 when the game went professional. Their ground still exists, but nowadays it is used for training by Leeds, the club that absorbed them when professionalism arrived.

For the 1914–18 war the *YRFU Yearbook* lists more than two hundred Headingley rugby members who enlisted – two hundred mostly young blokes, the same age as me when I first began to play, the same age as the men who surrounded me in the team. Many joined the West Yorkshire Regiment, but there were also naval officers, members of the Royal Flying Corps, the lot. Of those two hundred-plus, more than fifty were killed. Twenty-one gained military honours – the Military Medal, the Military Cross and a host of DCMs and DSMs.

It is incredibly moving to turn the page to the dead of Headingley RFC – each with an individual page and photograph, all showing them in pristine uniforms. Headingley was quite a middle-class club and so many of the men became officers, as shown by their officer's caps and stripes.

The photograph of John Abbott King, however, shows no such insignias of rank. He was a mere lance corporal, a bloke in plain khaki. He is smiling. He was in the Liverpool/Scottish Regiment and died on the Somme on 9 August 1916. There are no details of his death: he is simply listed as 'missing'. His body, if it was ever found, was never identified.

Yet he gets his own, lengthy eulogy in the yearbook, a tribute written by R. F. Oakes, a well-known official of the Yorkshire Union. In Oakes' words the full glory of this amazing Headingley man blazes through.

King won twelve caps for England, from 1911–13. Oakes wrote: 'How those critical but delightful Twickenham crowds cheered the great little man! And how the breasts of that little but enthusiastic hand of Headingley and Yorkshire supporters used to swell with a mighty – and a perfectly justifiable – pride at the great doings of their idolised "Jack" King.'

King seems to have been an extraordinary character, and completely selfless, with, Oakes wrote, 'the greatness of a soulful man'. He was helping to bring in the harvest on a farm in the summer of 1914, along with 'Busty' Lumb, another Headingley player, when Lumb raced out with the news that he had received his call-up papers from the Yorkshire Hussars. He had come to say goodbye.

There and then, King decided that he would go along, too, with his friend Lumb. At first the Hussars would not take him because he stood only five foot five inches. King's Regulations stated that a trooper had to be five foot six or more. King refused to take no for an answer and, after three days, possibly growing an inch in the interim, possibly not, he was accepted. He refused to try for a commission and thus stay in relative safety behind the lines. Oakes said that King told him that he wanted to serve among ordinary soldiers.

However, the Hussars were primarily engaged on patrol and police duty and, as Oakes has it, King was desperate to become 'more of a real soldier'. So he enlisted as an infantryman in the Liverpool/Scottish Regiment, therefore knowingly condemning himself to life in the trenches when he could have continued to operate in relative safety behind his own lines,

Oakes believed that this decision perfectly reflected the man all the Headingley players knew so well – 'brimful of mirth, kind, loving, generous, and absolutely unselfish, ever keen and very anxious to do his utmost in whatever he took in hand'.

King did not last long in France. On 9 August 1916, the Liverpool Scottish made three separate assaults on Guillemont, a German position heavily defended by a system of tunnels, dugouts and concrete emplacements. All the attacks were beaten back, with heavy casualties, one of whom was John Abbott King. Guillemont Road cemetery, one of the subsidiary cemeteries at the Somme battlefield, contains 2,220 graves, many of them unmarked. King's body may or may not lie there.

Colonel Davidson of the Liverpool Scottish wrote from the battlefield to King's next of kin, his two sisters: 'When I saw him, absolutely cool and collected under a murderous machine gun fire, with shells falling all round, one thanked God for such men to set such a priceless example. He was absolutely lionhearted and, had he come though, I should have promoted him on the field and recommended him for DCM.'

Colonel Davidson was aware that King was a well-known rugby player. 'It was a sad day for [rugby] football,' he continued. 'But if another game . . . is never played in Britain, the game has done well. After two years' command in the field, I am convinced that the rugby footballer makes the finest soldier in the world.'

Just before he took part in the attack on Guillemont, King wrote to Oakes. 'I am absolutely A1 in every way. But one can never count on the future. As long as I don't disgrace the old rugby game . . .'

It would be ridiculous to compare rugby and war: only one of them is a 'great game'. But I find it incredibly moving to read that rugby players had such a wonderful reputation during the war, and that the game is held in such esteem when it comes to characters and character building. The story of John Abbott King is something that affects me deeply, perhaps not surprisingly. For there is the link with my father and his services background, the services traditions of my family; there is the link with Headingley, the pride in the history of our club, and the courage of our young predecessors in the white, green and black hooped jersey.

'Jack' King was one of two players of that name who went to the First World War from the club – he was a forward – and the other was one A. King, like me a half-back. He was in a howitzer brigade and, thankfully, survived to return to play again for Headingley and Yorkshire. And to wear the jersey before handing it down the line, to me and then to others.

Sometimes, when I am dealing with players who behave like prima donnas or who complain about the harshness of their sporting lives, I would like to be able to refer them to that *YRFU Yearbook*, to the story of both the Kings and of all the rugby players, but especially to the incredible stoicism of 'Jack' King under 'murderous' fire.

But if there is no comparison between war and the sport of rugby, for me rugby is at least the ultimate team game; simply put, you are totally reliant on other people. You have to support your team-mates and you receive their support in return. When it works, the effect of that support is incredible, the bond unbreakable. Rugby still produces great men. If I had to go to the trenches I would feel sanguine about doing so in the company of someone like Phil Vickery, with whom I have great rapport, and for me a man who stands for so many good things in rugby.

The best examples of rugby as a team game have always stayed with me. The emotions you get are not so much enjoyable as extremely satisfying; aware that as a team you have all worked together to a plan and over eighty minutes you've got something right. It's not that you tell yourself you're having fun. It is just that you know you are in a special place, and the pleasure comes from the sense of achievement. I am lucky enough to have been inspired by people and things all around me.

There used to be an honours board on the wall in the clubhouse at Headingley. As well as the names of club members who had died in both world wars, it bears those of all players from the club who became internationals. Although, as I have said, Headingley RFC no longer exists in its original incarnation, I hope the honours board is in safekeeping somewhere.

That board was an inspiration to me from the moment I walked into the club until I left. I wore the Headingley jersey for more than fifteen years, but, once I had retired, it was gone, passed on to someone else; just like the Lions jerseys I wore in 1974 and 1977, handed to me for a brief moment of glory before being passed on to the next wearer.

On that honours board were the names of men you might have played with if you'd been born in a different generation, perhaps served with, even died alongside. They were asked many questions. Would I have been able to answer them in the same way?

Ken Dalby was, as I have mentioned, a huge influence on me not only as a maths teacher at West Park School but also far beyond the school boundaries. Ken was a local legend thanks to his exploits managing the Leeds rugby league team and in my midteens all the live rugby I watched was rugby league, and the great George Stephenson and Lewis Jones were in the Leeds team.

But we had a really good rugby union team at West Park and, after O levels in 1963, we were all going to join West Park Old Boys – it was normal for boys still at the school to play for the Old Boys. But then Ken got us together. 'Look,' he said, 'the best rugby club in Yorkshire is Headingley. Go and join the Colts there and see what you make of it. Because if you don't try, you will never know. If you don't make it, you can always come back to the Old Boys team.'

Things started to move so quickly that it was as if I had suddenly stepped on to an escalator. We had a really good Colts team that remained pretty much unbeaten for the two years after I entered the Headingley club for the first time as a member. It was to be a brilliant experience, because Headingley were a wonderful club, with a true amateur club spirit. As I look back at that time now after many years in the harsher fields of the professional game, I can see that for me it was indeed a golden era in terms of the sheer enjoyment I got from the game.

Unlike so many of the leading players today, who seem to have represented a galaxy of different teams in their rise up the ladder, I missed out on the whole lot. I did go for Yorkshire schools trials but when you came from a secondary modern school like I did, you were suddenly thrown in among all the boys from the big grammar schools, where everyone was on first-name terms, probably including those of the masters. People told me that I didn't have the right tracksuit. I didn't even have any tracksuit.

As it was, I made the jump from Headingley Colts into the first team, without touching the second XV, and ran out to play for Headingley First XV as an eighteen-year-old. In that first game, against Waterloo at Headingley, I immediately came up against Chris Jennings, who was an England international. I always used to scrutinise the match-day programmes to see where the asterisks denoting an international were, and there was one against Jennings. But we won, 21–3.

As usual, I was outweighed, but the *Yorkshire Post*, reporting on the game, was very loyal. 'Ian McGeechan was marking a man nearly twice his size in weight, and he was never second best. His defence was all that anyone could ever ask, and in attack, he allowed the ball a smooth passage along the line. He was always looking for work.' I hope I am not being immodest if I say that that description, of my first game in senior rugby, summed up the way I always tried to play the game thereafter.

It seems remarkable to look back on all this now, but at the time I was still at school and so I would play for West Park in the morning and for Headingley in the afternoon. There were so many wise heads at the club, so many individuals who offered encouragement and to whom I owe a tremendous debt. Men such as Ivor Lloyd and Pat Donovan would come to wherever the school XV was playing in the morning, park up and watch the game, and then whisk me away to play for Headingley.

In those days Ivor drove a Humber Hawk, an enormous estate car. He used to put on his flying helmet and away we would whizz. He would overtake by whipping the car on to the wrong side of the road, hit 70 or 80 mph, and then whip in again as all the oncoming cars were furiously tooting him. When we played Hartlepool Rovers one Saturday we stopped off in Yarm, where we had egg and chips for lunch. I thought this was fantastic, and the height of professionalism.

Imagine someone like Danny Cipriani, the brilliant young Wasps player, going up to the club in his early years and saying: 'Look, I'm going to play for the school this morning, and then I will be along to play for you this afternoon.'

People often ask me when it was that I realised I was a really good player. The answer was that I never did. I played in good teams, I had a good sidestep and I knew I could beat people. But I think it was only when I was in the Yorkshire team, and especially for a match when my mum and dad drove down to watch, that we all knew I could play a bit. 'I never realised how good you were.' Those words of Dad's again.

Headingley also looked after me wonderfully. I made the First XV originally because of injuries, I was youthful, and small, but they put experienced players inside and outside me, so if I was picked in the centre there would be an old hand at fly-half and another alongside me in the midfield. At the time I just felt it was all coming easily to me but, in fact, they were doing all the work and the ball was coming to me only when I could do something with it.

In one of the games in my first season I got smashed – absolutely smashed – and it was a good lesson, because I suddenly realised how well others had been playing around me, and how important it was to fit into a team.

Later that first year we beat Moseley at home, winning 9–8 against a team that had been playing great stuff. I remember being trapped at the bottom of a ruck in the game. In those days, if the forwards managed to get a back in a ruck they would really have a go. Peter Squires, our experienced hooker, must have realised what was about to happen. He came over and literally pulled the Moseley forwards off me. 'Nay, nay,' he said. 'The lad is only eighteen. Give him at least a couple more years.'

That was also when I first began to shy away from the big build-up, because of sheer nerves. I hated dressing rooms before the game. I do not like long build-ups and never have done. Sometimes I'd turn up twenty minutes before kick-off, get into my corner, change, do the ritual '1-2-3-4-5' warm-up, a quick sprint and then take the field.

It was just too much nervous energy. I was nervous anyway. I was nervous from eleven in the morning. I couldn't eat. I always tried to have lunch, tried to force down some fish from the fish and chip shop. I was always on the toilet, too. That's why I always empathised with Dean Richards, Leicester giant and one of the world's finest number eights, who felt the same as I did. He left the dressing room in the Second Test in Australia in 1989. He did not need it and all the pressure it generated. He went away alone and made his own quiet preparations for the game.

The roots of a coaching career, were, I suppose, there from the very start of my First XV playing career. I was so lucky because, as I have said, for a relatively small club we had an incredible number of wise rugby men. Along with Ken Dalby and Ivor Lloyd there was, especially, Bernard White, a lecturer at Carnegie College in Leeds and still one of the best and wisest coaches I have ever worked with. He was years ahead of anyone around at the time.

After games there was always a brainstorming session. I would talk to our forwards or to the opposition or, more especially, to Bernard. I would be the last one out of the bar, after endlessly talking through what we had or hadn't done, and how we could get better in the future. Sometimes you don't appreciate the wisdom of what you're being told until much later. But if you take it on board, piece by piece, then you suddenly see how it all fits together.

When I went to Carnegie College myself to train as a PE teacher in 1965, and partly because of the teaching environment, my thirst for analysis grew. The subject of my dissertation was the great New Zealand team which toured Great Britain and Ireland in 1967. They were fantastic, and I looked at how they started their play and how they developed it. I looked, too, at every try they scored, and how they got to the line. I examined the way they built their game from set pieces and worked back. I watched Fergie McCormick, the full-back. He would launch kicks 40 and 50 yards parallel to the touchlines, which would bound and skip sideways into touch. I told myself that I had to learn how to kick like that.

Judy typed it all up for me. It ran to about 10,000 words. I got a straight A for it and until quite recently it was still in the college library. Unfortunately it has since disappeared.

For all that, though, you learn most rugby lessons on the field. Ken Dalby was in large part responsible for my philosophy. He once watched me in a school game between Allerton Grange and Moor Grange. I always knew that we were going to win, and I was cocky during the match. I scored a couple of tries. During the game quite a few of their kicks went over my head.

When it was all over, Ken came up to me. I remember his words. 'You were fantastic with the ball. If you want to be a really good player, however, what you should be doing off the ball is just as important. After how many of those kicks that went over your head did you go back and help your full-back?'

The answer, of course, was none. It was a lesson that stuck with me. From then on I tried to make sure that I worked harder than any other player or opponent off the ball. In any backs move I used to try to get outside the wing and so I stepped up my training to five days a week to get fit enough to do it. Ken could easily have congratulated me on scoring three tries. But as he said: 'You should have done that, anyway. They were run-ins.'

He also taught me the key lesson that a centre must look after his wings. When I first came into the Headingley team we had a winger called Mike Booth. He was a giant, and we used to call him Hooligan Booth. On the field he would look for anything and anyone to smash and hit.

Hooligan wore glasses, and without them he couldn't see a thing on the pitch. Your passing therefore had to be accurate enough to enable him to catch the ball; if he did catch it, he was well-nigh unstoppable. It was exactly the same as in my school days when I played inside the great John Atkinson, who was to have a distinguished career as a Great Britain rugby league international. You realised that with these powerhouses on the outside, all you had to do was develop the skills to get the ball to them.

Hooligan looked at me when I first played with him. 'Make sure you look after me,' he said. 'I want the ball when I can do something with it.' There was me, ten stone and seventeen years old, and there was him, an experienced giant, and he wanted me to look after him.

But, again, it was a great lesson. I was gratified after one of those early games when Mike came up to me and said that he had really enjoyed playing outside me. Judy would always be annoyed if she felt that I had put my wing away when I could have scored myself, but it was just something that gave me great pleasure.

Bernard White, as I say, was years ahead of any coach I came across at the time. I always enjoyed club games immediately after returning from Scotland matches and, after one international, Headingley had a home game against Bedford, at the time one of the best teams around, and there was added spice because the game was to be shown on BBC2's *Rugby Special*. I was at fly-half and the open-side flanker for Bedford was the famous Budge Rogers, who for years held the record for England caps.

Bernard told me that I had to keep Budge Rogers interested in

me, that I had to stop him drifting across to take the man outside.
I tried to hold on to the ball so that he was having to come to me
and that meant that people outside me could play. Bernard said:
'Look, if he leaves you and moves out, just go.' And, of course,
Budge was trying to predict when I was going and when I wasn't
and it became the classic cat and mouse.

It worked. I even became a little cocky, and scored a try. That
sensation of planning something for a rugby match which comes
to fruition is addictive and I have never lost that thrill. Bedford
were the favourites that day and Bernard White worked out a way
of beating them.

An incredible amount of my career as player or coach was with
teams that were not dominant in the forwards. The Headingley
pack, for example, was never massive. We always had a good back
row and good backs, and a front five which had to fight like mad
for any scrap of possession they could win.

At Headingley we had to get the ball in play, and keep it in play,
and so we challenged ourselves to be able to shift on every ball, to
look after it and to work hard off the ball. In many ways it was a
microcosm of my whole career, because for Headingley, Yorkshire,
Scotland and even with some of the Lions parties, we had to cope
with not being fantastic up front. It was not until 2005, when I
moved to coach a Lawrence Dallaglio-driven Wasps, that I had the
luxury of formulating a game plan based on winning some possession. Otherwise, it was border reivers time.

We also had a northern chip on the shoulder about clubs that
looked down on us. We could only play Gloucester at Gloucester,
which we did every Easter Saturday, because they refused to come
north to play us at home. Bristol didn't deign to come to
Headingley either.

The third outfit who looked down their noses at us were
Blackheath. In 1972 they announced that they didn't want to play
us again (under the amateur code clubs could elect to behave like
that) and so, when we travelled down to south-east London to play
them it was to be for the last time. John Spencer, the England

centre, was with us then. For a time, we had a back division to die for. I was at fly-half, with Spencer and Chris Rea in the centre. Chris was another Scotland international, a great centre who had made the 1971 tour with the Lions. The confidence the pair brought to the team was incredible. We also had David Caplan at full-back and Bill Hartley on the wing. On our day we could be brilliant.

At Blackheath that afternoon we won easily; in fact, we smashed them, this team that felt we were beneath them. And then Spencer, as only Spencer could, took the mickey out of them remorselessly in the bar afterwards. 'These two-bit clubs that we would prefer not to play,' he said. 'I don't think you will be seeing us down these parts again until you can improve.' It was a hilarious night.

My seasons at Headingley coincided with a period when rugby was at its most sociable, although we took our game very seriously. There were so many Yorkshire and Lancashire sides playing each other, and that meant innumerable trips across the Pennines.

There was a pub right at the top of the Pennines called the Floating Light, and on a Saturday night there might be three or four teams in the pub at the same time. We never left any ground early, anyway; we would always stay drinking at the club until about 8.00 p.m. Then we would drive towards Leeds and stop at the top of the Pennines, or wherever was convenient on the way, and be back at the club in the early hours. We were rarely home before two in the morning, leaving a trail of happy landlords in our wake.

Headingley was also the source of the great milk float transport story. One of the players, Alan Hurdley, actually had a milk round and a milk float to go with it. We didn't have a car in those days, so as many as ten of us would just clear away the empties and go careering around in the float, with Judy along with us on the back. Happy days? It hardly needs saying.

In all, I played for Headingley's First XV for sixteen seasons, and for most of them we were one of the best teams in the north and

never less than competitive. There were so many highlights –
winning away at Leicester in 1966 with Paddy McFarland alongside me in the centre, at a time when Leicester were celebrating a
post-war record of twenty-six consecutive wins, and then, a week
later, winning at Gloucester on one of the very rare occasions
when they allowed us to play them at Kingsholm. I scored two
tries, and the lads dubbed me 'The Rabbit' after I scuttled over the
line. The *Daily Telegraph* recorded that Gloucester 'had no answer
to McGeechan and Arthur Binks in the centre'.

Soon after that we won away at the raucous bear pit that was
Coundon Road, ending a fourteen-match unbeaten run for
Coventry. While we were waiting for Coventry to take a kick at
goal, one of the spectators, a woman, started laying about Jeremy
Graham, our full-back, with an umbrella. They were not happy.

The next season we beat Wasps at home, and even though
Wasps had the England pair of Terry Arthur and David Rosser at
centre, we still beat them, said one paper, 'through the thrustful
running of the centres'.

Season 1970–71 was reckoned to be the best in the club's history. We played great rugby. The midfield trio of Spencer, Rea and
myself came together regularly. We beat Leicester at home with a
great try from Spencer, we won away at Bedford, and I can recall
dropping a goal right at the end. In fact, that season we did not
lose until April, an incredible record for what was still a smallish
club, and even though we fell apart a bit in April the final statistics were excellent.

My first representative game for Yorkshire was against the South of
Scotland in Melrose in October 1966, and even though we lost
19–3 it felt fantastic to have been selected. County rugby was a
huge part of rugby in that era and nowhere more so than in
Yorkshire. We went up on the bus on the morning of the game,
with me at fly-half outside Roger Pickering, the England scrum-
half. The South had David Chisholm and Alex Hastie, the doyens
of the period, the Scotland half-backs. When I turned up to board

the coach at Leeds some of the Yorkshire players thought I was the son of one of the selectors coming along for the ride. But to become a county player was a really, really big thing.

Selection for Yorkshire was another indication for Mum and Dad that I might become a decent rugby player. Headingley was very much public school: I had been secondary modern, council estate. I never had pushy parents, they were just very supportive. 'He must be reasonably good, if they are picking him for the County side,' I heard Mum say to Dad.

A month later I played in the County Championship, in those days the biggest domestic tournament by far in England, against Cumberland and Westmorland at Bradford. I was moved to centre outside Phil Horrocks-Taylor. All told, I played fifty times for Yorkshire, though I was often competing with England's Alan Old for the fly-half position. The highlight was probably the match against Cumberland and Westmorland in 1972, when both my wings, Peter Squires and Dave Hoyland, scored four tries.

It was not a vintage era for the White Rose county and the furthest we ever reached was the semi-finals of the County Championship in 1972, where we lost to Warwickshire by 7–6. In that run, I was played on the left wing. In an interview with *Rugby World* I explained that, on balance, I would rather play in midfield. That was putting it mildly. In another profile, I was described as 'a useful tidier-up'. Not exactly effusive, perhaps, but by this time I had embarked on the Scotland fast track and trials system, and my thoughts were turning northwards across the border.

It was while playing for Yorkshire against Cheshire that I suffered my only serious rugby injury. Jeff Young, the Wales hooker, was an RAF officer stationed at Harrogate and he played his county rugby for Yorkshire. He bit the ear of one of the opposition, a terrible thing to do, and there was blood everywhere. At a period during the match when the Cheshire team, to a man, was trying to get even, Phil Horrocks-Taylor, our fly-half, sent out quite a difficult pass to me. If I saw him tomorrow, no doubt he would still be apologising. I took the ball into contact, someone booted me in the head as I was trapped on the ground and my jaw was broken. I shared an ambulance with the prop with part of his ear hanging off.

At the time, I was on teaching practice up in Dormanstown, a really rough area, near Redcar on the coast. Thankfully I didn't have to have an operation, because everything had more or less stayed in line. They put a rubber contraption round my jaw to hold it, instead of it being wired, I was in hospital for three days and then it was back to teaching practice, talking to the pupils through clenched teeth.

One happy upshot of my time in Dormanstown was that I first realised what great places the staff rooms could be in a good school. The staff were superb and I also received a lot of damage sympathy from the pupils. I had missed two weeks of my teaching practice so, to get it signed off, I had to stay an extra fortnight, right up to Christmas. I went to the Christmas parties and they all really looked after me. Shame about the Christmas dinner, though. Complan through a straw.

At the age of thirty-three, in my sixteenth season, and by now a Lion twice over, I played in a testimonial game organised by Gordon Brown at Ayr, who had just retired from playing for Scotland and the Lions. It was the end of the 1979 season. During the match I damaged a cartilage. With the arthroscopic treatment available now I would have been back within weeks but at that time treatment was rudimentary, to put it mildly.

My knee locked for about a week, then released, but they told me that they could not operate until it locked again. So I went all through the summer training and, eventually, it did lock again.

I was operated on that September. They cut the knee open and stitched everything together and afterwards, well, I have never had pain like it before or since. I was not fit enough to play again until February 1980, and by that time, obviously, I had missed out on Scotland, missed out on Yorkshire.

It was time to take stock. I knew that, broken jaw apart, I had had a charmed career, and I decided that I wanted to finish in one piece. So I decided to train hard, to play until the end of the season, and then to finish on my own terms. And that's exactly what I did.

Those were the years when the fixture list was always the same each season. Fylde was always the last game and it was always fast and exciting – because their pitch was sand-based and a great surface, or because ours was always so worn that it was bare and fast but for a different reason. In April 1980 I wore the Headingley jersey for the last time.

It saddens me that a club with such great tradition, with so many characters and so many memories, no longer exists. When the game went professional, Headingley tried hard to cope. They sold their back pitches, so the area on which I once trained is now a supermarket. They used to have a squash club as well, and even a canoe club on the river. All gone.

Next they amalgamated with Roundhay, the other Leeds team, in an effort to try to pool assets and resources. None of it provided a sound base for running a professional operation; maybe it was not the sort of club that was ever suited to the new era, and in a way it did make sense to come together under the Leeds banner. Old Headingley men like David Jennings, Dick Oliver and Mike Lampkowski are actually involved in the professional club, so the flame still burns. Headingley made me a life member, and I still get season tickets from Leeds as a result. For season 2009–10, they are back in the Guinness Premiership.

The grounding Headingley gave me was invaluable, and the memories are still fantastic. It was often rugby played for sheer enjoyment and I am so happy that I played in that particular era, and not afterwards.

Sometimes it is the smallest things that leave the warmest, most lasting impression. For instance, we often travelled to matches by train. If we were playing London Scottish, for example, we would all board the train together at Leeds, get off at Euston and take the tube together out to Richmond. All as a team, sharing a sense of camaraderie even travelling to a match.

The club president always travelled with us (or near us, anyway, as he was up in first class, of course) and one of the great traditions was that the captain and president would take dinner in the dining car on the way back.

One day we were away at Bedford. Roy Southcott was the president that year and, together with the captain, I was invited to walk up the train and sit down at the president's table. Rattling through the countryside en route for Leeds, with the silver service of the old restaurant car, was a grand feeling.

Our usual home crowd was around five to six hundred but for the really big games we might play in front of two thousand or more. We might not have been the most consistent side, but on our day we could be so good, as good as any club in England. We always played decent rugby, so I think we must have been entertaining to watch, and the spirit at the club was a powerful one. I hope that in the way we played the game we honoured the memory of John Abbott King and those of all the other great men who went before us.

5

Braid Hills

Appearing on the Scottish radar

It was all going well with Headingley. I was twenty-one, I loved the club and the way we played, but, more and more, I seemed to be popping up on the radar north of the border. We were invited to play in the 1968 Middlesex Sevens as one of the guest sides and, for a club like Headingley, that was a great honour. The Borders sevens circuit at the time was absolutely huge; it was one of the biggest things anywhere in Scottish sport and, to get ourselves ready for the Middlesex tournament, we went up to train with Langholm in the Borders every Sunday for weeks.

We would drive up early on a Sunday, the trip would take three to four hours, then we would train, have lunch and drive back. It shows how seriously we took our rugby at Headingley because, strict amateurs or not, there was a professional approach to everything we did.

We reached the semi-finals at Middlesex, which was creditable, but then we were invited to the Langholm Sevens in May 1968 because of the link we had forged with them. At the time, Gala were *the* brilliant sevens side; they were going for the title of Kings of the Sevens and they had won every other Borders tournament before Langholm. They had Peter Brown, Arthur Brown, Jock Turner and a host of other internationals.

We met them in the final. They took the lead, but, quite simply, we were not overawed by them because we didn't know any better. We just went for it and in the end we won quite easily and Gala followers were streaming out of the ground before the end. We had a Gala lad playing for us at the time called Allan Bates. His family was still in Gala. They didn't speak to him for ages. Gala's attempts at a sevens sweep was ruined and they were not happy.

The following week, in his column in the *Glasgow Herald*, Bill McLaren made reference to me. Bill, justly famous even then as the best known and best loved rugby commentator of all time, was also an enormously influential newspaper columnist and to have my name in his column was very significant. Suddenly I was flagged up.

Headingley's away game against London Scottish in November 1968 was also significant. 'McGeechan scored a neat solo try,' said a report in the *Daily Telegraph*, although, because of the sensibilities of the time, they could not show the picture of me crossing the line. As I went past the last defenders someone grabbed the pocket of my shorts and they came off. I therefore ran the last 10 metres in my jockstrap. The *Telegraph* could not use it but they did send me a copy. The shorts-free try may have helped alert the Scotland selectors, who were present in force watching the London Scottish players. Maybe the name in the programme of one Ian Robert McGeechan alerted them to a possible Scottish qualification.

So, while I was still only twenty-two on the day I lost my shorts and scored a try, I was now being recognised, though it was to be another four years before I won a cap. In 1968 I was chosen for the Scotland Trial match as fly-half for the Whites, the junior side, with Colin Telfer at fly-half for the Blues. It was one of my first appearances on a Scottish rugby ground. I would have been delighted if I'd been able to impress the Scotland coach then, except that there wasn't one. It would be another two years before Bill Dickinson was appointed to the post of 'adviser to the captain'. Even with the 1971 Lions tour to New Zealand and the great coaching triumph of Carwyn James imminent, the Scottish Rugby Union could not bring themselves to call Bill simply 'coach'.

For the trial, I reported to the North British Hotel, the great railway hotel in Princess Street, Edinburgh, for lunch. The teams dining together in one big room, the Blues at one end and the Whites at the other, we had a brief chat, the forwards sorted out the line-out signals and that was that. We went down to Murrayfield on the same bus to play an international trial.

I was actually sounded out as to my availability for the Scotland tour of Argentina at the end of that season but not selected. I heard afterwards, though, that it was a good one to miss. Jim Telfer, who I knew at the time only by reputation, was the captain and he ran the whole show. Scotland lost the First Test and Ian Robertson and Chris Rea still talk about the aftermath as Telfer prepared the squad to try to save the series in the Second Test. He had them training and training and training. He said: 'We are not leaving this field until we can do a length without a mistake.'

But the boys kept dropping the ball or making other errors. The story is that the moon was coming up, but Jim would still not let them off the field and no one was going to complain. In the end, they slowed down the move so that they could do it without mistakes, which they did. 'Not quick enough,' Jim said.

I played in the Trial matches every year after that and also played for the Anglo-Scots and for Yorkshire. By the 1972–73 season I was captain of Headingley and the great looming threat of the season was that the All Blacks were coming. It seems remarkable now, looking back, but I played against the All Blacks three times in a very short period of time – I played for the Rest of Scotland against them, but I was also made captain of the North-Eastern Counties' team which played them at Bradford and it was another significant match along the road. We lost 9–3, with me in the centre with Peter Warfield, who was to play for England, outside Alan Old. Bill Dickinson came down to watch and I still think it was that game, even though I was eventually capped at fly-half, that persuaded Bill that I could play centre as well.

'McGeechan and Warfield buried their men time and again,' the report said. It was another of those occasions when, realising that I did not have the biggest frame in the world, I tried to smash my opposite number early in the hope that he might be persuaded not to come again. Sometimes it worked.

Ten of that New Zealand team had played in the Test against Wales the week before. I remember our match at Bradford as especially hard and it was played on a particularly dark and dismal Bradford day. But it helped me enormously.

At the time, as usual, I was training hard. Actually, I was training even harder than normal. I was doing five sessions a week outside the normal Headingley sessions because I had decided that there was no way anybody was going to be fitter than me and I prided myself on that. I had just moved to teach at Fir Tree School and there was a hill at the back. I used to run the cross-country course and then do hill sprints, run another lap of the cross-country and then do another set of hill sprints. Sometimes, I would have the pupils running with me, giving them a start and trying to catch them.

As 1972 wore on, Dickinson had to put together the team to play New Zealand at Murrayfield. Things began to go my way even though the Scottish papers, while not conspicuously anti me, were still asking the question, 'Who does this Yorkshire upstart think he is?' with the clear implication that Scotland should stick to their Edinburgh lads.

But at the time Colin Telfer was injured, Ian Robertson had retired and Chris Rea was injured. Fraser Dall was another contender at fly-half, but he had a poor game in a Scotland B match at Inverness.

So, one day in late November, a letter arrived in the post congratulating me on being selected to play for Scotland. It was a moment every bit as emotional as you can imagine. The letter also informed me that I would be provided with a jersey, but that I had to bring my own white shorts and navy socks. I cannot remember if it warned me not to lose the jersey; at the time you were only given one and you had to pay for a replacement – if it was needed. I still have that letter.

Frankly, I was still something of an outsider when I went up to Scotland to play. I vaguely knew most of the team from the Trials, but it was still awesome to come across Ian McLauchlan, Sandy Carmichael and Gordon Brown, all heroes of the Lions tour of the previous year. They had such an aura about them and there was tangible admiration for what they had achieved.

My first international was a great experience. For a start, in those days the Scotland team used to stay at the Braid Hills Hotel. The great thing about that place was that it had a fantastic menu and that we could eat à la carte. We could have fillet steaks, scampi, prawn cocktails. Alastair McHarg was one of the established players and his first piece of advice was that I should get to the hotel as early as possible to start off three days of great eating.

For all the Scotland experience, I have still spent all my life in Yorkshire. I was born and bred there and I have often been asked how I'd have felt if I had been born and bred in somewhere like Hawick or Edinburgh. Firstly, to be chosen for Scotland made me feel incredibly proud because of my father and his connections. On the way up, it was a strange feeling. I was representing my country and, in my heart, that was what it came down to. But I was also representing my father and the family and that was a fantastic feeling, too.

And I was, too, emotionally reminded of my father, as I have already said. The long road from junior rugby in Yorkshire up through the great years with Headingley and into the Scotland system culminated in me playing for Scotland against New Zealand at Murrayfield, the first of all my caps.

As I ran out at Murrayfield to play the All Blacks, a twenty-six-year-old who had lived all his life in Yorkshire, part of me felt that I had arrived. I had come home.

6

Culture of Awkwardness

Playing for Scotland, 1972–79

Members of the Scottish Rugby Union rarely lived at the cutting edge of popular culture, and there was no one quite so fastidious as they were when fighting to uphold the amateur code. They would supply one Scotland jersey for you to wear when playing in front of 60,000 at Murrayfield, and only one, so if you swapped it, lost it or if it faded in the wash, you had to pay for another. And also for your shorts and socks.

But they were occasionally mindful of team morale and also of the superb hospitality we in the Scotland team were afforded by the French whenever we played in Paris. The French rugby authorities entertained us at the Folies Bergère or the Moulin Rouge on the Thursday evening before the game. They were fabulous nights.

So the SRU decided that we would be given a night out on the Thursday evening in London prior to a game in the 1970s against England at Twickenham, and they set to work. Where should we go for our culture? They settled on what they told us was a musical with a religious theme, called *Let My People Come*. It was being staged at something called the Raymond Revuebar. 'It's a great musical apparently, about Moses,' said the organiser of the evening.

There was a series of sketches, of which the most unforgettable was a scene at a hairdresser's with typical hairdresser's chat, about holidays and general gossip, except that the 'customers' were having their pubic hair attended to, not the hair on their heads. The players thought it was hilarious, the committee men present less so. I can't remember if they were wearing their Scottish Rugby Union blazers or not.

Ah. The Scottish Rugby Union. This was the era of the all-powerful Union presidents. Alf Wilson, who had once managed a Lions party, was president in 1972 when I first played. After every match, after we had showered and changed, we would file into the presidential drinks reception in our blazers. The players would all be standing in little circles making small talk before going into the post-match dinner, and the president would instruct one of his committee to come and bring a particular player to an audience with him. 'Ah, McGeechan. Well played today, keep it up.'

Then there would be an announcement. 'Gentlemen, your president will now lead you to dinner.' He would go out of the room first and we would all trek in behind him like sheep. We were the lucky ones. The poor women, the wives and girlfriends who may well have sacrificed as much to the cause as any player, had to find somewhere in Princes Street to eat, dressed up in all their finery. They were not allowed into the dinner itself. They were permitted to attend the dance which followed the dinner, but we had to go out into the central foyer to collect them and bring them into the dinner. They couldn't just come in and join us.

The one-jersey policy lasted for decades. In passing, I might point out that for the 2009 British and Irish Lions tour of South Africa each player was given seventy-six items of kit (and their salaries). Peter Stagg, the Scotland lock of the 1960s, is said to have played for Scotland with large holes in his socks, but to save money he blacked up the areas of white skin with boot polish so that the cameras never noticed. Players who reappeared for Scotland after the Second World War were apparently asked to bring the jersey they had been given pre-war.

If we did swap jerseys with the opposition at the final whistle, which is, after all, one of the sport's grandest traditions, we had to pay for replacements. There were no exceptions. I think it was Sandy Carmichael, the veteran prop, who finally made the break-through and caused the abandonment of that policy. He had won thirty or forty caps and swapped innumerable jerseys but then he decided to strike a blow – he kept the same jersey throughout one season and by its fourth appearance, and after several washes, it had faded to a light blue from the normal dark blue, and it looked very scruffy. The SRU were embarrassed into changing their policy and, from 1974, we were given a brand-new jersey for every game.

I kept my first Scotland Test jersey, which was actually a white one – Scotland always seemed to play in white against the All Blacks. I also kept my first dark-blue Scotland jersey from the match away in Paris, my second cap. Sadly, I have mislaid the pro-gramme from the SRU's night out at the Raymond Revuebar.

When looking back on my Scotland career I have one real regret. I won thirty-two caps for Scotland from 1972 to 1979, twelve at fly-half and twenty at centre, was never dropped from the team and my first twenty-seven caps were won consecutively. I cap-tained Scotland nine times. But in all that time we never won a Grand Slam, or the Championship title or even the Triple Crown. The World Cup had not yet been invented and I made only one overseas tour with my country, to New Zealand in 1975. I played in what might be called an enormous black hole of more than forty years, between the 1930s and 1984, in which Scotland won nothing. Scotland finally won the Grand Slam in 1984, with Jim Telfer coaching, five years after my last cap. We did finish top in 1973 – and bottom. That was the year of the unique five-way tie between all the teams.

But I look back on it now as a fantastic experience. I loved play-ing for Scotland, and to do so was the fulfilment of a dream which was driven by the memory of my Glaswegian father, something which evoked a passion for Scotland and Scottishness in me despite my Yorkshire birth and upbringing and despite the fact that I played all my sport in England. Furthermore, we often played great rugby and what better men to play with than brilliant players like Andy Irvine and Jim Renwick?

At one stage, it seemed that I would never wear the jersey. I was twenty-six when I was first selected, and it was December 1972 that I crossed the Rubicon. Because I began late, many people always assumed that I was younger than I was. Because I had lived and played in England all my life, it took time to get on the radar in Scotland. But when I did, it was just the best of the best, and my lingering sadness that we won nothing starts to fade when I recall all the marvellous experiences I enjoyed.

I can also say that I played in the heyday of the Five Nations Championship and at a time when, with the victories of the 1971 Lions in New Zealand and the 1974 Lions in South Africa, our rugby was on top of the world. I was effectively the reigning Lions Test centre in 1974 and 1977, which gave me great confidence. I trained like a professional; I was incredibly fit. Possibly I may be wearing rose-tinted spectacles, but in that era I seem to recall that all the teams were very competitive. In those days I am sure there were no easy matches.

Wales were regarded as the best team of the period. They had some of the all-time greats, the best players ever to illuminate the Championship – Gareth Edwards, Barry John, Phil Bennett, J. P. R. Williams, Mervyn Davies – but we beat them in both 1973 and 1975 in wonderful occasions at a teeming, thrilled Murrayfield and the latter game was so enormous that it led to the establishment of all-ticket matches. Before 1975 you could still pay at the turnstiles for Murrayfield internationals and for the Wales game the crowd was given officially as 104,250, but the word was that more than 120,000 were present, many unable to see.

But look also at Ireland at the time – they had Willie John McBride, Mike Gibson, Ken Kennedy, Fergus Slattery. England had Fran Cotton, Roger Uttley, Tony Neary, David Duckham,

Andy Ripley, Alan Old. France were improving throughout the seventies, and they developed some frightening forward packs based around the forbidding Gérard Cholley up front and on what may have been the best back row ever seen in the Five Nations – Jean-Claude Skrela, Jean-Pierre Rives and Jean-Pierre Bastiat. It was not as if Grand Slams were easy to come by!

My time in the Scotland team may also have been the heyday of Bill McLaren, the legendary BBC commentator from Hawick, beloved by so many armchair viewers, respected and revered by everyone in the game. He brought his own aura and professionalism to proceedings. It was the heyday, too, of the travelling legions of supporters. The tournament is truncated now, packed into a small part of the season with double-header and triple-header matches, so not so many fans can travel to many games. But it was common for 40,000 Welsh fans to travel to Scotland for the Scotland–Wales match and, wherever we played, there would be thousands of kilted supporters cheering us on. They should extend the Championship again, in my opinion, and play just one game a week. But in the 1970s, the games were massive. Those were heady days.

If we were never dominant, we were at least always hard to beat. I was in my fifteenth game for Scotland before we lost by a margin of more than seven points, and that fifteenth was the famous water polo Test in Auckland, a lottery of a match played on what was nothing less than a lake, when to be trapped at the bottom of a ruck was, without exaggeration, to be in danger of drowning. The referee said that he would whistle up any collapsed scrums or mauls immediately because somebody might be caught under the surface. The ball often landed and just floated on water, and players aquaplaned through it. When we came back into the dressing rooms, they were flooded too, so our shoes and other items were just floating around. It was only played because we had return plane tickets for the next day, and they were non-changeable. Typically, the All Blacks adapted better.

These days there seems to be a rather callow and fresh-faced look to Scotland teams, but in those years the Scotland squad was packed with players of experience, character and edge. 'Scotland's Awkward Squad' was the heading on one article about us and that summed us up.

Bill Dickinson, a rather small, experienced and bespectacled forward who had coached successfully at Jordanhill College, was in charge of the team for most of my Scotland career. He was never called coach, as I have said, because that smacked of professionalism and trying too hard. He was called 'adviser to the captain'. He had taken up his post for the 1971 Scotland–Wales game, one of the most incredible Five Nations matches of them all, won with a last-ditch kick from John Taylor from out near the touchline and described by someone as 'the greatest conversion since St Paul'.

Bill was good. He was a college lecturer and therefore a good communicator, and the core of the team was formed by Bill and his relationship with Ian McLauchlan, the fierce prop who is still universally known as famous Mighty Mouse, and who became captain in 1972. They were both Jordanhill men. Bill was very methodical. We used to train at Murrayfield out on the back pitches. I can also recall sessions in the back dressing room at Murrayfield. The room was always freezing and unheated. Bill would lay out benches and he could stand there, with his glasses perched on top of his head, working a reel-to-reel tape machine, fast-forwarding until he came to the choice bits he wanted to show us. It was invariably useful stuff and it had an impact on me, fuelling a passion for analysis later on. Bill's analytical mind was perfect for the job, and for improvement. He was good on cause and effect, on the likely outcome of the improvements he was suggesting.

Ian McLauchlan, the Mouse, was a hard character. He stood around five foot seven, which is small for a scrum-half, let alone a prop. And when he arrived on the scene those who didn't know him well could not believe that he would ever make it. He went on the 1971 Lions tour, very much as a back-up to Ray

McLoughlin, the Irish loose head, but then McLoughlin broke a thumb and McLauchlan was catapulted into the Test series. He was outstanding and, by 1974, when he went with the unbeaten Lions, he was dominant against the massive Springboks. As one writer said, he 'took on all-comers with a rasping disdain'.

The Test series in 1971 gave Ian a terrific boost to his confidence. He was the best captain I ever had, the best of all my leaders. He set a terrific example and, as Jim Telfer used to say of him: 'If his granny was in front of him, if she was in the way of him getting the ball, he would have stood on her.' He had that focus, and it was famous in Scottish club rugby that if you played against the Mouse then you got away with nothing.

In the build-up to one of the matches against Wales at Murrayfield, Gerald Davies, who was playing for Wales on the wing, was quoted in the *Scotsman* as saying that he would 'like to be a fly on the wall of McLauchlan's team talk'. That suggested to me that Wales were being influenced by the Mouse as well, that they understood the strength of his character and that he was impacting on them before match day had even dawned. He became a member of the senior players' group on the 1974 Lions tour of South Africa, and he was a good influence on me. He would encourage me to keep working and improving, suggesting that there was a Test place in the offing.

With the Mouse on the loose head, with Sandy Carmichael on the tight and a hooker as good as Duncan Madsen, we had the basis of a worldly and aggressive pack. In the second row we generally had Gordon Brown, who made all three of the Lions tours in the 1970s and was seen before his untimely death (and after) as one of the great locks, and alongside him Alastair McHarg. This was well before the time when forwards were not expected to go into every breakdown; in those days they all went into almost every ruck and maul. But McHarg's preference for missing the odd ruck and popping up all round the back division was unique. It endeared him to crowds and I once named him the centre I most enjoyed playing alongside. He was a great character and player.

The team was built round that grizzled core, and also round another core of players from the Borders, led by Renwick, Alastair Cranston, Colin Telfer and others.

But with all that forward muscle, we needed a counterpoint, we needed spokesmen in the backs. I suppose Andy Irvine was the darling of Scotland rugby, then and even now. He was our talisman, and he made three Lions tours into the bargain. The essence of Andy was his confidence. Even in training, he was supremely sure of himself and for me that was absolutely fantastic. I tended to be quieter and more reserved, but Andy was full-on, he was quick and had fantastic ability, and he tended to infect the rest of the team with his optimism.

Maybe I couldn't compare in every way with him so the only target I set myself was to be quicker than Andy over 30 yards, which I eventually achieved. But Andy was pacey, he was quick over 100 yards, he was a bit bigger than me and unless he had one of those days when he tried to run too much and was caught behind the advantage line, he was superb. To choose when to run was the key for him.

He was also important in maintaining the balance in a team, with the strong forwards coach and the strong characters up front. The forwards could easily have dominated that team. Bill Dickinson was a big set-piece man and, forwards being forwards, they were essentially a conservative crew. So Andy gave us the voice. He would often tempt fate. When the session was starting with touch and pass, he would go up to the Mouse and say: 'Mouse. Do you want to touch me now? Because that's the only chance you are going to get!' You had to be good to say things like that to Ian McLauchlan.

But Bill Dickinson was very clever and very subtle with Andy. He had to persuade him to vary things by simply passing the ball on occasionally, and not trying to beat a man every time. Bill told Andy that he could do damage just because he was there, that he could often be effective acting as a decoy and a draw for the defence and that we shouldn't just look to launch Andy every time. But

Andy had an excitement and a freshness that was so different from the dour Scottish image. He made us bubblier and quicker and the truth is that in that team we played a hell of a lot of rugby.

Jim Renwick, the sidestepping genius of the midfield, was a diamond. For my money, he was one of those players loved throughout the Championship, no matter which side you supported. Jim was and is a quiet man, but he has a sense of humour and a razor-sharp mind, both for rugby and for life. Even now, I sit with Jim and Andy at some of the internationals and revel in their conversation. Jim is not directly involved any more but he still shows great astuteness in his comments on the action before him. Again, he had a strength of character which balanced up the influence of the forwards.

Our style was no mystery. We rucked. It was our trademark. We played quickly, at pace, and we were mobile. Our body positions were superb at the ruck, and we did it better at the time than any other team except the All Blacks, and they came from the home of rucking. Ruck ball tended to give you quick ball, and we were ready to have a go with it. I could sidestep, Jim could sidestep and Andy could sidestep. It meant that if one of us got into a bit of space, we would just have a crack. Billy Steele was a dangerous wing outside. If you half-beat somebody, if you were caught, the forwards were in behind you for the ruck, clearing the ball again, and off we would go. Someone once described our rucking style as 'just like a big *whoosh* here, a *whoosh* there and a *whoosh* there'.

It was a crying shame for Scottish rugby that so very few of these giants of the 1970s remained in the game, because they could have wielded enormous influence. But at the time, and also far more recently, you felt that the Scottish Rugby Union, being arch-conservatives, would rather that the players were seen and not heard, that if they won too many games on the trot then they would somehow become too powerful. It was almost as if they did not want the players getting too big and preferred them not to win too many games.

There was the same feeling markedly in 1990 after we had won our famous Grand Slam by beating England. You sensed that the committee were jealous of the credit so rightly given to the likes of Finlay Calder, John Jeffrey, the Hastings brothers and David Sole and the others. Back in the 1970s, I think that the SRU were quite happy when the Mouse and some of the others wrote books. At the time, if you took royalties from your book it meant that you were professionalised and could play no further formal part in rugby. Once those books were written, the SRU did not have to worry about the influence of those players; they could easily be kept at arm's length.

Too often, the SRU committee members were not former players with a grasp of the modern game, but long-serving committeemen who, by the time they reached grandee status, were very out of touch. There were some shining exceptions, but not many.

When I became a regular with Scotland, but was still playing for Headingley and still living in Leeds, Judy and I had it in mind that we might move up to Scotland, thus making life much easier. But in the end we stayed, and never again seriously considered moving north. Judy and I were very happy in Leeds, and I was in my first full year teaching at Fir Tree Middle School. At the time, the local education authority were developing a string of middle schools and they wanted some secondary school teachers to become involved in the middle school sector. So I went to Fir Tree from Moor Grange in September 1972, only three months before I won my first Scottish cap, and joined the staff with only two male teachers and around twenty women. My entire playing career was conducted while I was at Fir Tree and the school was absolutely superb with me, especially Ken Cobbett, the headmaster, who was always so understanding and helpful. I had briefly looked at the possibility of teaching in Scotland but different certificates were needed there anyway.

To illustrate the support the staff and the school gave me, I would miss school on the Thursday and Friday prior to inter-nationals, having travelled up on the Wednesday evening to

Scotland, and then head back on Sunday, to be in school first thing on Monday morning. I would train five days a week at school into the bargain. Once I had got into the Scotland team, relatively late at the age of twenty-six, I was absolutely determined that I would not relinquish the jersey easily, so I trained and trained.

Driving up to Scotland for my first cap, at fly-half, passing through the Borders and approaching Edinburgh, I realised then that I was about to cross my personal Rubicon. I can remember watching the sun set over Edinburgh on a December Friday and being struck by the reality that, when it set again the following day, I would be an international rugby player.

But before that, dinner. The Braid Hills Hotel, an old-fashioned, turreted building on the outskirts of the city, was our headquarters for many seasons, and it was fantastic. We were allowed to eat à la carte, and for some young squad men, notably those not earning much, it was a joy. The food was excellent: prawn cocktails, smoked salmon, fillet steaks, gammon steaks. Those of us who played our rugby outside Scotland used to check in on the Wednesday night to be ready for the Thursday morning training session, so we had an extra night there. Mention the Braid Hills scampi to any ex-Scotland player of a certain vintage and he will go misty-eyed. If you were dropped, it was a toss-up whether you missed the match or the food more.

To play against New Zealand as a new cap, on the day of high emotion in December 1972, was obviously a remarkable experience, although, as I have explained, my chief memory of the day is not the match, but the encounter with the pipe major of the band from Queen Victoria School in Dunblane. He had known my dad in earlier days. It was a sad reminder that Dad was not there to watch me win my first cap and, after speaking to the pipe major, it took some doing to switch on completely to the demands of playing the All Blacks.

And yet it was an incredible game in which to start. I dropped seven goals for Scotland in my career, and my first came against New Zealand that day, to bring us back to 6–10, with the game still in the balance. Players these days steady themselves to drop for goal but I tended to let fly with the drop when I was running at top speed. In fact, I took pride in it, and that is how my first points for Scotland arrived.

We were still putting the All Blacks under pressure in the last ten minutes of the game and trailing by only 10–9 but a pass from Alastair McHarg was intercepted by Sid Going and Going ran about 70 yards to score and win the match. It could so easily have gone the other way and yet I suppose that this was an early lesson in playing New Zealand – a lesson reinforced every time I met them as player or coach – that absolutely everything had to go right for the full eighty minutes if you were to have any chance of beating them.

There was another drop goal in my second match, this time away to France in Paris. People talk about the atmosphere generated these days in the Stade de France in the north of Paris, and it is certainly a beautiful stadium, but it is nothing compared to the hostility that we visiting teams had to encounter in the Parc des Princes, in the south-west of the city, where they used to stage the internationals. It was a real bear pit. Alan Lawson, our scrum-half, scored a try after I had put in a high kick but we were to lose 16–13 – more evidence that if we were not overwhelmingly brilliant at the time then we were still difficult to beat.

I dropped my goal in Paris from near the halfway line and, just in case, I chased it like mad after I hit it. I think that the origin of the drop kick on the run was in the games of kicking and gaining we used to play at Headingley, and if you caught the ball on the full you could drop for goal if you were within range. We were handicapped slightly in comparison with today's kickers and notably so compared to the new technology, which sees the ball fly long and true. We would be using the old leather Gilbert balls, which you had to clean and dubbin; they would also suck up water and become heavier. The more they were used, the less oval and the more round they became; I suppose towards the end of the season it was as if you were playing with a football.

In Paris, Jim Renwick, Alastair Cranston and myself had a big night out on the rum and Cokes. I think the feeling was that my stint was over. I had come into the team because of injuries, but Colin Telfer, the usual starting fly-half, would be fit for the Welsh game. But at this point I realised how much good I had done myself earlier in the season, when playing for the Northern Counties at Bradford against the All Blacks in the centre. Bill Dickinson had come to watch me and I had clearly made an impression on him, so when Colin came back for the Wales game, I stayed in the team in the centre.

But it was only in that game, which we won 10–9, that I felt I was coming to grips with the international game. My club rugby at Headingley was of a good standard, but it was a massive step-up to play international rugby. I knew that I was fit enough because of all the work I put in, I knew that my skills were good enough because we all worked so hard on the basics. So the only thing that I had to adjust was my brain, because I found that in internationals you had two or three seconds fewer to react than you did at club level. This made it a joy to go back to play for Headingley, because, suddenly, you felt that you had so much time. But those early games were a real learning experience.

Wales, the dominant team of the 1970s, found that day just how horrible it really was to scrummage against the Mouse and Sandy Carmichael. They were absolutely hammered in the scrum and this was also the day when Doug Morgan at scrum-half set out to climb all over Gareth Edwards, and taught me valuable lessons for the future in how to upset the opposing number nine – everyone from Gareth to Nick Farr-Jones of Australia to Joost van der Westhuizen of South Africa was to be a beneficiary of Doug's legacy. He stood on Gareth's feet, he nudged him, barged him and was all over him like a rash. So for the first time, and at the third attempt, I tasted victory in the Scotland jersey. And I also made a contribution. I followed up a kick ahead, and hammered J. P. R. Williams into the Welsh in-goal to set up a five-yard scrum. Colin Telfer started running diagonally, we executed a dummy scissors movement with me going back on the dummy line, Colin showed me the ball and dummied and went in to score, and his try won the match.

So I was embarked on my Test career. We had our frustrations, and we had our moments. After the defeat by New Zealand in 1972 it was well over three years before we lost at Murrayfield again which, for a country with the small resources of Scotland, was a considerable achievement. In 1973 we beat Ireland at Murrayfield for the first time in ten years, with another drop goal on the run from me. We then lost at Twickenham after leading until quite late on. I remember Peter Brown and I making a try for Billy Steele but also Ian McLauchlan playing even though he had broken his leg three weeks before the game. It was braveness in the extreme, but also a mistake, because he was nothing remotely like his true self and the knowledge that he was not really fit to play had an effect on the team.

In the next season, we beat England 16–14 at Murrayfield, when David Duckham fell offside at the end and Andy Irvine kicked a beautiful winning goal from 40 metres in injury time, and we played really well against France, winning 19–6. Andy launched a move from his own half, we moved the ball well and Lewis Dick scored. We were winning well at Murrayfield, we were competitive, and I was playing well enough to be mentioned as a possible Lion in South Africa in 1974.

The 1975 season really should have been our Grand Slam year, because we were the best team in the Five Nations. We beat Ireland by 20–13 at Murrayfield, with another drop goal from me on the back of another tremendous effort from the pack; maddeningly, we then lost 10–9 to France in Paris, when Andy Irvine missed six kicks at goal, including one from almost in front of the posts.

We beat Wales at Murrayfield in front of that mega crowd, with rows and rows of schoolboys in their caps being allowed to sit around the grass on the fringes of the pitch because of the crush in the terraces, something that would never be allowed today. Then we went to Twickenham, so often the graveyard of Scottish rugby aspirations. We were the better side, England were poor and yet we lost 7–6 – Doug Morgan missed a late kick this time, again from almost in front of the posts. The two wins at Murrayfield had been wonderful games, but the two away games, in which we were superior, had ended in sheer frustration. It was the last time we really came close to the title.

We did beat Australia later in 1975, however. It was one of the best post-war Scotland wins and it came at a time when I was playing as well as at any time in my career, with the confidence of the 1974 Lions tour in the bank. I was also heavier, at twelve stone three. In the first half, we moved the ball from a ruck and I passed across three players. I came round on the outside break and they had us covered. So I missed out the next two, passed long and straight to Lewis and he sneaked over in the corner. In the second half, I intercepted a pass, ran on and put Jim Renwick over and we had tasted the blood of the Southern Hemisphere for the first time. It became addictive.

Our run of success at Murrayfield ended when we lost to France in the first game of the 1976 Five Nations Championship and then we lost heavily in Wales in a bizarre match. André Cluny, the French referee, was injured early on but refused to be replaced. He probably concluded that it would be his only chance to referee a Test match (he was right) and he hobbled around yards and yards behind play. Sometimes, he might be 50 yards away while we hung around waiting for his decision.

We recovered with a tremendous 22–12 win over England and then won away in Dublin for the first time in a decade. And for my twenty-first game, sadly a 26–6 defeat at Twickenham, I captained Scotland for the first time. It was a milestone for me. Bill Dickinson had already asked me to run sessions, and to call the moves, evidence that he was trusting me more and more. The captaincy came reasonably easily to me. Wherever I had played I had always talked to players after games, and after five years with confidants such as the Mouse, Andy and Jim, I felt part of the senior group. I also remember that first match as captain for the look in the eyes of Jim Aitken, the prop. He had a macho image as a player, but that day he was incredibly nervous and you wondered when you looked into the whites of his eyes whether he would be there when he was needed.

The other memory of that season is a gory one. We played France in Paris, lost 23–3 and Gérard Cholley tried to punch us off the field. It was brutal. He felled Donald MacDonald, also punched Ron Wilson and Jim Renwick, and the referee, Meirion Joseph of Wales, opted out completely. It was a horrible running battle. One report said that 'Cholley went along a line of Scottish players punching them like a conductor collecting tickets'.

By now, though, the team was starting to break up; the influence of the Mouse was waning. That settled group that had been together for four years began to disappear, and we took a while to adjust. In 1978, as before, we never really lost badly, but we just couldn't win; we lacked the edge to snatch victory from the jaws of defeat. For example, we threw away a draw in Dublin when Doug Morgan, obsessed with the idea of going for the win and the Triple Crown instead of a draw, ran a kickable penalty towards the end and we were held out. That was not popular in the dressing room. We then led 13–0 against France but our excitement got the better of us and we were overhauled, Doug Morgan put us back level with a drop goal and then Jean-Michel Aguirre gave France the match late on, with a penalty.

The season 1978–79 was my last in the Scotland jersey. Bill Dickinson had gone and Nairn MacEwan, who had been a fine flanker, was now in charge. Ludicrously, he was still called 'adviser to the captain'. Scotland won only one of the fourteen games in which he was in charge and, by 1980, after I had left the scene, Jim Telfer came in as coach.

In 1978, we lost 18–9 to New Zealand, who won the Grand Slam against the four Home Unions. The margin of victory against Scotland was the narrowest. We scored a brilliant try at home to Wales, with the young and promising John Rutherford in at fly-half alongside me in the centre. Rutherford, who was to become one of the great Scotland fly-halves, made a classic break, I carried the move on with Alan Tomes, the new lock, and it ended with Andy Irvine scoring at the posts. But again, sheer frustration as Wales came back to win.

We drew at home to Ireland and then, in Paris, we led well into the second half after a try by Andy Irvine. The match may have summed up our history during that era. It was a cracking game, but we were not quite good enough to hold on and come through, and the chance of an incredible, rare win in Paris disappeared. In the final reckoning, I had won eleven and drawn two of my thirty-two Scotland Tests.

I had never intended to retire at that stage but I badly damaged my cartilage playing in a charity game at Ayr in the pre-season of 1979–80. The recommended treatment was that I carry on until the knee locked again, which it did in August at Headingley during pre-season training. In those days, it took a long time to come back from a cartilage operation, and it was only in the February that I started playing again. I was unfit for all the Scotland Test matches that season, my first long absence from the game.

I was determined that I would not end my career injured, however, so I got myself fit, played out the season with Headingley and retired from rugby altogether – from Headingley, Murrayfield, Braid Hills and from Scotland, from the jersey that I had sought in order to honour my Scottish father and my Scottish blood.

Four years after I retired, Scotland, under Jim Telfer, won a Grand Slam, beating France at Murrayfield to seal it, and restoring Scotland to the top table of the world game. It would have been tremendous to have been party to that achievement, tremendous to have had just something concrete to show.

Yet surely the criterion for a happy career, and the best way to reflect on things in later life, is to be able to say that you wouldn't have wanted to play at any other time, in any other era. It was all a magnificent experience, playing before gigantic crowds, sometimes thrilling a roaring Murrayfield, shaking the best teams to their boots, and doing it alongside some of the most colourful, rumbustious characters in sport.

And all for nothing? Well, we had one free jersey, and the finest memories.

7

The Wonderful Millar Men

The 1974 Lions tour of South Africa

When they sat down together, side by side, with their great weathered and battered faces and stiff movements, they looked as if they would be more at home on Mount Rushmore. The two massive Ulstermen, Syd Millar and Willie John McBride, coach and captain respectively and, between them, the core of the 1974 Lions, were almost slumped in the dressing room under the stands at Newlands, Cape Town. McBride, like the rest of us, was caked in mud; it had been a Test played on a bog, such a contrast to the brown, baked, arid, high-veldt fields where most of the 1974 Lions tour was played.

Dick Milliken, the Irish centre, and I also sat together. We had been the Lions centres that day, as we were to be for the entire four-match series, and in those heady months in South Africa we developed an almost telepathic understanding in the midfield, and a friendship off the field that survives strongly to this day.

It was our first Lions tour. Of course, Dick and I were well aware of Lions history, aware that, in fact, almost all the Lions teams that had ever toured had gone home defeated. So, in terms of history, I was not supposed to be confident, even after the 1971

Lions tour when those marvellous pathfinders has beaten the All Blacks and everyone in British and Irish rugby had grown a little.

But I *was* confident. As the tour progressed, every day was better than the last. I loved the whole wonderful experience, the special rhythm and glamour of a Lions tour. What a marvellous arena in which to play rugby, in which to train like a professional player for the first time in my life. Quite fantastic.

And I never thought for a moment that we would not beat the Springboks, even though we had never beaten them before British and Irish rugby was on top of the world, we had won in 1971 in New Zealand, and the Five Nations Championship was also in its pomp. These days there always seem to be a couple of teams in the Six Nations (Italy joined in 2000) going through a rough patch and therefore relatively easy to beat. In the 1970s, however, all the teams were competitive and some were outstanding.

The 1974 tour was to become the first ever unbeaten Lions tour. We won twenty-one of the twenty-two matches we played, and we drew one only because the referee, Max Baise, refused to award a perfectly good try in the last moments of the last match. 'Well,' he said. 'It's all right for you; you are all going home after this. I have to live here.' Statistically, it was the greatest Lions tour, a magnificent crusade.

The tour was brilliantly launched by that 12–3 victory in the First Test in Cape Town. Dick Milliken and I were both really pleased with the win; we were 1–0 up in the series, thank you very much. Yet Syd and Willie were quiet, and far more reflective. As I watched them I recalled my own career to date and realised that to reach this point, sitting weathered, battered but victorious in the Newlands dressing room, those two warriors had endured so many Lions defeats, had been beaten twice before with the Lions in the incredibly physical, even brutal arena of a Lions series in South Africa.

We both looked across at the two massive Irishmen. It wasn't anything that they said or did. It was just the look in their eyes. It was a look that was completely different, a look of elation, a look

I had never seen before, I suppose. The meaning of this Test and the tour to two first-time Lions playing in a great Lions team and wide-eyed at it all, and their meaning to two old warriors who had suffered and grafted for it was something on a different plane altogether. Maybe all we'd done was to win another game, another international match. Or maybe it was something really, really special.

It was not the last time we were to see that look of silent eloquence during our African tour. Syd and Willie were to enjoy that blissful moment again. And again.

But first, way before we even met, and the day the squad for the 1974 Lions tour was officially announced, I was faced with a tricky point of etiquette and manners. What *was* the correct way to address Gareth Edwards? Should you ask permission before speaking to him? I would have to check because I had just learned that I would be spending more than three months with a man who, to this day, I regard as the greatest player there has ever been.

For later Lions tours the squad was announced through the media, or live on television, or even with a kind of Hollywood-style fanfare with loud rock music. In 1974 they sent you a letter. I can't remember if the one I got was second-class. The waiting was the worst part, but once that letter landed on the mat you knew you could stop worrying and enjoy the thrill of anticipation. That long-dreamed-of day had finally arrived. You didn't need to open the letter. Surely they weren't going to drop you a line that said: 'Dear Mr McGeechan, you have *not* been chosen for the British and Irish Lions tour of South Africa' were they?

What most moved me that morning, standing in our hall, was not the wording of the letter but the Lions badge embossed at the head of it. Something mystical had become real, and it had become mine. Gareth had received exactly the same letter as me, after all. So had Willie John McBride, J. P. R. Williams, Phil Bennett, Ian McLauchlan, Fergus Slattery, Gordon Brown and all the other all-time greats. Their letters weren't any longer than mine either.

If anything, I was too excited. I decided that when I joined the party before the tour I would be the fittest I had ever been, and Judy and I used to go out into the fields near where we lived and I would do circuits and sets of sprints, endlessly repeated in all weathers, with Judy standing by holding a stopwatch. I continued this when we actually met up as a Lions squad; I was racing round the training field, trying to lead the field as we ran from corner to corner; then I tried to run the fastest in the touch-and-pass games we played.

Eventually, Ian McLauchlan, one of the senior men in 1971, came up to me. 'Hey,' he said, 'calm down. We are together for three and a half months. You don't have to do all your training in the first session.' Even when we got to South Africa and our training camp in Stilfontein, I was still rushing round. One of Syd Millar's favourite routines was to tell us to run right round the training field as a warm-up. This was fine when there was only one pitch, but when we trained at Stellenbosch there were around eight or nine rugby fields so it was a long way. Billy Steele, the Scotland wing, and I set off at the front, as usual. But Willie John and the old pros had seen enough. 'Hey, slow down and get to the back,' they ordered.

But this tour did indeed make me a professional rugby player for the first time – not in terms of a salary, but in terms of approach. We trained every day, I was the fittest I had ever been and for the first time, with the diet and hard work, I weighed in heavier than 12 stone. I also became very critical about my own game, something which stayed with me until I retired.

There were many great players on the 1974 Lions tour and a Welsh manager in Alun Thomas, but the two pillars of the expedition were those two Ulstermen, Millar and McBride, the captain. They, and more precisely the relationship they had with each other, were pivotal in the success of the tour.

Syd was an outstanding character, hugely influential. Big,

direct, fierce and intelligent, he knew how to deal with us players as people; he was very open. He would talk things through,
share his views, reach a conclusion. Along with Bernard White,
my old coach at Headingley, he is one of the people who have
most influenced me in my own sporting life. They are in the
same class.

On the tour, Syd wouldn't come in and take over a backs session – we were left to our own devices – but he'd come over and
watch us for a while. Then he'd say: 'Can you do that a bit
quicker?' or 'What if you stood a bit wider?' He knew how vital
Gareth was, so he'd give him time off occasionally, treat him like
the thoroughbred he was. Millar dominated that tour.

There are some excellent examples of Syd at his cunning best.
No Lions tour has ever passed without massive refereeing controversy and these were the days before neutral referees. We had
South Africans who, like the aforementioned Max Baise, had to
live there after we'd gone home. I never myself heard any ref say:
'Scrum down, *our* ball', so I am not sure if that was myth or
legend, but it is not entirely without foundation.

On that tour the procedure was that the Lions would choose a
referee for each Test from a list of four handed to them by the
South African Rugby Union. Max Baise had refereed the First Test
and, when the list came for the Second Test for the Lions to
peruse, Baise was not on it, even though we had been reasonably
happy with him. To our horror the name of Cas de Bruyn, who
had refereed one of our early tour matches very badly, was on the
list. No way would he get our vote.

So we were staggered when Syd told us that he was going to opt
for de Bruyn. A nightmare, we felt. Syd looked at us. 'Look. I'll
tell you why we are going for de Bruyn,' he said. 'It is because he
thinks he will never referee a Test match. He thinks that we think
he is a terrible ref and would never go for him. So when he hears
that he is doing the Test, he will realise that the Lions have chosen
him; he will be appreciative, and he will be honest.' Syd was right.
It worked.

And Syd Millar understood South Africa, too. On a Lions tour you have to take in everything around you and absorb it. Syd had been there, as a Lion under pressure and in defeat in 1962 and 1968 (and also in New Zealand in 1959) and he realised that, until you had been involved in something like a Lions Test, you had no idea what it entailed.

It was in South Africa that I first grasped the importance of coming to terms with the environment. Rather than fight it or be afraid of it, you had to make it work for you, come to terms with all its vicissitudes. There would be problems of climate, conditions, refereeing, even the peculiarities of the local culture, and so many other things, but they all had to be taken on board, without complaint. They had to be seen as part of the challenge. Bare, brown fields and odd, panelled balls? Get on with it.

In any case, the Lions were and still are absolutely massive in South Africa, not least for someone like me who had been used to playing in front of five hundred spectators at Headingley. Playing for Scotland, you had crowds of 60,000 or more but in South Africa it was way above even that. On that tour, and decades before the advent of sports ground safety acts, the stadiums used to hold vast numbers and there was an incredible raw intensity about the whole experience.

We went on tour long before the age of the mass media, the internet and satellite television providing wall-to-wall coverage. There were books and magazines about us, but nothing else. Yet everyone knew who we were, and they bought into the great adventure we had embarked upon.

It was also important to get into what might be called a tour mindset. All our loved ones were thousands of miles away; this was long before the time in sport when wives and girlfriends toured with their men. Ringing home was a rigmarole so letters from home, plus your responses, would go to a disembodied box number somewhere in Johannesburg. It was interminable.

It was all yet another amazingly useful lesson for the future. You do get homesick, of course, but you have to flick a switch and think about things in a different way. You have to tell yourself that for the next three and a half months this is your life.

Of course, this all wavers a little when you actually get letters from home, but those tough tours and even the shorter tours of today, when communications are so much easier, demand a tough attitude. In South Africa you might be playing at altitude one day, at sea level later in the week, and on the edge of the desert the week after. In 1974 we had that resolution, that mental hardness, to cope.

The priceless gift we had in 1974 was a winning mentality. The 1971 Lions in New Zealand had reversed history. Those 1974 Lions who had toured in 1971 by now expected to win; they *expected* to beat South Africa and in terms of mindset that was a hell of a thing. It is the kind of mentality that I have looked for in players when choosing squads for every subsequent Lions tour I have been involved with.

It was intense from the very first game in Potchefstroom, where Gordon Brown kicked off the tour with a try in the corner. I can still remember pulling the jersey on over my head for the first time, and standing there wearing the Lions kit. That sense of wonder was not diminished even a tiny bit by the knowledge that we had to give back the jerseys at the end of the match so that they could be sent to the laundry, a far cry from today when there is a pristine kit laid out for each game, each bearing the players' initials.

It is also important to remember that in those days we were not faced with a totally hostile environment. In recent tours of New Zealand, there has been a hostility and lack of respect for the Lions but South Africans have always bought into what we are. Just walking round the stadium in Potchefstroom in '74, we found that the home supporters went absolutely berserk. These were the days when children were still given half-day holidays when the Lions were in town. We were an event wherever we stopped. We went around schools and social clubs and there was an excitement and buzz and an appreciation whenever we were present.

And since then, too, I've always tried to get across to players the significance of what we are in their eyes, and in understanding that this is one of the biggest things they will ever be involved in.

Among all the big numbers and significant statistics on tour, another number loomed. That was the number ninety-nine. Amazingly enough, the ninety-nine call seems to be as much associated with the 1974 tour as the 3–0 victory itself.

We brought in the notorious ninety-nine call after the brutal match against Eastern Province in Port Elizabeth – and it is amazing how many tours in history have featured a brutal match against Eastern Province. Recently, one of the television stations in the UK showed that game and the thuggery now seems so out of place, and every bit as bad as I remember. The cheap shots came in torrents.

There had been talk in the senior players' group meetings about standing firm against South African intimidation and the need for this came out into the open after the Eastern Province game. We held a highly charged team meeting at which Syd and Willie John spoke bluntly. We were no longer going to take a backward step on the whole of the South African tour, they declared. It was us against South African players and referees, and we were going to look after each other. We decided that if their players wanted to try to intimidate us, then we would all get involved and stand together, and that was the basis of the ninety-nine call.

The idea was that the team leaders would call ninety-nine if they felt that one of us had been picked on. The other basis of the whole plan was the conviction that the referee would never send off all fifteen. And that was how it went. There is no question that some of the scenes from that tour were totally unedifying, although, as far as I can remember, the only occasion the ninety-nine call was used in a Test match was in the Third Test in Port Elizabeth, another brutal game when South Africa knew that if they lost they were dead in the series.

It must be said that Dick Milliken and I were not among the

most enthusiastic participants when ninety-nine was called, although I am pleased to say that we offered as much verbal encouragement to the forwards as we possibly could . . . There was also the problem of J. P. R. Williams at full-back. JPR was very keen on the ninety-nine call, and he was so anxious not to miss out on it that for almost every call made, even if it was for the line-out or a back move, he would come rushing up just to check that it was not the ninety-nine. 'He drove me nuts,' Phil Bennett said.

On one occasion, JPR ran about 30 metres to join in, threw a few punches and stood there with his fists raised ready for the next bout. These days such matters would rightly be castigated, but I suppose then it was just recognition that Lions teams had been pushed around for far too long and weren't going to put up with it any longer.

One big question that came out of the tour was whether or not we were the greatest Lions ever. Not everyone thought so. After the tour the British journalist John Reason published a book in which he played down our achievements, devalued our victory, first because he said we had kicked all the time and second because, according to him, South Africa were rubbish anyway and easy to beat.

Anyone who took the field on that tour knew how wrong he was. South Africa's selectors made errors, they threw out too many players after the First Test, but we thought that they had some great players, big men who were also clever. They could play all right. The South African back division in 1974 was every bit as good as the New Zealand backs in 1971, and the idea that there is any such thing as an easy Lions tour of South Africa is almost too ridiculous for words.

We also had a reputation for playing forward-dominated rugby, based on the rare sight of a South African pack under major pressure from the Lions. One or two critics seem to recall that we played totally boring rugby; it was almost as if we were expected to apologise for what we did. We knew we had to win up front, and

Syd worked hard on us keeping the ball off the ground, and keeping control of the ball in the mauls. We did have big line-out forwards and a really good scrummage, and we had hard men such as Roger Uttley in the back row. So we were taking the South Africans on at their own game, something which shook them to their boots because they had never contemplated it.

On the other hand, we did play some outstanding rugby and we did score incredible tries. We played rugby with the ball moving from forwards to backs, and backs to forwards, and the try count in the Tests in our favour was massive.

It was also on that tour that I received what was probably my greatest ever compliment. It came from J. P. R. Williams, who has probably long since forgotten that he ever paid it. The great Welsh full-back was on his second epic Lions tour. He had been a giant in the stunning Lions win over New Zealand in 1971, and in 1974 he was so outstanding that one book described him as 'playing with a towering command of his game'.

Dick Milliken and I had worked out between us that the opposition were going to be at least a stone heavier than us, but that not only were we going to be cleverer to make up for it, but we were not going to let anyone past us in midfield. As far as I can remember we did not let anyone through us in a Test match, and JPR never had to make a tackle on an opposing player who had cut through the middle. We just stood our ground, and if they tried to get outside us our fitness and pace came into it. I even remember making tackles wide out on the flank.

At some point during the tour, JPR addressed us both. 'It's great playing behind you two,' he said. At that point, Dick and I reckoned that we could die happy, secure in the knowledge that we had played for the greatest of all Lions teams. For that, in my opinion, is what the 1974 Lions were.

If the key men on tour were obviously Syd Millar and Willie John McBride, the record states that men like Gareth Edwards at scrum-half and JPR at full-back were also central to the whole endeavour. But there were many others and I am going to single out Fergus Slattery, a Dublin solicitor and the Irish flanker, veteran of the 1971 tour but in 1974 at the peak of his abilities as a player and tourist. Slats was an amazing figure because he played it ferociously hard on and off the field.

And he was quick. He would come and train with the backs because to run with the forwards would have been silly. Syd would have us sprinting ten sets of 100 yards, with thirty seconds rest in between. Then we would repeat the set again. Fergus would join in, he would keep up all the way, and then often at the end of the session you would either see or hear him throwing up on the field, as the beer from the previous night came up. Then he would bounce back up for the next set of sprints.

On the field he was absolutely brilliant. He underlined for me a defensive principle that I have stuck with ever since, and driven into all the teams I have coached. It is that the most important defensive player is the man just inside the ball and just inside you as you go up.

Fergus would not only talk to the opposition. He would say to the scrum-half: 'Don't run now. If you run now, I've got you.' He would also be screaming at us. When Dick and I were going up in defence, he would be bawling: 'I'm on your inside! I'm on your inside! If he comes this way, I'll smash him.' Dick and I were just so comfortable, absolutely confident that no one would get through by stepping inside.

There was a parallel with this on the 1997 tour, because Scott Gibbs was a latter-day Fergus Slattery in the way he dominated the middle. He would almost be dragging his inside man along, shouting, 'I want you with me, I want you with me. We're going to make some hits.' Defensive players with this kind of authority are priceless.

Dick Milliken was the perfect man to play alongside. He was much younger than me, and if he had not been injured in the year after the 1974 tour he would probably have been in the Irish team for many more years. He was great to work with because as a pair we would look after each other.

Although Andy Ripley was a terrific player, Mervyn Davies played in all four of the Tests. Mervyn was a player's player, so clever, silky even. He had a huge skill set, his hands were brilliant and he gave Gareth Edwards the space to play. He was not a heavyweight but he was very brave, and he would put his body over the ball. We had Andy Irvine and J. J. Williams on the wing, and it was JJ who scored some of the signature tries, especially with his party trick of chipping the ball ahead and using his great pace to get to it first. Fran Cotton was a fantastic rock at tight head. The list was endless.

The characters on that tour were also incredible. First, it was a squad without bad apples, without a corrosive element; it was only much later that I realised fully how much damage can be done to an entire tour and the environment by people who are disruptive in their various ways. Bobby Windsor has passed into legend for his exploits on that trip, because, like Fergus Slattery, he played hard on and off the field. The amazing thing is that all the stories about him were actually true, including his response to a waiter who asked him what kind of omelette he wanted.

'An egg one,' he said.

Bobby always found a way of reducing his bills or the cost of his calls home. He got hold of a key to the room of the manager, Alun Thomas, and would let himself in to make calls whenever Thomas was out. One day the manager walked into a team meeting brandishing a long bill. He asked who had been putting calls on his bill. There was dead silence.

The telephone numbers dialled were all listed on the bill. Thomas read out the number. It was a Pontypool code and number. 'Right,' said Bobby immediately. 'Which one of you bastards has been phoning my wife?'

Although, in the end, Andy Ripley just lost out to the great Mervyn Davies as number eight in the Test series, he was another amazing character – he was then and he still is now with his successful and inspiring battle against prostate cancer – during the trip. He was an absolutely incredible athlete. And a joker. He was once ordered by the manager to wear the regulation tour rig of bow tie to a formal function after he had turned up in an open-necked shirt. Ripley dutifully went back to his room and returned wearing the bow tie as instructed, but over a T-shirt instead of his dress shirt. On it were the words 'If you want a really hard drink, drink wet cement'.

Andy did not even take a case on tour. He stuffed everything into the Lions duffel bags that we were all given. Into those bags went his blazers, his kit, whatever. When I shared a room with him I discovered that he just tipped everything out in a pile in the corner. His pride and joy was a pair of leather boots. If he wasn't wearing them, he would tie them together and hang them round his neck, just to make sure they went with him.

It is also important to remember the kind of reserve strength that we had. Geoff Evans and Roy Bergiers were the other centres on that tour, and at the very start I was looking at them and I could not believe I would become a regular in the Test team. Phil Bennett was in excellent form on the '74 tour, far better than he would be under the burden of captaincy and homesickness in New Zealand three years later, and we also had Alan Old, a strong contender for fly-half in the First Test until he was injured. Gordon Brown was a fantastic lock, larger than life, and he achieved an ambition on the tour he had always cherished – he played golf with Gary Player. With a broken bone in one hand.

Life as a Lion could be glamorous. All sorts of delights were laid on for us, and there was a natural, warm hospitality. There was probably far too much in fact. They would have golf clubs just waiting for us to play their courses. On Sundays, we would accept invitations from families and groups of friends. Entertainment usually consisted of a barbecue in the garden by the swimming pool, spending time with people with seriously big houses. They would invite all their friends, so there might be fifty or sixty other guests there, against perhaps two or three Lions. We would have a good Sunday, and then, in the evening, they would drive us back to our hotel. I loved it.

How things change. You feel that modern players would run a mile before taking part in something like that. But remember that in 1974 we were away for nearly four months, and some of the hotels were not quite what they are today. So to socialise, or to go golfing or sailing or game-spotting, would be a fantastic diversion.

Naturally, in terms of absorbing the culture you had to understand that you never really won a game in South Africa. Each game was merely a preparation for another one somewhere else down the track. It was a case of 'Wait till you get to Free State'. If you won against Free State, it would be 'Ah, but wait till you get to Transvaal'. If you beat Transvaal, it would be 'Wait till you get to Western Province'. As it went on and the bandwagon grew bigger and bigger, people would travel hundreds of miles to the games. And perhaps best of all – and this is a tribute to South African rugby followers of the era – the atmosphere never became poisoned even when we were marching through the tour and even when we went 3–0 up in the series.

Less edifying was the evidence of segregation. To go somewhere like Bloemfontein or Kimberley was a very uncomfortable and unpleasant experience, because there you encountered all the petty horrors of apartheid such as separate doorways and counters. Seaside towns had separate beaches for blacks and whites. It was a little less rigid in places like Cape Town and Durban, but this was very much in the era when pressure was being exerted on foreign sportsmen not to tour South Africa.

In rugby terms, one of the results of segregation was that at every game, packed into the worst terraces in the stadiums and always looking into the sun, would be an enclosure of non-whites who would always give the Lions the most fantastic support. Everyone from Nelson Mandela down has recalled the fact that, because the Springboks as a whole were seen as an icon of apartheid, the non-whites always supported the opposition, and often noisily.

Before every match and usually afterwards, too, we would always go to the part of the stadium into which the blacks were crammed, to wave to them and to thank them for their support. It was both remarkable and encouraging to have this pocket of people cheering for you among a sea of raucous whites. We went to townships and other black areas to run coaching sessions. Sometimes we stayed to dinner and remained after dark, which at the time was illegal.

Twenty-three years later I was head coach of the 1997 Lions in South Africa. We were approached by a man and his family. They had with them a large book of cuttings containing the whole story of the 1974 Lions tour, really comprehensive and superb. The father spoke. He said that he had followed the 1974 tour avidly, had wonderful memories of the team and the rugby we had played, and he had brought his family along that day to thank us for coming all these years before.

The hotel managers were, of course, frightened to death of us because we were the first Lions to tour in South Africa since the infamous tour of 1968 with the Wreckers and the Kippers. The names speak for themselves, and nights often ended with massive bills for damage being presented to David Brooks, the 1968 man-ager, by the hotel. The Wreckers lived up to their name, whether in hotels, on trains or anywhere, and it was said that both Syd and Willie John were among their number.

In fact, by 1974 we were pretty well behaved. There were some antics, of course. One of the players took a girl out to dinner, and when they went back to his room they found that all the furniture had gone. It had been thrown out and so when he opened the door there were just floorboards. We reeled out the fire hose in a couple of hotels, but I don't think we lived up to the reputation of 1968. Not that Syd or Willie could say much if we had.

Probably the best diversion came when we went up to the Kruger Park for a few days after the Second Test; there were warthogs running across the training pitch and we stayed in ron-davels, traditional African round huts with conical thatched roofs, in the bush. We had a night of drinking and playing Fizzbuzz and some of the other usual games. Naturally, the players quickly realised who among their number were not so adept and picked on them. Poor Billy Steele had to take on so much beer in forfeits that he simply poured the final pint over his head and collapsed. He was never seen again at Kruger, and missed all the big-game expeditions that we went on. There were some antics, but it is important to remember that this was a time when the media operated in a different way, and things that happened off the field tended not to be reported.

This was also the era of self-help, when there was no giant and unwieldy coaching team or administrative back-up. Every day duty boys were appointed, and it was their solemn obligation to organise themselves and everyone else. If it was your day, you had to go early to the manager, pick up all the day's timings; make sure that everyone was up, that everyone knew where they had to be and when. You even had to supervise the kit bags so that they arrived safely at the other end.

There was not even a physiotherapist or a doctor. If you needed one or the other, you had to ask the local liaison officer and then you would find yourself sitting in a waiting room alongside members of the general public. Local liaison officers fixed golf, trips, game drives, everything. Syd was big on allowing down time, but only after you had worked to earn it.

The spirit of the players was amazing. We stayed solid together as an entity, even though some were frustrated that they had not made the Test team, and we kept that unity over such a long period. Perhaps one of the most famous picture on any Lions' tour was taken in the immediate aftermath of the Third Test in Port Elizabeth, when we clinched the series in brilliant style. We had always made a huge thing about it being the whole squad who were up against South Africa, regardless of who was chosen for the Tests. Willie John took us all across to the touchline on the final whistle, we located the rest of the squad in their seats in the stand, and we raised our hands above our heads and applauded them. The boys stood up in the stand and applauded back, and it was a tearful and unique moment. We managed to blend the Saturday and midweek teams so that players did move between the two and there was no drawbridge. And it was another lesson. You keep people involved, so that you are all Lions.

On 15 May 1974, in Potchefstroom, in those days a town with a frontier feel, I wore the jersey in anger for the first time, in the centre in a 59–13 victory over Western Transvaal. In all, I was to play in fourteen of the twenty-two games, so I was one of the busier Lions. In Potchefstroom, in match conditions for the first time, we experienced the way the ball flew further in the thin air. I missed the next game, up in Windhoek against South West Africa (now Namibia), but was back in the centre for the 33–6 win over Boland province in Wellington. I was only an onlooker for the next two fixtures and so missed two games significant in different ways – we beat Eastern Province 28–14, the brutal match which saw the birth of the ninety-nine call, then I missed the 97–0 win over South West Districts in Mossel Bay, when J. J. Williams scored six tries, looking dazzlingly fast.

The first really telling win – against a big team, that is – came next, 17–8 against Western Province in Cape Town and it was so satisfying to be chosen in the centre that day for what was an early indication of Syd's thinking just a week before the First Test. I missed the game in midweek against the coloured Federation XV, then came the agonising days and then hours and minutes before Test selection. Dick Milliken and I both made it. When you become a Lion for the first time it is an incredible feeling.

The team talk in our Cape Town hotel before the First Test was never to be forgotten– such as it was. Willie John McBride sat there puffing on his pipe and we waited for his words of inspiration. He didn't utter a word. 'I was just about to open my mouth and I realised that there was no need. We were ready,' he said later.

And we were ready. The First Test was played at Newlands on a really heavy pitch; it had rained in Cape Town for the entire five days we were there and it was waterlogged in places. It was a collision up front of massive and almost thunderous proportions and our pack gradually got on top. We spent an afternoon kicking and chasing, desperate not to give anything away. I just remember making big tackles on bigger men, and thinking: 'I don't know how many more times I can do this.'

As a smaller player, I always used to try and smash the opponents in the first few minutes, hoping that if I made my early tackles big enough they would tend to go and attack somewhere else. But I also remember looking at the clock in Cape Town that day, already feeling the effects of my big hits, and realising that there was still an hour of the game left, and that they were still coming. I suppose I wondered if I could last.

Famously, we won it that day with three penalties from Phil Bennett and a drop goal – Gareth took the ball from a line-out on the left, moved slightly to his right, looked up and fired over a drop goal. It was a great moment because it put us 12–3 up and two scores ahead and we held on well. Their pressure had come to nothing and, in a bog like that, at least we knew they weren't going to run round us.

It was a fantastic victory and when we had won it we all boarded the bus and went off to hospital. Alan Old, the Yorkshire and England fly-half, was playing really well on tour and, at the time, Phil Bennett was not playing quite so well. Old may even have had a sniff of the First Test but he suffered a horrendous knee injury in the match before the Test, against the Federation XV. We sat around his bed in hospital, laid out the beer and spent time with him. The hospital staff never knew what hit them but they were both brilliant and tolerant and more or less gave us the run of the place. It was an odd kind of celebration, perhaps, but it was the sort of feeling that we had in that group. By this time, South Africa was beginning to sit up and take notice.

I missed both the next two games. We beat Southern Universities in Cape Town 26–4, then, vitally, we beat the powerful and forbidding Transvaal in Johannesburg, 23–15. In its significance the result was almost up there with the Test match, and it was another game in which we refused to be intimidated.

One of the best off-field experiences on any tour came next, when we went to Rhodesia, now Zimbabwe. We flew up to Salisbury in a turbo-prop Viscount, with all our bags stuffed in canvas webbing underneath the fuselage. We had a magnificent time. We went to the Victoria Falls – absolutely incredible – followed by a boat cruise which saw us eating and drinking among basking crocodiles. On the way back from the Falls we had to endure a dodgy landing on to a runway with no lights, but, certainly in retrospect if not necessarily at the time, it was all part of the rich tapestry of that stopover.

In 1974 Rhodesia was still considered an illegal regime by the British government after its unilateral declaration of independence. Ian Smith, the Prime Minister, attended the game we played against Rhodesia on 18 June, and afterwards we chatted about politics, sport, life and apartheid. There was a different atmosphere in Rhodesia; it seemed much happier and more relaxed, in marked contrast with South Africa, a country which at the time bore all the hallmarks of a police state.

Before we left, Ian Smith said sadly: 'You know, if the rest of the world was to give us ten years we would show them how to succeed. We are trying to get people in the village schools educated, so that when they get to a certain standard in education they get the vote. What we want is for them to understand what they are voting for. But the world will not give us the time. I realise that.'

Despite the air of controversy, the Rhodesia game was one of the best of the tour. I played at fly-half that day, did a lot of running and I absolutely loved it. We won 42–6, against opposition which included Ian Robertson, the Springbok. As someone said at the time, if this was what supporting an illegal regime was all about, we were all for it.

The Second Test in Pretoria, on 22 June, was the one that made the rugby world realise that the old order was changing; it was a game in which we proved that we were indeed dominant and that the First Test had not been an aberration. There had been talk beforehand that I might give way to Mike Gibson for Pretoria, but

I stayed, for that match and right through the series, with Dick Milliken alongside me.

The pressure was massive on South Africa before that Test – pressure from the media, the public, everyone. The Springboks trained in a jail leading up to the match because they didn't want us to know what they were doing. They were banned from reading the newspapers by Ian Kirkpatrick, their coach, presumably so that they could suspend reality until the Test match.

We were now up at altitude, up on the high veld, home to brown, dry grounds. If you are lucky enough to get hold of a video or DVD of the match, you will see a pitch of almost startling brownness. It was a tremendous Test match, in which some outstanding rugby was played, but in a sense the Springbok selectors helped us because they made eight changes when it would probably have been better to let the First Test team have another run.

Again, the pressure from those big, physical and passionate Springboks was immense; again, our resistance was extraordinary. They moved the ball very early on and had us under pressure, but once more the sharpness of J. J. Williams rescued us. Gareth chipped back into the box from a scrum, the ball bounced wickedly, JJ hacked it on and reacted brilliantly to reach it first for a try, perhaps against the run of play.

In the second half we were immense. Fergus Slattery made a superb run down the right and found Benny (Phil Bennett). Benny sidestepped through, showed a decent turn of speed and sidestepped the last defender for a lovely solo try. The video shows Benny surging outside the cover, and he scored in some pain as the last defender stuck out a boot and the studs caught his shin as he went by. Benny didn't seem to mind very much although the leg stiffened up at the end and pictures of the match show him limping off as he is shaking hands.

We sealed victory with a try from Gordon Brown, created by our pressure. There was a stray kick out of defence and Gareth went snorting down the touchline with the ball. As he was checked, he popped the ball inside and Gordon Brown came up like a runaway train. He took defenders over with him and scored. Then, late on, after a drop goal from me, Dick Milliken was put almost clear, and, as the defenders converged near the line, it seemed as much as anything that they dragged him over the line, not away into touch. Dick scored, just to rub it in, and it meant that we could not be beaten in the Test series. A victory by 28–9 said it all.

The intensity of that tour was massive. We played five games inside twelve days before the Third Test, ideal if you were a South African trying to soften us up. I played in four of the five – at fly-half in three of them; we beat the Quaggas by 20–16, we beat Orange Free State with a late try, 11–9, one of the few times when we looked as if we might lose. It was another ferocious battle: the Free State captain made his post-match speech thanking us for the game with blood running down his face. But, once again, no one held it against us that we were so much on top of South African rugby. We had paraded into Bloemfontein from the airport to the city centre in a fleet of vintage cars.

I missed the next game against Griqualand West at Kimberley, site of the amazing Big Hole which reaches to the bowels of the earth, and where so many diamonds have been excavated. I was at fly-half again in another key win, 16–12 over Northern Transvaal at Pretoria, and then before the Third Test we had an easy run against the Leopards, the black team, in East London, winning 56–10.

The Third Test was surely one of the greatest days in our rugby history. A big ramp led down from the dressing rooms on to the field at Port Elizabeth. We jogged down the hill into what we hoped would be a place in history and stood there doing some exercises. Time passed. No sign of the Springboks. Were they going to turn up?

Suddenly, there was a huge roar, and we saw the Springboks absolutely tearing down the ramp, absolutely sprinting. Because they had built up so much momentum they only stopped when they were more than halfway across the field. At one time it looked as if they would keep going and disappear out of the far side of the stadium. I remember Dick Milliken and me looking at each other and thinking: 'Here we go!'

The Springboks were so undecided about who to choose at scrum-half for the game that they called up players from all over the country and had a sort of final trial for scrum-halves in the week before the game. In the end, it seemed that they wanted to add even more formidable power, so they chose Gerrie Sonnekus at scrum-half. A giant, he normally played at number eight; indeed, a full ten years after the 1974 Test he was back in the South African team in exactly that position, playing against a touring England team. He was not exactly the greatest passer or 'the new Gareth', I seem to remember.

Simply put, the Third Test was the hardest game I have ever played, and the first half was even harder than that! The Springboks were on a mission from history, and the pressure they put on us was incessant. It was big South African forwards and backs powering through at us, and for a long time there was nothing we could do to stem the tide. The psychology of it was difficult for me. Every time I played on that tour I was up against guys who were comfortably a stone, or even two stone, heavier than me. Sometimes I wondered how long I could keep defending against it all.

But, as happened so often in my career of playing for or coaching the smaller team, we were able to lay a honey trap. South Africans are always so intent on coming up and making the hit; they are very focused on pushing up in a straight line to smash the opposition. The honey trap we laid involved us trying to get them to come up and then we'd spring it and shift the ball late.

Whenever we were taking the ball up to the line, we were actually attacking two metres the other side, or to the left or to the right. We had to have players who could offset where they were running and where the ball was going. It was the basis of what we tried in 1974 and what we were to try in similar circumstances against another bigger side in 1997.

We would get as close as we could to the tackler, and make a really late shift of the ball. We were trying to follow each other in, and if our ball carrier took the defender one way, we would support him on the other side so that he knew there was somebody there. It reached its zenith in 1997 with Jeremy Guscott and Scott Gibbs, but even the forwards, if they were clever enough, could do it.

The Third Test was also full of verbals and violence. There were two or three sustained stand-up fights, there were torrents of abuse and, at one stage, Willie John told one of their players: 'Either you leave the field now or you will be carried from the field. It is your choice.' The call of ninety-nine rang out, JPR came rushing up to join in as the forwards pummelled each other.

A score of massive strategic importance came minutes before half-time after we had just ridden out some of the siege. The Springboks threw into a line-out near their line and Gordon Brown made a giant leap, caught the ball and almost literally fell over the line to score. It was a stunning blow because it left the Springboks with nothing to show for their pressure of the first half.

In the second half we just picked them off with some brilliant play, and we launched J. J. Williams twice for tries. We moved good line-out ball to the left, cashing in on all the work we had done in training on moving the ball quickly and accurately, and JJ set off, JPR backed him up on the inside, then, after JPR took the ball on, JJ switched back inside JPR and ran round behind the posts.

Later in the half we counter-attacked from deep, JJ did his chip-and-chase to perfection and scored again and Benny sealed it all with a drop goal. It was a towering second-half performance, and on the whistle, with Willie John on the shoulders of the forwards, we all moved to the touchline to salute the rest of the squad: that special Lions moment. Phil Bennett later described the hour we spent in the dressing room, drinking and chatting after our 26–9 victory, as the most emotional and satisfying of his entire life. We were the first Lions team to win a Test series in South Africa. And remember that it was to be twenty-two years before New Zealand won a series in South Africa for the first time. That is possibly the best indication of the magnitude of what we had achieved.

Four days later I was out there again, this time as fly-half in the 26–6 win over Border. I missed the 34–6 win over Natal, when JPR was involved in an altercation with the famous Tommy Bedford, the Natal and South African number eight, and then, in the last provincial game of the tour, against Eastern Transvaal at Springs, and in a 33–10 win, I scored my first and only try of the tour. I like to think that I had been a provider on tour rather than the executioner.

The Fourth Test, on 27 July, was an incredible occasion. At that time, Ellis Park in Johannesburg was all planks and scaffolding and there were around 100,000 people there. It was very noisy indeed and amazing to think that there was no kind of crowd disaster. As an interesting side note, pictures of the match also show that the numbers of the jerseys we played in were in a completely different style from our usual ones. We had run out of jerseys, and the set we played in had been run up in record time in South Africa.

Of that final Test, the most memorable and certainly the most crucial moment came towards the end, when Slattery's try was disallowed. We launched JPR through the middle and when he was stopped he found Slattery on his left. Slats went for the line and tried to force his way through a tackle by Peter Cronje right on the line. Slats probably went in just a little high and he tried to force the ball down between his legs rather than get outside or inside Cronje.

To this day I am still convinced that Slattery scored. I would have been a few strides away and he definitely got the ball down. After that, we were awarded a five-metre scrum which did not come to anything and after that Max Baise could not blow the whistle quickly enough to end the game. It was following that game that he made his priceless comment that *we* were all leaving for home, but *he* had to live in the place.

Earlier, however, Roger Uttley had been given a try when, as even he admitted afterwards, Chris Pope of South Africa had reached the ball first. The day of the television match official was still far in the future. The day of the Lions had arrived. Three-nil, with one draw.

The last act of the tour was to fill packing cases, specially supplied, with all the gifts we had been given by our most generous hosts. They were all freighted back home to us, and around six months later they arrived. We had all sorts of Zulu carvings, a copper coffee table from Rhodesia, leather gifts of every kind. And thousands of the warmest memories.

As usual, going home meant returning to reality. We had had to suspend paying the mortgage for several months at the time of the tour because, although Judy was working, I was not being paid in my absence. We were also fostering children at the time. There were additional benefits from the tour, though. We had been well served by the De Beers diamond company. On one occasion we had gone to their main office where they displayed the diamonds that had recently been cut; within reason we were allowed to choose one, had to pay virtually nothing for it. Syd knew that there was not much money coming in back at home. 'Don't worry, it's covered,' he said of my diamond. I selected a ring, had the diamond set and brought it home. I never went through customs because the head of customs was a rugby man.

There was a tour reunion in 1994, and there were four celebration dinners in England, Scotland, Ireland and Wales. My mother died during that period so I went to only two of them, but we had another reunion in 2004 when the whole party turned up. That is always a good sign – the sign of a group with a fantastic spirit. Long afterwards, Willie John spoke about the tour. 'When we came back,' he said, 'we were all better men.'

The debate continues to rage as to whether the 1974 Lions were the greatest ever. The 1971 tour of New Zealand was definitely the breakthrough and the confidence that gave to us all in British and Irish rugby was incredible. However, Colin Meads may have been finished by then, and we did things that surprised the All Blacks.

In 1974, however, we went through a tour lasting around fourteen weeks and twenty-two games, and we emerged unbeaten. We had a fantastic relationship in the squad; we had an unbreakable harmony. I have always admired the 1971 Lions, but I am in no doubt that the 1974 team are the greatest Lions and I cannot see their achievements being repeated.

It was a tour on which I developed a special feeling for South Africa and South Africans, because for four magnificent months we were part of what they were.

8

Clouds over Christchurch

The 1977 Lions tour of New Zealand

Our first morning in New Zealand, May 1977. 'The Lions squad awoke to a cloudless blue sky,' said one New Zealand newspaper. At this fledgling stage, it seemed just like the glamorous tour to South Africa of 1974, with its big skies a place where the sun always appeared to shine.

It should have been an even more dazzling prospect than that. Throughout all the decades of Lions tours, the Lions had consistently been overpowered by the forwards of New Zealand and South Africa. Every tour, every era, it seemed that the Lions had superb backs, even iconic backs, and yet it was always the forward muscle of the home teams that bullied the Lions into submission. We had been beaten mentally and physically. The trend had been reversed in 1974, when our forwards had been better than the Springboks'.

There were further indications three years down the line that the power of Northern Hemisphere forwards was increasing, especially in the scrummage. The 1977 Five Nations had been won by a monster French pack and, to be honest, the 1977 tour should have been not so much a watershed as a tearing-up of the history books. The forwards we had in New Zealand in 1977 were to dominate the All Blacks so completely that at one stage of the Fourth Test the Kiwis actually gave up on the forward contest altogether, held up their hands, at least in terms of the scrum battle, and surrendered.

Incredibly, they opted for a three-man scrum, effectively conceding that the Lions were too big, too good and too brutal for them. One commentator called this 'the complete humiliation of New Zealand forward play'. A newspaper report of the Fourth Test concluded that New Zealand 'had been shoved about like cows'.

All we had to do in this situation of apparent luxury was cash in on the forward domination. We had to use this domination wisely and to use the possession well. And how better equipped could we be? The head coach was John Dawes, who had been captain of the 1971 Lions, was regarded as a great backs coach and who had come to the fore developing exciting attacking play with London Welsh at the end of the 1960s and into the early 1970s. It was surely the basis for an historic Lions win, far more convincing than the celebrated 1971 victory, which had been won by two Tests to one, with one drawn.

But we lost. Calamitously. Absolutely nothing on that tour seemed to turn out quite as British and Irish rugby supporters had hoped. It was not the glorious moment; it was a grim, doomed, endless slog. It was interminable, not enjoyable in the slightest.

The weather for the first day was indeed glorious. It was also the last time, almost literally, that we saw the sun in a tour of twenty-six games and thirty-five flights which lasted well over three months. We went up to the holiday areas of the Bay of Islands in the far north, which the brochures described as 'beautiful, and winterless'. It rained incessantly. The sun reappeared for tour match twenty-six, when we stopped off in Fiji. We may have awoken 'to cloudless blue skies', but it was a pitch-black tour. Welcome to New Zealand.

Following in the footsteps of newspaper themes which never quite came true, another report greeted us by explaining that we were going to campaign against dirty play. 'The Lions intend to make their tour a *jihad,* or holy war, against rough and violent play.' Cynics may say that the tour did indeed turn out to be a war, but with very little holy about it.

Even the backdrop was gloomy. New Zealand was struggling economically, too. A survey of the time reported that the outlook for the New Zealand economy that year was 'the blackest since World War Two'. The rugby outlook seemed to be similarly black. The All Blacks had lost that famous series in 1971 and, the year before we arrived, they lost in a highly charged, violent and bitterly controversial series in South Africa.

There was one way to cheer up the country, sport and the economy included, and that was to gain revenge on the Lions and lift everybody's spirits. New Zealand players and the public became fanatical about it, and their fanaticism ensured that the welcome they gave the Lions ranged from unfriendly to appallingly hostile and rude – with a few exceptions. For me, still basking in the warmth of the memory of the tour of South Africa three years before, and the reception we had received, it was both salutary and disappointing.

The first match against Wairarapa-Bush, at Masterton, set the tone. It had been pouring for days, the pitch was a quagmire, and at the final whistle we were caked in what seemed like inches of mud from head to toe. We shook hands with the opposition and headed for the dressing room. There was no hot water. The showers were freezing cold. Shivering, soaked and still caked in mud, we wrapped ourselves in blankets, boarded our bus and were driven back to the hotel for a shower.

Occasionally, there was not enough mud for our hosts who however foul the weather or terrible the state of the pitch would play curtain-raiser games before the kick-off or big domestic games in monsoons the week before the Lions match. We had to win the Second Test, which took place at Lancaster Park, Christchurch on 9 July 1977. It had been raining there for what seemed like months, yet the week before the powers that be had allowed a minor game to be played on the Test pitch, which cut it up hopelessly. As we arrived for the Test, a helicopter was hovering above the field, trying to dry the pitch out with the downdraught from its rotors. The helicopter seemed to follow us everywhere, and buzzed over most of the pitches on which we played. Or perhaps it was a different one. The weather on that tour was absolutely ghastly and it was a grim trip in other ways. For me, a confirmed Lions lover, to have come back from a tour grateful that I would be too old to make another probably says it all.

The Lions were to lose the Test series by three matches to one. If the 1974 tour really is seen as the greatest, the 1977 tour was certainly the most heartbreaking and frustrating. In the lounge at Auckland airport before we left for home, Fran Cotton, the Sale and England forward, paused at the entrance to the aircraft. 'We smashed the All Blacks. I cannot believe we are going to walk though that door having lost the series.'

It is still hard to believe what happened, even after so many years. The basis of our failure, I suppose, is that the forward power and domination, which began fairly early on in the tour but which grew and grew, went to our heads. And that we were not clever enough. Tactically, we were absolutely hopeless. We messed up the First Test, when our selection was odd, but smashed them up front throughout the rest of the series and throughout most of the tour games. Terry Cobner, the Welsh flanker, effectively took control of the forwards after the First Test and they became in most respects a superb unit.

But we never got the ball back from the forwards at the right time. They would take the ball on and on, but then they would wait until the momentum stopped before giving the ball back. I kept chipping away at Cob. 'Look, it's time. You have got to let the ball go when we are on the front foot. Don't wait till you can't do anything with it any more and then give it back.' Thus we looked really impressive, but only up to a point. It may have been humiliating for a New Zealand forward, and old All Blacks forwards were probably turning in their graves, but we never cashed in on our forward superiority.

Typically, as they always were, the All Blacks were incredibly smart, and Jack Gleeson, their coach, outsmarted John Dawes. They didn't bother committing too many forwards to the forward play; they almost gave it up and not just when they did their famous three-man scrum in the final Test. Their back row held off and that meant that when we won the ball we were outnumbered.

They made the game fast and loose, and they played with their back row out in the backs. They played off rucks and loose play, they played after we had won the ball but they had arrived in numbers and turned it over.

But when we did win the ball, we found Phil Bennett, the captain, and a hero of 1974, struggling at fly-half, diffident and running laterally, so that when I got the ball I always seemed to be running towards the touchline, not the goal line. As I say, we found that we were outnumbered because they had their back row out there. In the end, we may as well not have smashed them up front because, in terms of results, it meant absolutely nothing.

We were unlucky in so many aspects. The whole tour was massively stacked against us, and we were still then in an era when the home New Zealand referees tended to even up the matches for the home side, but we nonetheless should have won at a canter. I learned so many tactical lessons from the whole experience.

The tour was firmly rooted in the amateur age. The management consisted simply of Scotland's George Burrell, John Dawes and a New Zealander called Doc Murdoch, the masseur and baggage man, whose job it was, as far as kit was concerned, to supervise every piece of baggage at every location and make sure it arrived at the next stop. Someone once counted the pieces of baggage. There were 110. Doc was so dedicated and such a friend to the players that we all chipped in and paid for him to come on to Fiji with us at the end of the tour, with his wife. Doc also provided some basic medical treatment and hours and hours of massage but, if you were injured, it quickly became clear that things hadn't moved on much from South Africa three years earlier, under Alun Thomas and Syd Millar. You simply found a local physiotherapist, and sat in his waiting room along with all his other patients; if you moved on halfway through a course of treatment you had to find the local physio in the next town, and explain your injury all over again from the beginning, and hope for the best.

Even with the players we had we should have won with a lot to spare because we were not up against a great All Black side. When you consider the individuals who did not make the tour – Gareth Edwards, Gerald Davies and J. P. R. Williams were all still playing Test rugby but, for various reasons, none of them toured (maybe they knew something we didn't know) – it makes you realise that it could have been one of the greatest Lions tours ever. Roger Uttley, the 1974 stalwart who would have been a great asset, had to withdraw injured; Fergus Slattery was not available; and the mystifying choice the selectors made in the centre would have been better if they had chosen a crash-ball merchant in that position with Jim Renwick as a brilliant runner. They chose neither.

Indeed, the party was wrong from the start. Wales had had a mediocre Five Nations in 1977, yet, of the party Dawes chose, half (fifteen out of thirty) were Welsh. Three more came out as replacements. Some played well, others were simply not good enough, some were dire, and John Dawes seemed considerably to overrate a few of his own countrymen. Some accounts of the tour saw that as the chief weakness.

John Dawes disappointed me as a coach. I was looking forward to learning from him. It may seem remarkable to say it now, but he was the first backs coach I had ever had. I was expecting a lot, but, very strangely, he didn't say a lot. He talked mostly in generalities, and he was never really specific about what he wanted. He would sometimes call, quite gently, for 'quick hands'. But it was no more than a slogan.

Before long, the backs had made up their minds to go off on their own to work on things. We *wanted* it to work. We would stay out for twenty minutes or so after training, working on handling or sorting out our moves. Some of us – Andy Irvine, J. J. Williams, Phil Bennett and Mike Gibson – had been there in 1974 so we tended to do the same things we had done then, running through basic things to make them work better, trying to search for that same understanding from our charmed lives in 1974.

Perhaps John, a natural player and leader in his time, was just not so good at putting things across; perhaps in his heart he was telling himself that this '77 lot were not as good as the '71 team, that we couldn't do what they did then. I got the feeling there was a kind of 'Oh well, I'll tell you this bit but really you're not good enough to execute it' attitude about it all.

One example of insensitivity I still recall with a shudder came after we lost 9–21 to New Zealand Universities on 14 June. The game took place on the Tuesday in Christchurch and on the Wednesday, well into Test week and with an urgent need both for proper preparation and rest, we were to fly to Wellington. Before we left for the airport, Dawes decided that we should all train in Hagley Park, the area of woodland and parkland near the centre of Christchurch.

It was not a rugby session, it was a beasting, a naughty boy punishment for losing to the Universities team in a match which was not in any case directly relevant to the Test. There was not a rugby ball in sight. For two hours we just ran and ran, often from one tree to another. There was no technical element to the session at all, even though it was three days before the Test. It was merely insensitive and a waste of time, to the point of being brainless. If you mention Hagley Park to any 1977 Lions, they will roll their eyes.

After I had been dropped for the Third Test at the end of July (David Burcher, the Welsh centre and a strange man, very difficult to warm to, had played well against Auckland before the Test), I decided to stop playing to orders and just go for it. We were playing North Auckland at Whangarei, home of Sid Going and all the Going brothers. The match commentaries sound like a bunch of auctioneers in action. It was my chance to stake a claim for a return to the Test side. I said to the players: 'Right. Bugger it. I am just going to have a real crack at them every time I get the ball.' I think that attitude got me back in – it was a match played in appalling weather and filthy underfoot, as usual, but I sidestepped through for a try and my strategy worked.

John Dawes was hard to reach. We had a senior players' committee on that tour – myself, Fran Cotton, Mike Gibson, Phil Bennett and George Burrell, the manager. We would talk things through, but not an awful lot changed. The party was not well managed; Burrell was not strong enough to stand up to John Dawes.

At the end of season 1975–76, the great Mervyn Davies had been struck down by illness, and while, thankfully, he recovered, he never played again. Dawes said after the tour was over that Davies would have been his first choice as Lions captain. Instead, he chose Phil Bennett, and by the end of the 1977 tour the confident and impish Benny of 1974 had become a withdrawn and struggling figure, as he himself later admitted. Benny was and is a very good man, but he was not cut out to lead that tour. He was desperately homesick for Wales throughout, he was put under pressure by the New Zealand defence and especially flankers, and he tended to move crab-like across the field, pulling the New Zealand flankers on to us. John Bevan, the other fly-half, was probably playing better but they could not bring themselves to drop the captain. Bevan was more direct, and very brave and, unlike Benny, he played flat, and with aggression.

We therefore had to develop ways of getting around the fact that Bennett was crabbing across field. I started trying to stand wider, to go in a square and then go up the outside. I thought I played quite well on that 1977 tour. Luckily I escaped injury and I was heavily involved, playing in thirteen of the twenty-six tour matches.

Phil also felt the pressure off the field and found it very hard to relax. 'I thought long and hard about whether I should make that tour,' he said long afterwards. 'We had just had a beautiful baby boy, and quite often on the tour, which was incredibly long, I was wishing I was back at home in Llanelli with my family.'

In 1974, Syd Millar had taken the pressure off him. In 1971, apparently, Carwyn James had the gift of deflecting the pressure from Barry John and his other key men. John Dawes didn't seem to have that gift and Benny was therefore a rabbit caught in the headlights.

Some of the selections were strange, and so were some of the players. In 1974 I had teamed up with Dick Milliken, alongside whom I played all four of the Tests. We became, and remain, soul mates.

In 1977, the choices at centre, as I have implied, seemed random. One day I'd be playing alongside Steve Fenwick, who was on great form; the next, Mike Gibson, such a blood brother to Dawes in 1971. By 1977, however, the relationship between Gibson and Dawes was odd, considering that they had been so close in 1971 when they were the Test centres and combined so brilliantly, with Gibson playing his best ever rugby. By 1977 the pair were clearly not so close. Mike was still good, though not the player he had once been. We played together only three times on a twenty-six-match tour in which there were only four centres. Mike's wife flew over too, which the management didn't like at all, as wives were not supposed to join their husbands. He only played in the minor games, really, and sometimes I felt that it was such a shame that he never found the consistency which had marked his play in 1971

There was also Burcher, already mentioned, one of the Welsh players who seemed to have come from nowhere. He may well have been delighted to be on tour, but he rarely showed it. His favourite ploy was to approach one of the many Kiwi heavies at the post-match dinners and then, when that individual was about to say something, turn his back on him. Very amusing. I have no idea what motivated him; his whole attitude was a mystery to me. I felt that he did play well against Auckland and justifiably won a place in the Third Test team, but he and some of the other Welsh lads on the tour were not really up to the challenge. They did not have the mentality of a winning Lion.

The other sad aspect about the tour was the ill feeling on and off the field. There were some very bad incidents in quite a few of the games, the worst of which came when Bill Bush, the All Black prop, kicked Graham Price in the head in the First Test at Christchurch, when Price was prone on the pitch. It seemed to me that much of the old respect for the home nations and the Lions tradition was no longer there. There was an arrogance, and some of the ill feeling was downright ugly.

John Dawes and George Burrell did not help matters or the way that the team was perceived. We could be rude ourselves. We once trained at East Tamaki RFC, outside Auckland. Burrell and Dawes were in a bad mood as the coach made its way to the club because they had demanded that the trip be cancelled and that we should simply train at Eden Park, where the match would be played in a few days.

The liaison officers with the party said that to change the schedule would be impossible, since the Lions' appearance at East Tamaki had been flagged up for weeks, that schools in the area were giving their pupils a half-day to go to watch the session and that the members of the club had laid on a feast for us. There were about two thousand people there when we arrived, we did the session and when we went into the clubhouse a fine spread had indeed been prepared for us.

Burrell, however, told us to get straight on the bus. Six of us refused, and the management had to wait in the car park. We stood and talked to the people who had gone to so much trouble and even when we left there was a ton of food left. It was not the only example of bad public relations, and it was another lesson for the future.

John Dawes had his own endless private skirmishes with the media. He conducted a running battle with them, claiming that the press accompanying the tour had no power, but that he had. According to one account of the tour, he told one particular journalist that he would 'destroy' him. It was all so unnecessary and took up so much time.

The home media conducted what was often a nasty, even a bitter, campaign, which I could not understand. *Truth*, a misnamed New Zealand paper, notoriously printed an article under the caption 'They're lousy lovers' which purported to tell the story of a woman called Wanda from Wanganui who claimed to have got off with some of the players. She was the most obvious plant you could imagine. That was the standard of the home press on that trip. They were paying women to come into the hotels to try and get off with players. Welcome, Lions.

But there was still evidence of the old civilities and good contact between the hosts and the team, and parts of New Zealand rugby still impressed me. Bruce Robertson, the centre, had played against me when I won my first cap at Murrayfield in 1972, we played each other again in 1975 and struck up an easy relationship. He was teaching in a primary school at the time, and one day we both went to visit the school, where we had an impromptu question and answer session. Doug Bruce, the fly-half, was also easy to get along with, and at the 1987 World Cup I went to Doug's fortieth birthday party. Brian Lochore, who had played against the 1971 Lions and then became the All Blacks manager, took us out to dinner at his farm, and he also took us duck shooting. So we had a decent chat and some kind of relationship after the games.

In that era of touring, one of the great Lions traditions was still in full swing. Schools all over the country would adopt individual Lions. The Lion would go to a particular school, perhaps speak at assembly, meet the children, take a training session, answer questions. Once he was adopted, the children would keep a scrapbook of that player's exploits on tour and present it to him at the end. It was a brilliant tradition, it pulled players and local communities together, and it is a shame that on tours today, when we only really ever go to major centres, it rarely happens any more.

It was so well organised in 1977 that we all knew our schools before we even left our training camp at home in Richmond, Surrey. I went to Buller High School in Westport, way over on the

West Coast. On the appointed day I travelled with Bruce Hay and Doug Morgan for support. We did a question and answer session and we had tea with the staff, and it was then that I realised that staff rooms are the same the world over. A few weeks after I got home at the end of the tour, my scrapbook arrived. It was excellent, and I still have it safe. Doug Morgan's, prepared for him at Rosehill College, Papakura, measured 30 by 12 inches, was two inches thick, weighed a ton and was bound with a nut and a screw. Does any other sport have a tradition like that? It was another of the little touches that make a Lions tour so special. It was such a shame that there was so much antagonism in the air and that at the end of it all we were just delighted to be going home.

Indeed, the rain almost created a stage of siege. The golf courses were flooded, and there was almost nothing to do. Andy Irvine, Bruce Hay and Doug Morgan, the three Scots, and myself spent hours playing snooker, usually in ex-army or navy clubs, potting away, while back at the motel our drying kit was steaming on the radiators. Our snooker improved out of sight, but I am not that sure our rugby did.

We had to find diversions, any diversions. I loved flying, and the New Zealand pilots were really good with us. They used to let us sit in the cockpit, in the jump seat. I put my new expertise to good use because the party contained some terrible flyers, and anyone who has been to New Zealand will tell you that in a wild, wet and windy winter, flying can be a very unnerving experience.

The white knuckles were to become whiter. We were descending into Wellington one day when the pilot announced that there was a hydraulics problem and that he couldn't get the flaps down. He told us that he was going to fly back out to sea, execute a really tight turn and hope that the G-force released the flaps. The curve was steeper than steep but the ploy worked. On another occasion we were coming in to land at New Plymouth in a Fokker Friendship, the propeller aircraft which were such a familiar sight at every airport throughout the country. The pilot announced that we'd be landing on one wheel, because of the crosswind, and the wing would be tipped into the wind so that it wouldn't flip us over. That raised a few hairs on the back of the neck, too.

On yet another occasion, one of the pilots who flew us decided that he wanted to give us a great view of Hamilton after takeoff. He banked incredibly steeply and the plane seemed almost to turn over. It would have been nice if he had told us before the manoeuvre. 'Just thought you might like a closer look at Hamilton as you leave,' he blithely announced.

That was the last straw for the likes of Terry Cobner and Bobby Windsor, the Welsh lads, who hated flying. Thereafter, they appointed me their flying adviser. I used to talk them through the flight, and explain everything that happened, every odd noise and whine, swoop and lurch.

'What was that noise, Geech?'

'What happened then?'

'Is everything all right with the flight, Geech?'

But the best flight of all was when we visited a farm in Hawke's Bay. Our host had a biplane in a shed. He just dragged back the doors and there it was. He wheeled it out, and up we went. We assumed he knew what he was doing.

Considering that we ended with a reputation of being a forward team and not much else, and considering the weather, we started by playing superbly against Wairarapa-Bush at Masterton. We won by 41–13, and kept the ball moving really well. There was a reality check in the next game, when I watched as we beat Hawke's Bay by only 13–11. George Burrell always made a speech at the post-match function, and he invariably included a very ribald joke. At the end of his speech on this occasion, however, bearing in mind our somewhat lucky win, he said simply: 'John Dawes. Get cracking!'

For the third game, against Poverty Bay/East Coast at Gisborne, somewhat off the beaten track but against a competitive side, I captained the Lions for the first time. It was such an honour, and the sense of pride that I felt was carried with me for years afterwards, when I sat down myself to appoint captains for future Lions matches on future tours. Even better, we won 25–6 and I scored two tries. Therefore, inside the first few weeks of the tour, I had doubled my grand total of one try scored on the whole of the 1974 tour in South Africa.

Then we began to work up towards the First Test, even though it was clear that some of the focus of a Syd Millar in 1974 was missing. In the game against Taranaki in New Plymouth, where we won 21–13, we played for the third match in a row against King County/Wanganui, home-town team of Colin Meads, still regarded as the best and hardest lock who ever played, on a day when Andy Irvine scored five good tries and we showed what class we had in the backs. I missed the game against Manawatu/Horowhenua, an 18–12 win, and also a 12–7 victory over Otago in Dunedin.

By now we were in the deep south of the country, so far south and so deep that the next landfall was the Antarctic, and Mike Gibson and I teamed up in Invercargill for a 20–12 win over the appropriately named Southland. But then, to my immense sadness, my first ever defeat in a Lions jersey, and with me as captain. We lost 21–9 to New Zealand Universities in Christchurch. Doug Rollerson, their captain, kicked Willie Duggan in the head during the match, then complained afterwards about our alleged illegalities even though the referee had awarded a massive total of penalties to the students. They played well, we were very poor and it was the first time the Lions had lost a provincial game on tour since 1968. Out we went on to Hagley Park as our punishment.

It was now Test time, and, while I was thrilled to make the team, it never felt well planned. We went out with an odd-looking pack, with Allan Martin and Moss Keane forming an unlikely second row, Steve Fenwick and me were in the centre outside Phil Bennett and Brynmor Williams and, bizarrely, Fran Cotton, the pillar of 1974, on the bench. Andy Irvine was at full-back. Athletic Park, Wellington, perched on the edge of a valley and with a howling wind the norm, was heavy, wet and dark.

The game was a disaster for us. We could have won, and should have won. We allowed Sid Going a soft try in the first half, which gave the All Blacks encouragement when playing against the wind. Going went back to pick up a loose ball and hesitated, but then he accelerated through a huge gap and scored. It was a shocking try to give away.

The wind was so strong that, with it in our favour, Andy Irvine had put us ahead with a penalty from five yards inside his own half. But our kicking was poor, our line-out was poor, and although we took the lead to make it 9–4, we then gave away another try when Bryan Williams kicked for goal for New Zealand, the ball fell short, Phil Bennett could not gather and Brad Johnstone, the prop, followed up and scored. We turned to face the wind a point behind.

However, a penalty from Phil Bennett put us back into the lead, and we started finding ourselves. And then the hammer blow fell. We launched a superb attack from our own half, with Steve Fenwick and Trefor Evans, the flanker, at the heart of it. It created a four-man overlap and Grant Batty, the All Black wing, was the only defender left. Batty had been suffering from injury, he was nothing remotely like the player he once had been, and his only chance was to sell himself and come in for the interception.

If the pass from Evans had beaten Batty then any one of four of us would have scored. But Batty did intercept, and he set off completely in the clear. He had lost pace and so he was almost caught from behind by Graham Price, the prop, but he scored and we were not able to come back. It was the original twelve-point try; it could have been 18–10 to us but instead it was 16–12 to New Zealand, which was the final score. Devastating, and yet another indication that on any Lions tour you need every last scrap of good fortune.

As we licked our wounds I was meant to miss the next tour match, against South/Mid Canterbury at Timaru. However, John Bevan had played cards late into the night before the game, and his foot went to sleep during a good run of hands against Bobby Windsor. He was in such pain that when eventually he went to bed he could not sleep, and he pulled out on the morning of the match. I played at fly-half.

Of the next four games, I played only in the 13–6 win over Wellington, another significant provincial scalp, and missed the wins over Canterbury (14–13), West Coast/Buller (45–0), and Marlborough/Nelson Bays (40–23), at Blenheim.

By this time a sea change had occurred. Terry Cobner had taken charge of the forwards, often in consultation over the telephone with Ray Prosser, the coaching guru back home at Pontypool. And by the time the Second Test came round, hard men such as Fran Cotton, Peter Wheeler, Gordon Brown and Derek Quinnell had forced their way in, and so too had Bill Beaumont, who had joined the tour late. We were gradually becoming formidable up front. The Second Test, at Christchurch, loomed as the tour saver, or wrecker.

The helicopter made its usual appearance to try to dry out the ground, but by now our powerful forward play suited the heavy field. The Test must have been a very poor game to watch, it was not played in a good spirit and there was a major brawl after Kevin Eveleigh, the All Black flanker, late-tackled Phil Bennett. It was far from the only outbreak of violence.

Yet this time our line-out was better, we were tougher up front, Phil Bennett and Steve Fenwick had good days with their kicking and we scored a good try. As part of a sweeping back move, I put J. J. Williams away as we moved the ball towards the right, JJ held on to it and stepped inside a cover defence that was racing across to try to cut off Andy Irvine. The try put us ahead by 13–6 at half-time, the only score of the second half was a penalty for them by Williams, and we held on. We had to defend really desperately towards the end. It was deeply satisfying, but it had been an awful, violent Test. J. J. Stewart, a former All Blacks coach, said afterwards that he would have preferred the band to have kept playing for the full eighty minutes.

The tour rolled almost interminably on, criss-crossing the country, mile after mile, flight after endless flight, muddy session after muddy session. Our excellent record against the top provincial sides continued. In mid-July we beat the New Zealand Maoris 22–19 and I was in the centre for the wins over Waikato (18–13) and New Zealand Juniors (19–9). That match was famous as probably the muddiest ever played. Photographs show players almost unrecognisable under inches of mud, and that was the day that the iconic photograph of Fran Cotton was taken, probably the most famous rugby image ever. Fran looked like some creature from the primeval swamp.

David Burcher played well in the centre in a very fine win in the next game, over Auckland, by 34–15, and was chosen for the Third Test. It was the first Test I had failed to start in seven, though I did come on for the injured J. J. Williams after thirty-two minutes.

The Third Test should have been our finest hour. The All Blacks panicked, and dropped a host of players after the Second Test, among them Sid Going. The momentum was with us. The helicopter was above us. We had all the power up front and, that day in Dunedin, we should have guaranteed ourselves at least a share of the series.

We dominated the line-outs and scrums throughout the game, we were too good up front. Colin Meads was quoted later as 'feeling sick' up in the stands because we were so much better. But we had stopped being wise enough to make use of it. Phil Bennett and Brynmor Williams really began to struggle at half-back. The All Blacks cleverly lived off their wits. They kept their back row disengaged, so that we were outnumbered whether we won the ball or they did (which didn't happen often). They began to find more and more counters and we started to make poorer and poorer decisions and seemed to become infatuated with our own power. It went to our heads. It was forward domination for its own sake.

It all started badly. Ian Kirkpatrick, the All Black flanker, scored a try in the opening seconds after we failed to clear a kick ahead by Bruce Robertson. Willie Duggan did score a close-range try for us based on our scrum dominance, but Andy Haden scored a driving try for New Zealand and it was 10–4 at half-time, which made a mockery of our control of the forward play.

But we subsided, nonetheless. Our kicking at goal and out of hand was bad, we fumbled behind the scrum against superior numbers, our tactics were poor, Bevan Wilson kicked two penalties for them and Bruce Robertson dropped a goal. We managed just one penalty by Andy Irvine and lost 19–7. In terms of possession and territory, we should have killed them and it was a dreadful feeling afterwards.

Phil and Andy Irvine had missed six kicks at goal between them and the result can have done very little to ease Benny's homesickness. It was by then eleven weeks since we had left Britain and he had sent 231 postcards home. The 232nd did not contain good news. Now two-one down, we could not win the series.

Considering the grinding length of the tour, our record in the provincial games was excellent. We completed the non-Test programme by beating Counties/Thames Valley at Pukekohe, I threw caution to wind against North Auckland, forgot the constraints and just went for everything. I scored an individual try and played myself back into the Test team, then I came on as replacement for Gibson in a 23–16 win over Bay of Plenty at Rotorua.

For all the dominance we had, in some ways, looking back, the result of the Fourth Test had always been written. We had to win to draw the series, and it was a day of infamy for New Zealand when, because we smashed them in the scrum, they packed down three forwards against us. We were in complete control for the first hour and were leading 9–3, with Doug Morgan, in for Brynmor Williams, scoring a try after a well-executed line-out peel and quick ball from the forwards – a rare thing.

Then we started making mistakes, the tension grew, but we held on. Once again, it could not have been much of a spectacle. Doug Morgan had a glorious chance to put us 12–6 up with less then five minutes left, and safe. But he missed from around 30 metres in front of the posts. Yet, by now, only injury time remained and we led 9–6.

The disaster, when it came, was late and devastating. We won a turnover and Benny ran into midfield and simply kicked the ball up the middle of the field. Bill Osborne caught it. He ran down the touchline, chipped ahead and hit Steve Fenwick as Steve was about to pass, jolting the ball loose. Peter Wheeler caught it, but he in turn was hit by Graham Mourie at the same time as the ball arrived. The ball bobbed up, Lawrie Knight, the number eight, caught it and ran on to score in the corner. It was a lucky try. And it killed us.

The All Blacks had been there for the taking. It really could have been a series won, and by 3–1. They played well in Dunedin, in the Third Test, when they had made all their changes. But really what I remember is that we should have beaten them in the First Test and we should have smashed them in the Fourth.

'The All Blacks were out-thought, out-fought and out-played,' said John Dawes afterwards, but what he said was only part of the truth. We had dominated some of the areas of the game, we should have won. But the All Blacks were not out-thought. They played smart rugby, considering that half their team had been obliterated. Despite that, we failed because of the lack of wit we displayed, because of the lack of quick ball and because of our obsession with being dominant for the sake of it up front. Fran Cotton's words of disbelief and disappointment as we boarded the aircraft home were echoed by all of us.

On the way back, we stopped in Fiji to play a Test. The weather was warm and sunny, and the Fijian people were thrilled to see us. We had a team talk round the swimming pool and the replacements sat on the bench eating ice creams. That was when Fran Cotton came out with his famous observation: 'Hey, they've got this tour all wrong. It should have been three months in Fiji and three days in New Zealand.'

Fiji won 25–21. The penalty count against us, from a referee who was a local schoolmaster, was astronomical. Towards the end, we set up a huge driving maul. It just went and went, and there was nothing they could do about it. We'd covered about 50 metres and were just about to score when the referee blew his whistle and penalised us for collapsing the maul – we'd come 50 metres and obviously weren't going to collapse it in the last yard! Still, like Max Baise in 1974, the referee had to live there. We were going home.

In the final analysis, and now that I had something to compare it with, I realised that 1974 had been a charmed tour, and that such a comfortable victory in the Test series might turn out to be a once-in-a-century experience. I realised that everything – absolutely everything – had to go right, even go brilliantly; you had to have all the breaks too, every bounce of the ball and no injuries. And even then you still might not win.

There was also the lesson that you had to absorb the culture of the host country completely. There was no point in trying to escape it. In New Zealand, rugby was king; there was a different response from the man in the street to us as rugby players. We had to become Kiwis for a few months. We failed to do that in 1974.

You also realised how hard the New Zealanders worked on their game, how much it meant to them in a country that often lacked counter-attractions; that all the schools played it, that everyone (including the waitresses) understood that when you played New Zealand on the field you were playing the entire country.

They had skills, running fitness and competitiveness. They competed hard at every level and age group. They had more people coming to watch the All Blacks train than we ever had at Headingley for a First XV match. For myself, I redoubled my training. I knew that no longer could we compare ourselves with our own kind. Whatever I did after that grim and gloomy tour was aimed at trying to match what they were doing 1200 miles away in the Land of the Long Dark Cloud. It was the start, I suppose, of a lifelong search. And the other point was that the crop of

All Blacks we met was far from vintage. It was force of will and the strength of their background which won them the series.

We were away for four months, and, as I have said, flew on thirty-five different occasions. It was a murderous schedule, and the last of the long, crusading Lions tours. At least the Home Unions officials realised that it was too long. Never again, was the feeling. We didn't so much tour New Zealand as zigzag madly round the place, hopping to and fro between the two islands with no obvious coherence. It was midwinter, dark and depressing as hell. Nigel Horton, the English lock, had only been there for three weeks when he broke his thumb throwing a punch. When he left the party to fly home, I don't think I have ever seen a man with a bigger smile on his face.

I had left Judy in the lurch at home, not for the first or last time on my travels. For some reason we moved into a new home, in Adel, Leeds, the day before I left to tour for four long months. The house was never meant to be finished so quickly but the builders pulled out all the stops. It was our first detached house in a development of about thirty but when we moved in there were no facilities. Only a couple of other houses in the complex were occupied, there was no gas connected, no street lights, nothing. We moved in the day before I left for New Zealand. I sanded the floor. That was my sole contribution. When I came back Judy had transformed the place and for months I had to keep asking where she had put things.

Judy summed up the feelings that my long absence had engendered. 'I kept all the letters Ian wrote home. They show that he was miserable, I was miserable. His letters were miserable.'

The flight home was in keeping with all the others. We flew from Fiji to Honolulu to Los Angeles, which was long enough. Then we were told that, because of a strike at Heathrow, we would not be able to land, and Air New Zealand were not allowing any flights to take off. We waited about twelve hours, then they got us on a Scandinavian Airlines flight to Seattle. We had about three hours there, then they flew us to Copenhagen; at Heathrow, way after all the other flights had stopped, they found us a landing slot for three in the morning. The chief controller was another rugby man and he kept the tower open for us.

We eventually landed at 4.00 a.m. We were not exactly mobbed at the airport. We may well have been the most powerful Lions ever but we were also the most savagely frustrated.

9

Inline, and Organised Chaos

Coaching philosophy, and hunting the English

One of my favourite rugby photographs ever was taken looking over the shoulder of Jonathan Davies, the Wales fly-half, during a Test in New Zealand in 1988. Wales were thrashed on that tour and the picture shows Jonathan standing his ground and looking upfield.

All you can see approaching him is a wall of black. There is no red anywhere else on the picture. Steve McDowell is carrying the ball and running at Jonathan. You see half a shoulder right, half a shoulder left, and right down through the camera lens you can see what seems to be the entire All Blacks pack.

Now, it may only have been pure chance that those players were in those positions, but what that picture did was put a thought in my head. If you are a defender and you see such an intimidating picture, then that's what you should be trying to re-create all the time as the team in possession.

It reinforced what I had been thinking about at the time and have been since – inline work in attack, with the ball carrier at the head of a group. I was still doing this inline work with Wasps as recently as season 2008–09. Earlier, when I went to Northampton in the mid-1990s, I had already refined it, so that the group coming in behind the ball carrier was working in a cone shape, with those nearer to him fairly narrow and those further back, wider.

What happened was that, depending on whether the carrier broke through, or made just a half-break, or was stopped and stayed on his feet, or was tackled to the ground (the levels of contact in a descending level of desirability for the attacking side), the next men on the scene from the cone would have to make a series of decisions under pressure – whether to carry on the move by following the carrier through the contact, linking up with him if he was stopped, or, failing that, clearing out at the ruck.

Inspiration for coaching, for attack, defence, coaching philosophy and everything, comes from all kinds of sources. This one came from a photograph, and set me thinking. Not just about coaching. I wondered why there was no brown patch on Jonathan Davies' shorts.

In April 1980 I played my last match, for Headingley against Fylde. I was thirty-three. That same summer I became Headingley's coach and within nine years I was coach of Scotland. It would not be quite right to say that I took over as Headingley coach, because at the time there was no one really to take over from. In the previous year, possibly because there had been some kind of falling-out of the committee, the players had pretty much run the team themselves.

Nor would it be true to say that I took over simply because I was there, or against my better judgement. I wanted the job; maybe there was even a sense of destiny. I grew to love it. Nearly thirty years later, I am still excited about coaching.

I had always been fascinated by the concept of improving individuals and a team, and in the thirty years since I took my first session with Headingley I have always had continuous involvement as a coach, in charge of some rugby team, somewhere – be it Headingley, the Anglo-Scots, Scotland B, Scotland, London Scottish, the Hyatt Regency XV, Northampton, the World XV, the Barbarians, Wasps or the Lions.

It is also a little-known fact that I came very close to adding England to my CV, which would have caused quite a media storm had it happened, not least in Scotland – had I ever been allowed back there. In 1997 I was coaching at Northampton and had just come back from the Lions tour of South Africa, one of the great experiences I had as head coach. Fran Cotton was manager. Fran was then the powerbroker in England rugby and England were keen for a full-time head man. Jack Rowell, the coach at the time, was a successful businessman and did not want the post full-time. I have a cutting in which Fran says: 'Ian McGeechan is the only one to coach England'.

The official line I came out with at the time was that I could not see myself, as a former Scotland player and coach, preparing an England side to go to Murrayfield. It is true that the age of country-hopping coaching was in its infancy but my reaction was only intended to keep the hounds at bay. A few had crossed borders already and, later, Graham Henry, Steve Hansen and Warren Gatland were to coach Wales. Matt Williams coached Scotland, Andy Robinson has recently, as I write, been appointed as Scotland's head coach and we now have Robbie Deans coaching Australia. They are all cross-borderers and there are many more examples. By 1997 the game had gone professional, and things were changing. The England job was arguably the biggest job in rugby. Judy was desperate for me to coach England. 'Bloody Scotland,' she kept on saying.

Talks were held with Fran and Bill Beaumont, the two grandees of England rugby, and I also went to Marlow to speak to the RFU's Don Rutherford. I was very keen. But it was badly handled, and before anything firm had been offered it was leaked to the media. For a time, we were under siege from reporters demanding to know if it was true. Keith Barwell, the owner of Northampton and my employer, declared that if the RFU wanted me, then I was on a six-year contract with Northampton so it would cost them around half a million pounds.

It all became very messy indeed. More relevant to the whole thing being aborted was the fact that the RFU wanted to pay me less than I was on at Northampton at the time! And that Jim Telfer subtly found me a consultancy role with the Scottish Rugby Union for a year.

Frankly, I would have got my head round coaching England at Murrayfield, for it would have been a fantastic opportunity. I was a product of the English system, not a product of Scotland rugby. At the time, I had just had Martin Johnson, Lawrence Dallaglio, Matt Dawson, Neil Back, Tim Rodber, Jason Leonard and Richard Hill with me in South Africa. We had a strong rapport. People were asking whether I could coach that group? Well, of course I could. I already had.

Frankly, I did sense that things were not that well organised behind the scenes, that the RFU did not have their ducks in a row. Clive Woodward was eventually announced as the new coach, at a media conference in Marlow, near where I had met Don Rutherford. I rang Clive and said, 'Look. Now you've got the job, make sure you get what you want. Make sure you get the structure and that you get a proper agreement before you take it on.'

All water under Marlow Bridge now. But for the media leak and the attendant fuss, it might well have happened. Consider the dramatic effect on the rugby landscape. Would I, and not Clive, have taken England to the 1999 and 2003 World Cups? Where might Clive be now, but for that leak? And how would my life have changed? We will never know. Frankly; in all the years since, I have been too busy to wonder. Well, mostly.

Teaching was the perfect background for my coaching career. So many times I have looked back and given thanks for the preparation teaching gave me for the years ahead. It was more than that; it was a calling to which I was dedicated for twenty-three years. I was always teaching in tandem with either playing or coaching rugby, and there was the added boost of my Carnegie College years, perfect for the aspiring rugby coach because of the discipline that Carnegie instilled.

It must be remembered that rugby coaching then was largely in its infancy. Carnegie offered experience in other sports where the art of coaching had gained maturity and so it was invaluable to me.

Teaching and coaching are essentially the same. You have something that you want to achieve with a group of people, and you work out how you are going to approach it, depending on the personnel at the time. And the most refreshing thing is that it is cyclical. People mature and they move on, leaving or retiring, and new people come in at the other end. And the anticipation at the start of the new season is the same as at the start of term. You are beginning a new experience, with a new mix of characters and experience.

The great thrill is the light bulb moment, where they pick up on what you are showing them, and realise the effect it can have, and, in rugby terms, when it changes the way they play. And for me, that is what coaching has always been.

The best advice I ever had from a teacher came when I had just started, after leaving Carnegie. 'After twenty years, make sure you have got twenty years' experience, not one year's experience that you have just repeated twenty times.'

And I have always tried to extend that into coaching. I always stick to key principles, the core values, which hardly ever change. I have always written them down somewhere. At Wasps, they were up on the wall to remind us. They always remained roughly the same and my teams always practised them frequently. But, on the other hand, I have never repeated the same coaching session, not with any team, anywhere. I have notes on every session I have ever taken. I will always make myself think what I am trying to do, what I want out of the players and what has come out of speaking with the other coaches. Some of the outer framework will be the same, but it will always contain fresh elements.

Sometimes there will be a real intensity about it. Sometimes it will be far more concerned with technique. Also, while I usually have the session all prepared and written down on a piece of paper, only very rarely have I gone out and followed exactly what I have written. Somewhere in the session, a player or coach will suggest another possibility, and the emphasis subtly changes.

In the 1987 World Cup with Scotland I always used to come up with an alternative move or something different to throw at the backs. I'd say: 'Try this. We can do this.' Then John Rutherford would chip in, 'Can we try this?' It was great. Some of it would never have worked but what I had was my backs excited about trying things. I still believe that there is nothing so dangerous as a confident back.

But ideas can come from everywhere; the search for the edge is ceaseless. So much of it over the years has come out of conversations. Even as a young player I used to talk rugby and strategy at the bar. As I have said, Bernard White, the coach of Headingley, used to talk through things with me and I was always keen to come up with strategies to try to outwit opponents. When Judy came to pick me up, even when I was still a young player, most of the others had already gone home.

Sometimes it is a solitary process, which is why I have always walked the dogs on the morning of a match whenever we are playing at home. And always walked out somewhere if we are away or on tour thousands of miles from home. That is when your head becomes clear. Except when, as happened in Durban in 2009, I was mobbed by around two thousand Lions supporters.

Of course, you worry about forgetting things. I always have a little notebook in my pocket, and it is often next to my bed. When I come back from a game or even a training session, I write down everything in my head on a sheet of paper. Then, after a while, I will go back to what I have written, cross out those things which do not seem important any more, circle the stuff that is still valid and extract it for the future.

In the professional game, the only difference is that you now have more formal time for planning and analysing from one game to another. There are more tasks and more people to achieve them. I've always thoroughly enjoyed the rugby equivalent of the boot room conversations at Anfield, the home of Liverpool Football Club, as well. The boot room was an integral part of Liverpool's success in the 60s and 70s under Bill Shankly and Bob Paisley. I have been in so many coaching groups that I have really trusted, and I drew so much from them. We might be in the team room, we could be in an airport lounge or an Indian restaurant. The chat was brilliant then. It still is now.

If you spoke to Jim Telfer, Doug Morgan and Derrick Grant about our days together with Scotland, they would immediately start twirling their hands as if they were moving pepper pots and knives and forks on a Saturday night when we were sitting down and talking rugby. There was rarely anything remotely like a specific agenda. Everyone just made some contribution. Saturday night dinner was a fantastic time.

Jim and I worked together for years. He was famous for his testiness and short temper with those who, he felt, were falling down. He realised that with some young Scots players, especially the forwards, they had to cover so much ground so quickly, and needed a toughening-up process. But I have never seen him so happy in his coaching, and so relaxed as he was on the 1997 Lions tour. He was anxious because he had been away from coaching for six years, but he was still superb on the tour. I am sure that the basis of his enjoyment was the respect he gave and received from the English forwards. He knew that they were exceptional, and gave them their heads.

There have been other figures. Some of the best rugby talk has been with Norman Mair, who hooked for Scotland in the early 1950s and who went on to become a wonderful writer on rugby and golf for the *Scotsman*. Journalists testify that his match previews were legendary and made wonderful reading. Norman joined Jim Telfer and me one night after Scotland B had played Italy near Naples. We were still talking rugby at three in the morning.

Normally, I would talk to Norman for at least ninety minutes in the week after games, and when he rang Judy would hand me the receiver and know that she would not hear from me for the next hour and a half. Norman has such a rugby brain, and we'd talk through what Scotland had done, about the opposition, absolutely anything. He was a tremendous sounding board, and a great second opinion. He helped give me clarity.

I have been so lucky with all the coaching groups I have been involved with. At Northampton, I had Paul Larkin, who was working with me in the first team; I had Jack Wright, an old Northampton forward, and I had Brett Taylor, who was running the academy. We'd go out after home games with all the coaches of all the club teams, and that was how 'the Northampton way' began to evolve. Again, it was all down to principles.

More recently at Wasps, Craig Dowd, Leon Holden, Shaun Edwards and others have formed yet another invaluable group and there was more of the same in particular with Messrs Gatland, Edwards, Howley, Rowntree and the others on the 2009 Lions tour. Simple talk about rugby is such a source of ideas.

And it has carried on. Wasps recently brought in a management company to look at how we operated. They expressed concern that we didn't have enough meetings, that we didn't have enough agendas. 'Our agenda is up there,' I said, pointing to a board on the wall of our training headquarters. We posted the fundamentals of what we were doing on that board and they rarely changed. We might add a bit but only occasionally. If it was a principle that we were working on, and if it worked really well, it was always there.

Then we had another board on which we set out what we wanted for that week, so that one did change. But otherwise that was it; it worked, we had the trophies to prove it and it is possible that the management company went away a little disappointed when we decided that we would not go along with all their meetings and agendas.

But if you are on the same wavelength, do you also have to like the people in your coaching group? What is far more important is honesty. I have worked with people who are known as spiky characters – Jim Telfer and Shaun Edwards spring to mind. But from that honesty comes respect, and the most important thing is respect for differences of opinion. We don't all try to think the same thing. Part of the challenge is when you realise that you are thinking from opposite corners; that's when I have had some really good answers.

But as for friendship, Roger Uttley and I are still close, twenty years after the 1989 Lions tour; Dick Best and I have been close friends since 1993, and Jim Telfer since 1997. Derrick, Doug, Richie Dixon and the others from Scotland are men I may not see as much as I used to, but they are people with whom I feel a special bond because of what I have been through with them.

There was a time, when I came up from Yorkshire to join the Scottish coaching set-up, when I was wondering what on earth they and I had in common. I was a secondary-modern kid from Leeds, had never lived in Scotland, certainly never gone to public school. Jim and Derrick were men from the Borders. But we found that we had rugby in common, because rugby had formed us in various different ways. You were not there essentially because someone had appointed you to a coaching post. You were there because you had lived through something. I can honestly say that with all my coaching colleagues respect and friendship have gone hand in hand.

There are also quite a few coaches who I have grown to respect in opposition ranks over the years, people against whom I know I have to be on my mettle because of what they might throw at us. I have always respected New Zealand rugby, ever since I toured there for the first time as a player in 1975 and realised, with something of a shock, how much people knew about the game down there. I remember when Derrick and I were coaching Scotland in the 1987 World Cup. We had just drawn with France in our opening game and everyone said that it was the match that very much kicked off the World Cup.

We moved up to Wellington where we had a training session

and then Derrick and I went into Wellington for coffee. While we were there, a woman came in holding two shopping bags. She recognised us.

'Great game at the weekend,' she said. 'I thought Scotland were really good. Your back row were superb, getting off the back of the line-out. Your scrummaging stopped the French and you took the French back row out of it. But why didn't you tie them in at the back?' She went on for about twenty minutes. Then she finished her coffee, wished us all the best for the rest of the tournament and thanked us for the chat. Derrick and I looked at each other. There are not many coffee bars anywhere in the world outside New Zealand where you could have had that sort of encounter.

The New Zealand environment impresses me so much. When a player becomes an All Black, he has already faced so many challenges, from his parents, his school, his early coaches, from his very background. If you put a new young Scottish player in a Scottish jersey for the first time, you have to keep your fingers crossed; you know that there may have been weaknesses in his background which will come to the surface and you are thinking: 'Bloody hell, he has got a hell of a lot to find out, he is still learning.' But young Kiwis appear to be mentally tougher; they appear to have a deeper innate understanding of the sport.

But there were others. I always respected Bob Dwyer, although I suppose we did cross swords in 1989 with the Lions. Bob was at Leicester when I was at Northampton, and you had to respect the quality of his work. I also thought that Bob Templeton, one of the father-figures of Australian coaching, was superb. I coached a world team with Tempo and I really rated him.

I also felt that Geoff Cooke did a good job with England from the late 1980s. His was probably more of an organisational than a coaching task, because they were disorganised for such a long time and I still thought that England could have done so much more with the players they had in the 1990s. I feel that we frightened them in 1990, when we won the Grand Slam. That stopped them playing a more expansive game, but they knew that they could beat sides up front and they won two Grand Slams playing less rugby than they might have. I cannot criticise them for that.

More recently, I have grown to admire Andy Robinson as a good coach. I have always rated him, and I would like to have spent more time with him when we were ostensibly together on the 2005 Lions tour in New Zealand. I was delighted when he was appointed Scotland coach in the summer of 2009 and will be fascinated to watch his progress.

But there is also coaching progression. Shaun Edwards, who won trophies for fun as a rugby league player for Wigan, is a remarkable character, driven, sometimes anxious, always engaging and with the respect of the players. He has matched his success in rugby league as a coach with Wasps and Wales and the Lions. I'd like to think that Shaun has still been improving as a coach in my time at Wasps, and that I helped him to do that over the past four years. I take a lot of pleasure in seeing how he has progressed.

As for players, well, they are all individuals, they are all at different stages. In any team you have to be prepared to absorb those players whom some consider to be difficult, even prima donnas. I can't say that there has been anyone in particular whose wavelength I couldn't get on to, and it is often the apparently difficult players who can add so much to a team. Undoubtedly I have made sure that certain players moved on from clubs I was coaching, or I omitted people from Lions tours because I had a concern about their character, but that was primarily because they had an off-field behaviour problem or a bad attitude that affected others.

In playing terms, I am always less critical of players who make mistakes than I am of those who are given a chance and don't take it. I've always told players: 'If you believe it's on, all I ask is you go 100 per cent and use 100 per cent of your ability to make it work. And then I'd never criticise you. I would only criticise half-heartedness. So even if it's the wrong decision, if you do 100 per cent then we can always play off it.'

Some people do get the reputation for being a loose cannon, for whatever reason. They have to understand that ultimately the team has to be able to rely on them. But I also very much like the observation of one French coach: 'The genius has to learn to play with the team first and *then* the team learns to play with the genius . . .' Your talent *will* show because everybody else will do the right things to give you the opportunity. It's being able to respect that that is important.

Danny Cipriani, who was with me at Wasps from the start, is one of those who causes controversy and makes some coaches nervous. He appeared to be going through a tough time in 2009 and it is clear that those who are advising him have a huge responsibility. But Danny is a good man, potentially a great player, and he would listen when Shaun and I took him to one side. Wasps were good for him, we looked after him, we gave him a season at full-back, a great position for a young fly-half to learn about the game. Genius playing with team, then team with genius. Over to you, Danny, and England.

We may not have held too many meetings at Wasps. In fact, I have never been big on management summits. However, as will now be clear to readers, I have always been big on analysis. 'Mr Meticulous' I was once labelled in a Scottish paper. I liked that. I like to think that I have been ahead of the field in aspects of analysing the opposition. I used to sit in the freezing dressing rooms at Murrayfield as a player, watching as Bill Dickinson, the coach (sorry, 'adviser to the captain'), manipulated his reel-to-reel contraption so that he could show us some particular nugget of information. It was usually worth the wait.

My first such procedure involved filling in giant hardboards with paper held firmly in place by giant clips, which Judy would buy me. I would sit for hours in front of the television analysing international matches, what teams did in certain phases and in certain positions, and fill up the cards with an avalanche of information. There was no remote control then; I had a system whereby I would make my analysis notes live, as the game was being played.

So Judy and I thought it was the height of sophisticated technology when, as Scotland coach, and despite a lack of funds at home, I bought a four-headed video recorder, the bee's knees. That made it possible to freeze the frame, and the picture was better because, when you stopped it, you could still make out detail from the picture, which was perfect. On the older machines the frame that you froze to examine would shake like mad. I could be sitting in front of it six, seven or eight hours a day and I would do that for every Test match that was relevant to the opposition Scotland were facing. It was a laborious process but it was rewarding. All my notes of analysis, from every training session, could probably fill a double garage.

For me, then, analysis began with a big hardboard with clips. But after the four-headed video recorder, things became a little more advanced. By the time I was at Northampton, there was a system which, although it was not digital, tagged the tape of the match at the spots where you had put something in, so that you could quickly whizz to the part you had marked when you wanted to examine it further or illustrate something to the players.

We then brought in a new system in Scotland, something converted from a non-sports concept which the medical profession used to log symptoms of illness. It was absolutely terrible, and it was all I could do not to throw away the laptop in frustration. But by 2002 someone had briefed me on something called Sportscode, which was being used in Australia. I flew down there in 2002 on a recce for Scotland's World Cup campaign and I spent time with the Sydney Swans, the Australian Rules club. They were really impressive, they introduced me to Sportscode and soon I was a convert.

Sportscode is very coach-friendly. You can tag everything that happens in a game – a tackle, a pass, a line-out, a scrum, anything. You can then collate the information so as to spot trends at the various phases; you can make a small film showing every scrum or every short line-out, or every kick or every line-out. It is so sophisticated and so good that, in South Africa, Rhys Long, our analyst, was giving me information from it from a game at half-time. We used Sportscode, for example, to track our way through phases. We once discovered that, while South Africa were competing very hard on the first two breakdowns, if we could be very efficient through the first two phases and keep playing so that we could get to phase numbers five or six, we were flying, we were going for it. Most times, if we got that far the Springboks struggled to hold us.

Whatever the system, the knobs and buttons, the main idea has always been to highlight the players that the opposition played through, the keys, the springboard for the other team. That is still the idea today. I am still looking for the same edges and advantages and still spending hours on analysis, perhaps just to give a presentation to a team or player that lasts only a few minutes.

But the four-headed video is now a museum piece and the techniques and equipment are developing rapidly. It is an indication of all the possibilities that exist today that the 2009 Lions took two analysts, and yet I was still spending sometimes three and four hours a day on further analysis.

Sometimes, such analysis can have a decisive impact. In 1997 with the Lions I came up with a short list of players who the Springboks played through, and, because we knew what to expect, we were able to shut them down – especially Henry Honiball, the fly-half, who made them click. By denying him his normal space, we made him look ordinary.

And we won. We coaches and analysts cannot play the game. Only the players can do that. But I suppose we can take away just a little of the unknown.

When I started coaching, at Headingley in 1980, the infrastructure was interesting. There was just me. I am not sure that the other teams in the club had coaches so I took the entire ninety players for the pre-season, and can't remember if I knew all their names. In one of my earliest sessions, I found nine different activities or exercises in which ten players could each be involved. An hour before training I went out and hammered nine posts into the ground and on each one I fixed a little card with what they had to do when they reached that post, and they went round all the posts like a circuit. There would be passing, kicking, tackling, some contact, some competition stuff, simple two-on-one and three-on-two work.

Then I would put a defender on each side of a square, the attacker started from the corner and the defenders let on to the attacker which one was going to come for him. What he had to do was get across the square and beat the defender who was coming at him. Then I would build it up and two defenders would come, so that what you were getting was defenders coming from his left or right or maybe head-on. I would walk round all the posts checking everything, though I tended to spend most time on the decision-making exercises.

The numbers fell away as winter advanced, the team captains would have been appointed by then and they would take charge of the lower teams, so I was left with about the thirty best players. I was teaching PE at the time so the organisational aspects came easily to me, and I enjoyed it right from the start. Carnegie taught you to be disciplined in your preparation. I still have my books from Carnegie, which split the coaching into introduction, preparation, objective of your practice, outcome. I would take aside the players who were best at assessing the sessions, asked them how we could improve them, what they thought about them. It was a practice I maintained and one I have always found rewarding. I would be very surprised if any players I have worked with ever found me a soft touch, but even more upset if any players have considered me a sergeant major.

Peter Winterbottom was probably my crown jewel in my Headingley years. John, his father, was a club stalwart. Peter was to come through like a meteor in the early 1980s, when he played for England for the first time and also played in the Tests for the 1983 Lions. Before that, I got him a club exchange so he had a season with Hawke's Bay in New Zealand. Peter was always going to make it.

He also liked American football so I introduced an exercise which he loved. We'd practise defence by setting down against each other like linemen and trying to force each other off the defensive line. Winters lapped it up, and he made big hits, just like the American football defenders.

At the end of my first season as a coach we had a good record. We opened with a huge win over Broughton Park, and also beat Waterloo, Sale and Harrogate, and everyone seemed to be reasonably happy. The influential *Rothman's Rugby Yearbook* said of Headingley: 'The team was better organised than previously, largely owing to Ian McGeechan taking over coaching responsibility.' I never missed a *Rothman's Yearbook* until it stopped appearing.

It took a year or two to bring home my first trophy, however. We struggled for a season but in 1982–83, even though we were often without Winters, who was away on representative duty, we played some really good stuff, as usual with the backs and back row heavily involved and the front five scrapping for whatever possession they could claw back. We won the Yorkshire Cup for the first time since 1921, which was a really big thing. Tim Sinclair, our captain, also made the England squad and Paul Huntsman, who went on to prop for England, was just emerging as well. The satisfaction of seeing players win representative honours never left me, even if in the later professional years it could be aggravating, especially at Northampton and Wasps, to play without half your team. In 1982–83 at Headingley we lost only thirteen of our forty-three games (no easy life as an amateur) and we averaged around eighteen points a match, which in that era was good.

Season 1983–84 was my last as Headingley coach. We retained the Yorkshire Cup, finished sixth in the Northern Merit table and we reached the third round of the John Player Cup, where we lost 17–0 to the mighty Bath, who went on to win the final. These were great formative years, and we played a really good style of rugby.

But by now I was on the Scotland radar. Jim Telfer had been Scotland coach but he moved up to coach the 1983 Lions in New

Zealand. Colin Telfer moved up from the B team to coach the national side, and, after some games in charge of the Anglo-Scots, I was made Scotland B coach. Judy may have thought that the years of the long trips up to Edinburgh were a thing of the past. She was wrong.

At least a couple of my B games provided wonderful experiences. We beat Ireland by 22–13 at Melrose and then we beat France B away in Albi, a very rare win on French soil. Alastair Campbell and Gordon Hunter from my B team forced their way into the senior team in 1984. Also in that B team with me were some other likely lads – Gavin Hastings, Finlay Calder, David Sole and John Jeffrey. No wonder we were successful. In that B crop, therefore, I had respectively two future Lions captains, the captain of Scotland when we won the 1990 Grand Slam, and one of the best flankers the country ever had.

In 1988, I was appointed Scotland coach, obviously a brilliant moment for me. I coached them for 33 games until 1993, when, after the Lions tour to New Zealand that year, I left to coach Northampton. In 1997, Jim asked me to take a series of coaching clinics for professional players and club coaches. Eventually, he approached me to help with Scotland in April 1999. I assisted him till the end of the 1999 World Cup before taking over the reins in January, 2000. I then took charge again for another forty-three games, leaving after the World Cup of 2003 in Australia had ended in defeat by France. In my first stint my record of success was 60 per cent, which might have meant the sack for an All Blacks coach but in the context of Scotland's rugby history was excellent. Jim and I felt that the period between 1989 and 1993, when we had an excellent Five Nations, through the Grand Slam season of 1990, a two-match tour of New Zealand in 1990 when we were fiercely competitive against the All Blacks and should have won at least one of the Tests – plus the 1991 World Cup when we finished fourth – represented the high point of our rugby fortunes.

We were not nearly so successful in my second stint. The

professional era had done us no favours whatsoever, bickering over the administration of the game and the professional set-up was rife, we had no real development system for our players in place, and we won just eighteen of forty-three games for a less impressive 43 per cent success rate. Sadly, the rate was still falling for years after and has yet to recover. With rather frustrating symmetry, therefore, my overall record from seventy-six matches as Scotland coach stands at W37, L37, D2, for an average success rate of 50 per cent.

There is no challenge bigger than a Lions tour, but in my career and for any Scotland coach the pulse quickener has always been the match against England. And often the most difficult to win. How could it be otherwise? In my lifetime England have always been far bigger and more powerful, and in some ways more sure of themselves. Players have been selected from far greater numbers. England teams have been able at certain times to strangle the life out of Scotland, to establish their pattern and to try to crush us.

And as I have said, it was Border scavengers time when we played them. We tried to be really quick about what we did and actually maintain as much broken play as possible. That is why, after the famous Grand Slam series of 1990, the high point of Scotland rugby and whose culmination was one of the best days of my career, it was Eddie Butler who remarked that it looked like organised chaos. Now to me that was a compliment because that's exactly what I wanted to create: it wasn't structured, it wasn't set-piece orientated; it was ball in play, game broken up.

At the time I used to say to our players: 'Look, this is the game we are wanting to play; if we get into another game, it doesn't suit us – because that's the game that we're not good at.' In my time with Scotland we had three famous wins over England, which in many ways defined what we were trying to do against them.

In fact, the best example of the philosophy emerging triumphantly, the most thumping defeat of the English with which I was ever involved, was probably the 33–6 win at Murrayfield in 1986, when I was assistant coach. We kept the ball moving. John Rutherford was superb at fly-half and we forced England to play at a pace higher then they were comfortable with. I think one of the headlines at the time was 'England dinosaurs' since they based everything on the set piece.

And we played with such accuracy, such pace, for eighty minutes that we were taking out a good team, with good players, but with a completely different philosophy, with a high-intensity game. If you had the smaller players, if you didn't have the strengths right through it, you had to break the game up.

We lost 32–13 to Australia in my first game in 1988, but at least I had the bonus of giving a first cap to a tough lad from Jedforest called Gary Armstrong, one of the best and most wholehearted players I ever coached. For the 1989 Five Nations, I made Finlay Calder captain, and also capped for the first time Sean Lineen in the centre, Craig Chalmers, who struck up a long and fruitful partnership at half-back with Gary, and also hooker Kenny Milne.

This was the start of what some have said is the best few years that Scotland ever had. We beat Wales by 23–7 at Murrayfield, we were unlucky to come out with only a 12–12 draw at Twickenham and we beat Ireland 37–21 at Murrayfield. We played some great rugby.

The season after – and therefore following the 1989 Lions tour under Finlay's captaincy – we were not so good and it was the confidence gained in the previous season that pulled us through. We beat France, Scotland and Ireland, and yet went to the Grand Slam game as massive underdogs. In our hearts, though, we knew we had a fighting chance.

It is surely now the most famous match in Scotland rugby history. Both Scotland and England were going for the Grand Slam but up to then England had played all the rugby. Will Carling's men were in town and full of confidence. I forget what the betting was, but we were long odds against. England were coming to complete their Slam by playing fantastic stuff. There was a bite and a tension in the air, there was the thing about Margaret Thatcher's poll tax and the fact that there were so few Conservative MPs in

Scotland. The build-up was mammoth and it was a mammoth occasion, incredibly charged and emotional, and I have never experienced such fervency or support from a Scotland crowd.

The signature that day was 'the Walk'. David Sole, a fantastic Scotland captain, led the team on to the field at walking pace. It seems old hat now, since so many teams do the same. But in 1990 it was traditional for teams to run on to the field, even to sprint. There was a latent menace in David's walk and it was very effective.

But the hours of analysis, of delving into England's play, had given me confidence. I knew exactly how to beat them. We found that England tried to play so much off Will Carling. With line-out ball off the top, it would go through Richard Hill and Rob Andrew at half-back, and then Carling would take a flat ball and take it on. Sometimes, he got through because he was a strong player. If he did he offloaded to Peter Winterbottom and they kept it going.

But if they were stopped they would recycle and the forwards would come round and play off Richard Hill at scrum-half. Then, after another phase, it would go out to someone like Rory Underwood. They were beating teams by twenty and thirty points, and yet no one was trying to stop them at those first two breakdowns, so Carling would come up, the forwards would play short next time and then the ball would go wide.

But not only did we have to smash them at the early breakdowns, we knew that we had to keep the ball as long as we could, so that they could not even begin to establish themselves. In the end, we did it brilliantly. It was nearly fourteen minutes before they had any effective possession. I was determined that we would raise question marks in their heads, we would keep ball and, if they won it, we would smash into Carling and their midfield whenever we had the chance. And smash their forwards as they came round.

It worked brilliantly. England were knocked out of their stride and you could see them beginning to look quizzical, trying to work out what was going wrong. During and after the game, a certain amount of bickering broke out in their ranks as to who was responsible, who was meant to be leading, and so on. Scott Hastings and Sean Lineen defended incredibly and it is hard to recall a single time when England's attack plan came to life.

We were 6–0 up after our outstanding start, with two penalties by Craig Chalmers. They did score a try through Jeremy Guscott, but we scored early in the second half when Tony Stanger ran on to a chip ahead from Gavin Hastings when we worked a move from a scrum, and we won 13–7. It took England a long time to recover from that defeat. They drew in their horns and played narrow rugby for some seasons, grinding out the wins. We had won the Slam that had always eluded me as a player: the feeling was the most satisfying I had ever had.

In many ways we were even bigger underdogs for the third of the England trilogy, at Murrayfield in 2000, than we had been in 1990, because, in fact, we had lost all our games in the season to date and they were going for another Slam. The papers recorded astronomical odds against. So, once again, it was a combination of breaking up the English pattern, concentrating on the things that made them tick and also convincing the Scotland players that we could do it. And, also, the analysis.

We worked out that the key to opening the door to England's play was in the person of Matt Dawson, who was captain. He had been taking a lot of tap penalties during the season and bursting away on his own, and I found, on analysis, that this was injecting a great deal of pace into the England attacks. We had to stop him as soon as he took his taps, and the key was Glenn Metcalfe, because, as he was the full-back, the probability was that he would always be 10 metres away, while our players nearer to Dawson were out of the game. I told the referee that this was what we intended to do, just in case he thought that Glenn, or whoever made the hit, had started too close.

We also had to confront England as quickly as we could; we had to keep the ball behind them, and stop their expansive running game. The good news for us was that it poured with rain from just after the kick-off until the end of the game. This helped us defend against another of their ploys. They were trying to copy France, who had flankers on the wing so that when the ball came into play they would stay out there and the front five would go in the middle. England had a variation and, whether or not it was just something to show off, they stuck Neil Back out at outside centre. I said to Gregor Townsend, who was in our midfield, that first of all he had to smash Back if it was England's ball and if he got possession then he really had to have a go at Back. As it turned out, we strangled England all over the field, and the longer the match went on the more hesitant they became.

But on the Thursday before the game there was still the battle of the mind to win with the Scottish players, whose confidence was low, and we had nothing remotely like the steel and experience of the David Sole side in 1990. The players turned up expecting the normal hard session. I told them that we were going off together for an afternoon of outdoor activities, and we went shooting, Land Rover driving and the like. And we followed that with afternoon tea as a squad. I just wanted to make the point that we knew how to beat England, and therefore didn't need another two hours of training, boring the pants off everyone. We saved our energy and did the job when it mattered. I also felt that we had played some good rugby that season, and had a video made of the best plays, set to music. It clearly had an effect.

England took a 10–3 lead in the first half but the weather was deteriorating and Scott Murray and Richard Metcalfe were disrupting their line-out. We didn't give Matt Dawson a yard all day and the remainder of the match was played in their territory. We overhauled them when Gordon McIlwham got to within feet of the English line for Duncan Hodge to score. They crumbled. Another England Grand Slam dream had died. I tried to keep a straight face afterwards when remarking that we had won the Calcutta Cup, but England were still champions so everyone was happy.

*

Of course, it did not always work out like that. England were generally on top in that era. But we did keep playing well after 1990, and in New Zealand on tour that summer and in the 1991 World Cup we were often a really good side. There is no doubt that the best two games of rugby in 1990 were the two Tests against New Zealand. I was so disappointed we didn't win the Second Test, I still am today, but we lost because the referee failed us. We didn't lose any provincial games, an outstanding achievement. We beat West Coast, Nelson Bays/Marlborough, Canterbury, Southland and Manawatu and drew with Wellington.

We lost the First Test by 31–16 in Dunedin. We scored three tries, by Chris Gray, Sean Lineen and David Sole, and to score three against the All Blacks was a rarity. We played some great stuff, but our defending was really poor. We leaked five tries and were beaten in the line-out. It was encouraging up to a point. In the Second Test at Eden Park, we scored two tries to one but were beaten by six penalties from Grant Fox awarded by Derek Bevan, who may have become frightened of refereeing an upset.

We kept our form through the World Cup. We came through our pool after a tough game against Ireland, we beat a really good Western Samoan team who had beaten Wales, but we were overpowered by England in the semi-final, a very different, ultra-conservative England with none of the flair of their 1990 side. Gavin Hastings missed an easy penalty when they led us by 3–0. We finished fourth in the tournament, losing the play-off to the All Blacks by 13–6 and yet we were competitive against the best sides in the world and it was a very, very good feeling. I felt that, on our day, there were no teams we could not beat.

We never quite had the numbers or the experience to repeat our Slam in my years as Scotland coach, especially in the second period when we lost power from our domestic game. England got their revenge at Twickenham in 1992, and the team was now breaking up – Finlay had gone, Gary Armstrong was battling injury and David Sole retired in 1992. We had a shot at the

Triple Crown at Twickenham in 1993 but England were too good.

When I came back in 2000, we were very inconsistent, and we welcomed Italy into the new Six Nations Championship by losing to them in their first match; it was a huge relief when we beat England in the rain, showing that we could still pull it off. The best result of my second stint was the 21–6 win over South Africa in 2002, at a time when the Boks were gearing up for the World Cup under Rudi Straueli. But in the 2003 Six Nations we were beaten heavily by Ireland at home and France away. We did bounce back again and played some great stuff in South Africa on a short tour in 2003 (we lost 29–25 and 28–19 but were in contention for both).

There was no real improvement going into the World Cup. We were heavily beaten by France in the major pool game of the 2003 World Cup in Sydney, we had to fight hard to reach the knock-out stages against Fiji, who scored two tries through Rupeni Caucau on the wing, and Australia beat us 33–16 in the quarter-final, which was my last game in charge.

The word rollercoaster just about covers it. We missed the hard men who had given us authority back in 1990; we did not seem to be developing players of authority; the conveyor belt of talent moved fitfully. After the World Cup, I removed my tracksuit for what could possibly have been the last time as a professional coach, and I became director of rugby at the Scottish Rugby Union, a prospect which (I tried to tell myself) I relished. I had been a rugby coach for twenty-three years, and a professional coach for ten. It seemed a long time. I did not know then that the suit would never feel comfortable.

What is the ultimate coaching thrill? Winning, of course. But for me it is when you know you can step back, perhaps not a situation in which I often found myself in Scotland. I believe that when you put new players in or a relatively new team together, you've got to be pretty direct in your coaching; you have to give them a framework, and a thinking and an understanding, because if you haven't got one mind, and one overall idea of what you are trying to do, that's when you fall between two stools. Once you've got that base right, once you've got all the basics, you can do anything; you can mix and match and that's where the decision-making and the talent shows, and then they bring the best out of each other.

It is a priceless moment when the players take over. Warren Gatland tells the story of taking a Wasps training session before one of the big finals. Actually, it was being run by the players – they had indeed taken over. One of the office girls came up as Warren was standing there and asked, 'Excuse me, I don't want to sound rude, but what is it that you do?' Warren thought it was a terrific compliment. Sometimes in training, when you have taken the team to a certain point, you are just about to say something when one of the players finishes your sentence. It is fantastic to reach the point when you are actually saying less and less. That for me is the ultimate coaching thrill, when the words and action are coming from the players.

You want your players to have confidence in the game you want them to play, in the game that you know is going to be a problem for your opposition. Whether it's the best defending in the world, whether it's keeping the ball, whether it's being able to keep it chaotic, as we did with Scotland; whatever it is, everybody has to understand this is the game we want to play – because it is the biggest problem you can give your opponent.

And when all else fails, what's the plan? Go forward, and win the contact. If you do that, you will probably win.

10

Pathfinders

The 1989 Lions tour of Australia

Looking back, the 1989 tour to Australia seems almost quaint. We only played twelve games, and two of those were afterthoughts following the final Test. Compared to the grandiose Lions crusades of old it was also very short. None of the previous post-war Lions tours until then had consisted of fewer than eighteen games, and many of them far more. There were only three Tests, another record low. And there were also three policemen.

It also seems odd to look back from the viewpoint of 2009, when Lions tours are bigger and more popular than ever, to grasp that in 1989, only twenty years ago, there were question marks over the entire concept of the Lions themselves. This was a trial tour. It was the year that apartheid in South Africa began to crumble, along with the Berlin Wall, but it was to be three years before South Africa emerged from the wilderness years of the sporting boycott. New Zealand was the only Lions venue left, and it had been six years between tours, the longest gap since the Second World War. Jim Telfer had coached the ill-fated 1983 Lions in New Zealand. After that, silence.

The four Home Unions, which organised the Lions, decided

that they had to try to create a new Lions venue. Australia. This did not sit well with grand old Lions such as Willie John McBride and J. P. R. Williams, who saw Australia as merely a stopping-off point en route to New Zealand, which is exactly how the country had been treated several times by the Lions. 'These are not real Lions,' said JPR, a view shared by a number of others.

Was Australia really up to hosting a Lions tour, and would interest in the Test matches be high enough? It was only two years since Australia had reached the semi-finals of the inaugural Rugby World Cup, which they part-hosted. Their semi, a famous match against France which they lost to a fantastic try scored by the great Serge Blanco in the last minute, was staged at the charmless Concord Oval, a mediocre ground tucked away in a long suburban street of endless car lots and fast-food restaurants.

The Oval seated only about 18,000 and yet the semi was not even sold out. There were rows of empty seats: vast areas of the nation seemed not to realise that a rugby union World Cup was taking place. The land of the great outdoors was outdoors all right, but at cricket, Australian Rules, rugby league and the beach.

But did the other games on the 1989 itinerary – Queensland B in Cairns, New South Wales B in Dubbo, New South Wales Country in Newcastle – have the ring of a true Lions tour? They did not; but was that simply because no one had tried them out yet? No one really knew. To win 100–0 in front of a hundred spectators was not a true Lions occasion, in any way.

So not real Lions, then? A half-hearted rugby tour to a half-hearted rugby nation? Very, very far from it. The 1989 Lions tour was a remarkable trip, deeply satisfying in its outcome and one on which, obviously, I learned an incredible amount to store away for future tours. It brought a great Lions triumph by a team that also realised, at the end, that it was playing within itself, and wanted to carry on to test its upper limits. It was a fantastic experience.

So much for a half-hearted series. The truth is that any confrontation between Australians and the old country in any arena will always be fierce. The Wallabies had achieved a thumping Grand Slam over the Home Unions in 1984, when they had never looked like losing any of the four games. They had been knocked out by France in that semi in 1987 courtesy of that famous late try, and, the year before we toured, England had been hammered by Australia in a two-match series. The vociferous Alan Jones had departed as Australia's coach, leaving Bob Dwyer, perhaps marginally less vociferous, perhaps not, in charge. The perspective of history also tells us that Australia were to win the World Cup two years after the Lions tour. It was therefore a monumental challenge.

Clem Thomas, in his Lions history, wrote: 'It was as physically demanding a Test series as any I have witnessed or heard about.' Coming from a man as hard and rumbustious as Clem, who had seen and done it all, that was some observation. The effects reverberated for a long time. I feel that in 1989 we established Australia for all time as a worthy Lions touring venue, and when the Lions returned in 2001, under Graham Henry, it was one of the biggest events of the year in any sport. In many ways we put Australian home Tests on the map for the country itself, because, inside two years, the 18,000 or so crowd at a 1987 World Cup semi-final had become a 44,000 sell-out at the Sydney Football Stadium in 1989.

The tour saw harsh and sometimes brutal play, and such ferocious controversy that some Australians, in my view anxious because they could see the series slipping away, and goaded by a major home media campaign, compared the controversies and dislike of the Poms (plus Irish) to those of the Bodyline series. If it meant that the Lions were winning, I had no problem being seen as Douglas Jardine.

Bob Dwyer, the Wallabies coach, said after the series that his team had 'been beaten up by the English coppers', a reference to the fact that our squad, for an extremely physical series, contained Police Constables Dean Richards and Wade Dooley and Inspector Paul Ackford. There was a hard core of England heavies including those three, the edgy Brian Moore at hooker and the famous Gloucester flanker Mike 'Iron Mike' Teague, who was deservedly to be made player of the series.

On the field, it was huge. I am very much of the opinion that in demonstrating to Dwyer and Australia that their team had a soft centre, notably up front, we helped them to begin a weeding-out process which saw a different Wallabies team win the 1991 World Cup. And they never even thanked us.

Ultimately, we won, becoming only the third post-war Lions out of twelve to win a series, and we became the first Lions ever to win a series after losing the First Test (and remember that previous parties had a four-Test series, not three, in which to stage their comeback).

We were said to be a forward-dominated team but the signature moment of the whole tour did not come from a forward. In the previous home season, sifting likely talent, I had gone to Bath to watch their young uncapped centre. After the match, I told Clive Rowlands, the manager, 'I'd love to take him on the tour.'

Jeremy Guscott made it. We originally chose Will Carling, who was then well on his way to becoming one of the most famous and highly publicised players in the world, predicted for all-time greatness. But Carling had to withdraw, with shin splints, although there may have been something of taking his bat home after Finlay Calder, at the time my Scotland captain, had been made tour captain. Rather oddly, Carling hung around the Oatlands Park hotel in Weybridge, where we gathered before departure. He said he was in some kind of media role. I thought that was strange.

Instead of Carling we brought in the rough young Bath diamond who had never played for England apart from an end-of-season jaunt in Romania, where he scored three tries. At the time, as I am sure he would not mind me saying, Guscott was difficult, even truculent. On tour, he and Chris Oti, the Wasps and England wing, hit it off very badly. They were highly intolerant of each other and the ill feeling reached boiling point when the pair had a fight in a car park after one of the games. Oti had to go home injured (not as a result of the dust-up), which may not have been the worst thing. But as for Jerry, I knew he had a fantastic talent.

At the time of the Second Test in Brisbane, which we had to win or die, he was still an apprentice bricklayer, having given up a job as a bus driver. At the end of the match, when we were leading by only two points and were desperate to seal it, Jerry typically took responsibility. He backed himself. He set off on a famous individual run, chipped the ball between two Australian defenders, accelerated smoothly, picked the ball up as it hopped, and ran on to score the try which decided the match.

Lions legend has it that a supporter at the ground in Brisbane turned to a friend as Guscott dived, and said: 'That boy will never lay another brick.' He never did. Jerry's father, watching at home in Bath at dawn, was so excited and full of adrenalin that he left his house, walked through the deserted streets to Jeremy's, and demolished a wall with a sledgehammer. Luckily, it was part of a planned rebuilding.

Jeremy Guscott's career soared. He played in two Tests in 1989, all three in 1993 and all three again in 1997, when he produced another devastating late score. He became a great Lion, one with whom I have enjoyed a terrific relationship.

Will Carling toured unhappily in New Zealand in 1993, then withdrew from consideration in 1997 (therefore becoming the only player I can ever remember opting out of a Lions tour, a sad decision). Some say that you only go down in history and become a true great if you succeed with the Lions. Guscott succeeded. History may judge that Carling did not.

Amazingly, the size of the tour management team was seen by some at the time as almost an extravagance. There were all of five of us. You could still have fitted the lot of us into a family car – and in that age of amateurism I am surprised they didn't try it. The management group on the 2005 tour of New Zealand was to total thirty. In 1989, we had manager Clive Rowlands, two medical men (Dr Ben Gilfeather and Kevin 'Smurph' Murphy, the physiotherapist), Roger Uttley and myself.

Roger Uttley, then England coach, owner of one of rugby's great craggy faces and a fellow 1974 Lion, was appointed assistant coach. Assistant coach? The reaction of some was almost as if we had announced that we were taking a Martian along with us. Looking back, it might seem a rather obvious move. At last there was someone to look after the forwards, if I was away with the backs. In 1971 in New Zealand by all accounts, when the celebrated Carwyn James, the sole coach on the tour, was taking a session with the forwards, the backs would go and kick a soccer ball around.

The concept of big coaching squads with specialists was still years in the future, and it was not so many Lions tours before 1989 that the idea of taking a coach at all was held to be a form of cheating, of taking it all too seriously. The 1966 Lions took John Robins as coach, but this revolutionary concept was so alien that, apparently, Robins had no real role and Mike Campbell-Lamerton, the captain, tried to do the job himself. I had Uttley and was very happy.

Clive Rowlands was ahead of his time. If you read any Lions history you realise that old traditions, political considerations and rugby's old committee system so often intervened to scupper tours, especially when it came to choosing the squad. Not only did Rowlands offer me the job as tour coach without interview, but he told me from the start that I would get the players I wanted – there would be other selectors, but they would give great weight to my own preferences.

Even after that, he gave me two wild cards – meaning that I could disagree with up to two of the final choices and they could be changed. This was a freedom that was withdrawn from me in 1993, something I always regretted, and a freedom I insisted upon by the time of the 1997 tour. Without it, I would not have accepted the post of coach. The idea that a Lions party should be chosen by a group, as individuals without a holistic philosophy or with scant regard as to how it might all fit together, is anathema to me.

Rowlands could be restless, and may sometimes have come across as rather loud and impulsive. But he was an excellent manager and he was very considerate on the personal front. I was still teaching at Fir Tree Middle School, in Leeds, where I had always been fortunate. I had been given time off with pay by my headmasters, both when I was playing for Scotland and in my early coaching career.

But by now another, younger, headmaster had come in, possibly a little jealous of my profile, and who was not nearly so well disposed to me. From then on, my coaching career had to be conducted in time off, without pay. For some years, to be a rugby coach used to cost me around a third of my annual salary, because on Scotland duty I was away for roughly a third of the year. We were struggling quite badly at the time. I have to say that the daily tour allowance with the Lions, of around £1.25 a day, did not alleviate the problems very much.

To help tide us over, Judy first had to go out to work, then decided to take a degree in music and PE. During the build-up to the Lions, she was doing a really difficult teaching practice. One day, I had to meet Clive in Cardiff for a selection meeting. The following day was a huge one for Judy's teaching practice. We stayed up all night, making sure we'd gone through her lesson plan, and all her preparation. I must have gone to bed in the early hours, had about two hours' sleep, then drove from Leeds to Cardiff to pick the Lions team.

Clive must have noticed something. Soon afterwards he rang again and told me that we needed more meetings. I was thinking: 'Oh no! What am I going to tell Judy?' He said that I should report to Tenby, way down in West Wales, over Easter. However, he also told me to bring Judy and the children.

It was a long, long way. My battered Ford Capri had gone well past the second zero point on the clock, from all the chugging from Leeds to Edinburgh and back. At the time, the Scottish

Rugby Union had a sponsorship deal with one of the big car makers. They had a spare car. I was coaching on time off without pay, I had to travel hundreds of miles on a round trip to Tenby, but, as I was an amateur, they said that I couldn't use the car.

Then, because we presented it to them that it was Lions business and therefore in some way different, they relented and decided that I would not be professionalising myself by driving it. What a relief.

Judy remembers the journey as a nightmare, with the motorways snarled up by Easter traffic and accidents, and that we weaved on and off the motorway down packed side roads. When we got there, however, things improved rapidly. We found that Clive had spun us a line. He had booked us into a hotel right up on the cliffs above Tenby, he joined us for dinner on the first night with his wife, Margaret, then he left us to it.

'What about the meetings?' I asked.

'You and I have had a chat over dinner. That's it,' he said. In the end he wanted us to relax, and I think he wanted to reassure Judy that I would be in good hands while I was away.

On the tour, he was exactly the same. He could sense when the pressure was on. Roger and I would get together mid-evening to plan the next day. 'When you've finished,' he'd say, 'come on up to my room.' He would have beers poured for us, ready and waiting on the table. If there were any issues, he'd take them on board and fix them for us. He was a really good Lions manager. It's impossible for a tour to be harmonious without one.

And, equally, it is impossible to win without an inspirational figure as captain. I had toured in 1974 under Willie John McBride, who was made for the job, and endured the tour in 1977 under Phil Bennett, who was not. I knew just how critical the choice of captain was.

For my first Lions captain I looked no further than Finlay Calder. There were other contenders. I suppose that there was something in Finlay that I also found in Gavin Hastings, Martin Johnson and Paul O'Connell, my other three choices in the future.

There were two alternative approaches in 1989. England at the time had a huge and experienced pack, and played to it. Probably too much. The captain was either going to be one of the England heavy gang, or someone from outside altogether, a counterpoint – in other words, Calder. Yes, I wanted those powerful England heavies in there to underpin the tour; they were a luxury I have not often enjoyed in my coaching career. But the England way was not the way I wanted to play.

Finlay was, and is, a really impressive man and an odd combination. He had a real hard edge to him. If he could hurt someone, within the laws, he would. I remember when Scotland played a tour match against Canterbury in New Zealand in 1990, he drove into a ruck, perfectly legally, and broke the ribs of someone who was hanging on the fringe of the ruck. He knew exactly what he was doing.

But, rather strangely, he sometimes lacked confidence in himself. Several times in Australia he asked me if I thought he should be dropped in favour of Andy Robinson, the other open side. He was always questioning whether he was worth his place. He once got up in front of the squad and raised the subject of his being left out. It took a good talking-to from senior players, who pointed out how effective he was in what he said behind the scenes as well as on the field, to reassure him.

He could also be off the wall. He would have a whisky school on the evening before a home Scotland Test match. One Friday at the Scotland team hotel on my way to a team meeting, I knocked on his door. Finlay opened it.

'Can I have a word?'

Finlay stood back and I walked in. Inside were Derek White, John Jeffrey and David Sole. They each had a glass of whisky.

'What are you doing? There's a team meeting in ten minutes.'

'This is our Friday night whisky,' he said. 'It sets us up.'

He poured me a glass, we had a drink, chatted, and all set off for the team meeting, smelling of whisky. It was the kind of rapport I had with Finlay. I could be honest with him, and he with me. Essentials.

Some of the glamour had been taken from the party in the autumn of 1988 when Jonathan Davies, who would have been the Test fly-half, switched codes and joined Widnes rugby league. I remember thinking how big a blow that was – it loomed ever larger as time went on because Rob Andrew, England's fly-half, had a poor Five Nations in 1989 and he didn't even make the original squad.

Of the two fly-halves we did take, Paul Dean of Ireland was cruelly injured in the very first game in Perth, and was invalided home, and Craig Chalmers of Scotland did not quite find his best form. Andrew flew out, probably for us more in hope than expectation.

Even without Jonathan Davies, the party gradually took shape in my mind. So did the type of character I looked for then, and have done ever since. At hooker, the two men we chose were Brian Moore of England and Steve Smith of Ireland. Smith was huge, a good lad and a good player. He could carry the ball powerfully and with pace, and throw very well. Moore was far smaller, not nearly as good an athlete – but he was to play in all the Test matches.

It was another Lions lesson. Moore displayed a harsh attitude in his rugby, he was indomitable, he was a winner, whereas Smith was far more laid-back. There is such a thing as a Test match animal: Moore was one, and the trick on all future Lions tours was to uncover the others. Such men have the extra, crucial, edge over the normal international player. They are different beings.

Another selection was also rewarding. The Irishman Donal Lenihan was not quite in the same class as the other three locks I chose – Robert Norster, the great line-out technician, and Dooley and Ackford. But Lenihan became a highly significant figure on the tour, and underlined another lesson. The midweek team is vital, especially for tour morale and momentum. If the midweek team goes badly, it casts a pall over the whole trip.

But the midweek team can save the whole thing, can create a

fantastic buzz, as Donal's Doughnuts, many of whom never really came close to selection for a Test, were to do in 1989.

Even this early in my Lions coaching career I knew that one bad apple could spoil the whole barrel. Clive had given me those two wild cards in selection and I wasn't going to waste them. I used one wild card, and so one particular player who was judged to be something of a social risk did not become a Lion in 1989.

It was a delight to coach in those dry, balmy Australian conditions and it helped me understand why Australian basic skills are so good. There was a curtain-raiser before one of the up-country games in Dubbo, out in deepest New South Wales. Some of the skills in that game, the speed at which the youngsters were transferring the ball, were marvellous. This was only a country side, not even an elite team. Very impressive. I loved the environment we had come into.

People made a lot – before, during and after the tour – of conflicts between England and Scotland players and philosophies. In the seasons before the tour England had a good side, but I thought they were poor tactically and never became as good as they could have been. I thought the worst rugby match I can ever remember watching was in 1988 when England beat Scotland 9–6 at Murrayfield. Will Carling said afterwards: 'It's not about rugby, it's about England winning.'

Derrick Grant, the Scotland coach, hated it, and not just through sour grapes. 'Enough is enough. If that's the way it's going I am not associating with it,' he said and left the post soon afterwards. Roger Uttley came into the dressing room afterwards and Derrick was so upset that he wouldn't speak to him. He was incensed because England had such a good side, and yet wouldn't play. They were booed from the field.

When I took over, in the aftermath of that game, I said that I would make no excuses for beating England any way I could. England were so powerful at the time, and I knew that the Lions strength would be based on their outstanding forwards. Wales

were all over the shop then, anyway. But, as I have said, the
England style was not the one I wanted to adopt on tour. I wanted
to use that strength and take things on.

There was also, at least among outsiders, a major stylistic argument – would we use the Scotland rucking game, or the England
mauling game? Others tried to claim that Roger, since he was the
England coach, had fallen out with the Scottish forwards on tour
and was almost sidelined. Frankly, none of it was true; it is just
something that seems to be accepted wisdom when outsiders are
talking about the tour.

It was never, for me, a choice between rucking and mauling. I
knew that if we could control possession, and if we could produce quick ball, then it did not matter if it was coming back
hand to hand through mauls or from the ground with rucks. We
did a lot of really powerful driving. I told the boys that it was fine
to maul it, as England preferred to, just as long as they released
the ball when we were still moving forward. Otherwise, it was a
waste.

Also, I think this suited players such as Dean Richards. People
thought he was slow and one-dimensional. In fact, he had power
and very good hands. If we could get those big forwards really
powering through we would be in business. I used players like
Dean and Brian Moore as sounding boards throughout the trip. I
trusted their judgement implicitly. Dean might say that we had
trained enough one day, or that the lads could have done a bit
more the next. Whatever he said was good enough for me.

We had to change things a bit after the First Test, following
what I can only describe as a light-bulb moment when, in the
wake of heavy defeat, I was convinced that I knew how to beat
the Wallabies. It was deemed at the end of the tour that we had
not invested in back play, or what people call open rugby. I did
admit at the end that I regretted not being able to develop the
back play more, but there was simply no time, though it is significant that near the end of the trip, and notably in the final
match, against an ANZAC team containing a number of All

Blacks, we started playing some good rugby, and the players were full of regret that we were not going on to New Zealand to show what we could achieve.

But in my opinion the style came together pretty well. We had to control the ball, control the release, and in that context it didn't matter whose style we followed. If there was anything between Roger and the Scots players I was totally unaware of it. Roger wasn't a Jim Telfer sort of figure, he was his own man, and we got on very well.

He was also a good man. During one of his team talks, he was talking about precision – being really precise about what we wanted to do, precise about how we did it. To illustrate what he had in mind, he gave us an example from his own playing career. 'I remember the Second Test in 1974,' he said. 'Or was it the Third . . .?'

There was also another balance to achieve. Off the field. There always is, even in the modern, ultra-serious professional era of today. Lions tours of old were fantastic social occasions with close contact between the tour party and the host country and the people. Clem Thomas tells the story of the 1955 Lions tour to South Africa where he was invited to stay on a farm way out in the hinterland.

The farm had been menaced by a leopard but the host was so keen to show his hospitality that he delayed the hunt so that Thomas could shoot the leopard himself when he arrived. Even in 1974 and 1977 it was not unknown for old-style drinking sessions to prevail – and not completely unheard of long after that, either.

It was impossible, even in such a glamorous country as Australia, for the players to spend their days sightseeing and social-ising, but we wanted to strike a balance. It's important to enjoy the tour, and find out something about the host country, although you must never forget exactly why you are there.

The Great Barrier Reef is a must-see if you are staying anywhere on the east coast of Australia. I suggested a compromise. We trained at 7.30 a.m., got back to the hotel, breakfasted, changed, they held up the boat for us for half an hour and we had our day of downtime on the wonderful Barrier Reef. That is the sort of accommodation I have always tried to make for the players. It was a brilliant day, so much so that in my next letter home to Judy I wrote that it had been the best day of my life. Such subtlety. I don't think she has ever forgiven me.

There was more downtime in Cairns, in far northern Queensland, after the midweek game there. Roger and I went out to a bar with some of the players and we simply got caught up. That's my excuse anyway. There was John Jeffrey, Finlay Calder, Brian Moore, Dean Richards. It was a hard school.

We were drinking Test Tubes – they would fill a row of tubes with different cocktails which we had to down in one. I recall that one of the drinks was called Slippery Nipples. Bizarrely, there was a television crew from England there, including a young Carol Vorderman, until quite recently the star of *Countdown*. Can't remember why she was there. I can honestly say that in my whole life I have only been horribly, seriously drunk about five times – and this was one of the times.

Somehow, much later, Uttley and I got back to the hotel. The room was spinning wildly all night. Next day, I woke with an uneasy feeling in more ways than one. There was an early morning session. I rang Roger's room.

'Roger. You'll have to take the session. I can't. I am wasted. There is no way.'

Uttley's tone was heartrending, a plea for mercy. 'Geech,' he said. 'I can't.' I staggered out and took the session. I cannot remember what I said or what we did. Afterwards, John Jeffrey told me it was one of the hardest sessions he had ever done. And for me, the longest.

We began our lives as Lions in Perth, Western Australia, on a warm day against a team comprised almost exclusively of Kiwis, and we won 44–0. Good. It showed we could play rugby on hard fields, and Brendan Mullin, who was a really clever player in the centre, scored a hat-trick. Sadly, we lost Paul Dean for the tour, a terrible blow for Paul and the squad. Not so good.

Next stop was Melbourne, where we came back to beat Australia B, a team cunningly packed by Dwyer with Test possibles, with a young Tim Horan at fly-half and a very physical pack, including the giant Tom Lawton, the hooker, and Scott Gourley, a highly-rated man in the back row. We showed we could play in wet weather, too. Gary Armstrong, one of my favourite players of all time, had a terrific game, and it was Gary's extreme misfortune that he was on the same tour as Robert Jones, who was another class act.

The pace of the tour was picking up. We had a session at Melbourne where I told Roger that I wanted to see the lads crawling from the training field at the end. They did just that.

We had by then moved on to Brisbane to play Queensland, and the tour was never the same after that game. The Queensland match was dirty, quite brutal. I judged that it was started by Queensland and there was a terrible incident when Julian Gardner, their flanker, kicked Mike Hall time and time again as Hall was trying to get out of the back of a ruck. It was as if he was frantically treading grapes. After the game, Hall and Mike Teague had livid weals criss-crossing their backs from the flailing boots. One reporter who saw the marks described them as 'latticework marks'.

Remarkably, while Australian TV kept replaying other incidents in that match, and throughout the tour, in which they judged the Lions to be the culprits, I never once saw that disgraceful incident with Mike Hall replayed. However, we had set out our stall not to complain. We didn't.

All I remember after that game is insisting that, for the rest of the tour, we could not be seen to be taking a backward step. It was not the time or place for the ninety-nine call, the sign for an all-out brawl in 1974. I just called the players together and insisted that we should have a collective presence on the field that told the

Australian sides that, if they wanted to start anything, they were taking on the whole Lions team. I specifically said that we should not start anything, but that we should finish it.

Robert Jones scored a try and we beat Queensland 19–15, but it was a thoughtful time on tour. Bill Campbell, the giant Test lock, was their captain, and was quite vocal after the game. Our forwards gave him some cause for thought, too. They hinted that they didn't think he was as hard a forward as some made out.

We then had the Cairns interlude, up in far north Queensland, warm and humid, the home of the cane toad, with access to the Barrier Reef. Just to emphasise the value of the tour from the hosts' point of view, the match against Queensland B saw Jason Little and Tim Horan paired in the centre, therefore gaining crucial exposure, and experience, on their way to forming one of the great partnerships in rugby.

But there was also a good ground and atmosphere, it was a decent match which we won 30–6 and it showed that there were places off rugby's beaten track where successful games could be staged. I think it was during that week that people realised that commercially the tour was going to make an impact.

That gilding of the concept of a Lions tour to Australia, and the sense of occasion it engendered, continued. The biggest game before the First Test was against New South Wales. It was to be played at the non-lovely Concord Oval but there had been some incredibly wet weather and the place was unfit for play. So we were switched to the North Sydney Oval, in reality a cricket ground but a really good arena.

We won it. They scored a really good try from Marty Roebuck, the full-back, we scored two, by Gavin Hastings and Bob Norster, but we needed a bit of drama at the end – Craig Chalmers dropped a goal in the dying moments.

New South Wales were a powerful team led by Nick Farr-Jones, the Wallabies captain. We were not playing that well – although we did cruise past New South Wales B in Dubbo in the next match – but in terms of the significance to the tour the main point of interest was that Rob Andrew had arrived as replacement for Paul Dean, and he played his first game. Immediately he seemed to me to have a ring of confidence about him. Test match animal? We would see.

Yet for all the high hopes and the build-up, the First Test was a salutary experience. We lost 30–12, the Wallabies scoring four tries to nil. It was one of my heaviest defeats in a big match. There were few excuses – we picked an unbalanced back row with Derek White on the blind side, since Mike Teague was injured. We had Mike Hall and Brendan Mullin in the centre, as Scott Hastings and John Devereux were unfit. I don't think the selection was brilliant.

Nor, probably, were our tactics. We went into the Test intending to play as we had played on the tour to date, with a mix in our game; we had not played expansively, but we had played consistently. However, we were turned over far too easily and we lost focus. Farr-Jones and Michael Lynagh, their half-backs, were dominant. They manipulated the game. The Wallabies back row, led by Gourley, who excited the country, were all over the field.

We also let the game get far too loose – this suited their back row, and it suited Campbell and Steve Cutler, their locks, who were good line-out men but not heavy forwards. They scored early, they had momentum. I was incredibly disappointed afterwards. In fact, I was very, very low. One Test, one heavy defeat. I apologised in the media for the performance. I promised everyone, and especially all our travelling supporters, that it would be different the next week.

This was neither desperation nor wishful thinking. The light-bulb moment had already occurred. It dawned on me that their forwards were not so fantastic after all. We had to change some players, but, far more important, we had to change the emphasis. Physically, we had to take them on front-on, attack their front five and nullify their middle five of back row and half-backs.

If we could make the back row work really hard, make them

tackle and tackle our power runners, then they wouldn't be able to run round the field. And, in the likes of Teague and Richards, we had the runners to do it. We had to make their back row tackle a lot.

As for their generals, I knew that Nick Farr-Jones needed space, and I knew too that he could become flustered if he lost that space. I was aware that he was critical. I was quite ruthless. I just said to the players: 'We have got to play him out of the game. You've got to hit him late, hit him early, but hit him! Just whatever it is, just take him out.' Robert Jones was a fairly reserved character on the outside, but he sat and took it all in. He was key.

We also had a blueprint to work to. I told Robert how Dougie Morgan, the canny old Scottish scrum-half, had targeted Gareth Edwards in a match at Murrayfield in 1973. He crowded his man at the put-in. He stood on Gareth's foot, nudged him at the put-in, invaded his space. Dougie just irritated Gareth for eighty minutes. The video still makes fascinating viewing. You'd see Gareth try to push Dougie out of the way. Dougie was real wily, a tough nut.

But before the Test there was a match to be played by the mid-week team. I found out something that I had suspected from my tours as a player and which was double-underlined in red ink for the remainder of my tours: that the midweek team could galvanise or shatter morale, that players who never appeared in Tests could affect the series. This knowledge was exactly why, after the win in the Third Test in South Africa in 1974, those of us on the field had gone over to applaud the rest of the squad in the stands, who had backed us so selflessly throughout the tour.

Between tests, we moved from Sydney to Canberra, the national capital, home of the wonderful Australian War Memorial where the names of the Australian dead in every war are inscribed. We were playing Australian Capital Territory, although, unfortunately for them, the marketing men had labelled them the Canberra Kookaburras. They even had a silly song.

It was a day when we looked to our non-Test players for a lift and, for some time, it looked as if we weren't going to get anything. We just didn't play. At one time we were 18–5 down, a massive deficit. We were not keeping the ball on the field; we were disorganised.

Then, suddenly, we started to put some play together. Two or three things started to go well. We were still way down at half-time, but then Jerry Guscott started playing; he gave a performance which won him the Test jersey. Donal kept the lads going, we broke out and scored a glut of tries, and we won, by 41–25, a match that had seemed lost.

The press still gave us a hard time at the press conference for our first-half performance, but I was thrilled by the team's attitude. There is always, always, a key game like that on every Lions tour. At the end, the Test squad came into the dressing room with their congratulations and that momentum carried us on.

We went back to Brisbane, for the match that saw the tour hanging in the balance. We made changes to our personnel. We brought in Wade Dooley for Robert Norster, who was a great line-out exponent and did not take kindly to being dropped. But it wasn't a technical decision about a second row, and Dooley, who'd missed the First Test, came in alongside Paul Ackford, a great player, and the tour saw one of the best pairings in Test rugby of that era.

We added something behind, too. Scott Hastings came into the centre and, alongside him, young Master Guscott. Craig Chalmers had failed to impose himself on the First Test, he hadn't kicked well, and so we brought in Rob Andrew, whose domestic season had been so forgettable.

In the preparation we covered almost every blade of grass. On the Friday, Rob, Robert Jones, Roger and myself took a car and we went to Ballymore, the Test venue. We walked on to the pitch. It would be an exaggeration to say that we walked every blade of grass. But we only missed a few.

We walked to almost every position on the field. We asked

ourselves: what are the options from here? What do we expect
the forwards to be doing here? What moves have we got in this
situation? Where are we going to play to next? We walked right
up the touchline, stopping frequently, and then down the other
side.

We went through it all again in the evening. I wanted to make
sure that our understanding of what we had to do was complete –
the every-blade-of-grass session is not something I necessarily
repeated, but occasionally, before a big game, I did it again.

And on Ballymore that Saturday we saved the series. 'Welcome
back, Lazarus' read one newspaper heading. We played well, the
pressure we put on Australia grew and grew, our big forwards like
Dooley and Teague were brilliant, but in our hour of victory I
refused to single out anyone from one of my most satisfying
games.

And yet, it is almost a shock now to recall that into the last five
minutes of normal time we were still 12–9 down, and had still not
scored a try in the series. Tight margins.

We allowed the Australia half-backs and back row far less leeway
and space; we made the Wallabies forwards tackle and made them
run and work and gradually, *gradually*, they started to falter and
the spaces appeared. Slowly, but surely.

It appeared when Rory Underwood and Rob Andrew sent
Jeremy Guscott away – he cruised about 50 metres, found Scott
Hastings inside him and Australia had to defend well to stop
them. From that position we scored the first try, took the lead and
everything on tour was once again possible – we won a ball down
the left, Andrew set the line moving, Scott Hastings threw a pass
off his left hand, it bounced, Gavin took it on the bounce, dummied and scored and we were leading by two points.

Then we came right back from the kick-off. Campese took his
eye off a high kick, Andrew recovered it, Finlay made a big charge
and when the ball came back, Brian Moore of all people acted as
scrum-half, and Rob sent Jeremy on his way. He chipped low,

chased at top pace and it bounced up into his hands and he scored. Finlay said afterwards that, when he saw that Jerry was going on his own, he was completely dismayed.

But not for long. Jerry said later that, as he ran back, still a young man and with the Test won, all his rugby life up to that point, from mini-rugby onwards, flashed through his mind. In about five seconds. Some of us probably felt the same. It was 19–12 at the end.

There was a powerful new strand to the story, however. In the aftermath, the Australians, being Australians, were bitter, and another storm about rough play blew up. Let's just say that Robert Jones was quickly into action, fulfilling the game plan. He nudged Farr-Jones at a scrum very early on, trod on his foot, Farr-Jones reacted furiously and the two bantamweights went at it. Most of the other players joined in and the match continued to simmer, with the two scrum-halves never far from coming to blows.

Not long afterwards, David Young, our tight-head prop, kicked Steve Cutler, who was on the ground at a ruck. This proved to be an incendiary device. Tom Lawton touched off a major punch-up by throwing a flurry of huge punches which then led to another mass brawl. In those days there were no citing procedures, no trial by television camera (except in the media), but the resulting Australian media campaign only just stopped short of calling us murderers. It changed the stakes. Paul Ackford made a good point. 'When you hear the Southern Hemisphere complaining, you know you've done well.'

For the record, I blame myself for Robert's loss of control. I knew how key Farr-Jones was, and I wound Robert up too much. We should also have said something in public about the Young incident. While media hell was breaking loose, we refused to comment; nor did we complain about Australian dirty play. It was our way. We should, however, have put something on record about Young.

In private we said plenty. Clive Rowlands and I gave David a major dressing-down. He was only twenty-one, incredibly young for a Test prop, and his impulsive act was out of order.

Soon after the game, the Australian Rugby Union put out a press release which the Lions history describes as 'intimidatory'. It said it was preparing 'a video depicting certain incidents which occurred during the Second Test at Ballymore . . .' They sent it to the four Home Unions. We realised that none of the 'certain incidents' depicted would show foul play by the Wallabies.

Nick Farr-Jones said: 'I think that the Third Test could develop into open warfare. As far as I am concerned, the Lions have set the rules and if the officials are going to do nothing about it then we are going to have to do it ourselves.' Nothing inflammatory there, then.

Some of the reaction was gross. There were hints in papers comparing alleged violence by our policemen to racist attacks back in Coventry, where Dean Richards worked. They hinted that all police back home were thugs.

To be honest, we in the Lions party felt then, and still feel now, that the Wallabies realised where our strengths lay, that we were too much for them and that there wasn't much they could do about it. They knew it, and they knew that I knew it. Bob Dwyer and I got on fine on that tour until the Tests. He would travel round watching us and watching home players, we'd have a chat in the hotels in which we were staying when we came across each other and I had enormous respect for him when he came to England to coach Bristol and Leicester. But I still feel in that last week, as the insults flew, that he knew that if we got it right there was nothing he could do.

As the storm raged, and the Australian media dug up every retired gunslinger in the country to give his opinion, there was a lone voice of sanity. Bob Templeton, the Australian assistant coach, is arguably the most liked and respected man ever to come out of Australia rugby and we decided to get together to talk.

We met in a hotel in Sydney, in our casual clothes rather than our team garb. We spoke about managing the players, about the need to avoid open warfare, and, apart from that, there was no real agenda or action plan. We had a drink and chatted amicably.

What did we agree, and did it make any difference? I suppose we agreed not to have a stand-up fight, and to try to bring some discipline into the situation. They knew we were not going to back off physically. I did tell the players that the final Test could rest on one penalty conceded and that it was in our interests to be more disciplined, but I said the same as usual. Do not start anything, but, if something does start, do not back off.

That week there was no midweek game, which was great. We went to the Gold Coast for a few days. We had already obtained the tape of the Second Test and we put it on in the team room. Lunch was already waiting. But the players sat and watched every second, no one moved, and lunch went cold.

And we almost lost our assistant coach. On the Monday we gave the lads a day off and we all went to a fun fair with those horrible frightening rides. I told Roger that we had to have a go on the biggest dipper in the park. I think it was called the Corkscrew. We took our turn, and it wasn't very pleasant.

But as we got up to leave, some of the heavy mob sitting in the seats behind us held our arms and pinned us down. We had to go round again. I think Roger was ill with motion sickness for about three days afterwards. But it was a break, we resisted any urge to put them through a heavy session and trained only lightly prior to returning to Sydney. I went out with Gavin Hastings for a while. He had been dropping a few high kicks so we did a session with him starting under the posts and me trying to drop the ball on the crossbar above him so that he could practise his catching. That was that.

The Third Test obviously had everything on it. One paper called the action 'almost fanatical'. By this time our pack was dominant. For Australia, players such as Gourley, Campbell and Cutler were not nearly so prominent. In the first half, we hardly gave them the ball. We had all the possession and field position, but we simply could not cash in on our superiority. We'd play so well, go through some phases, then make a mistake.

So, although Gavin was kicking some goals, we were pegged right back. Michael Lynagh made a really good break and the Wallabies scored through Ian Williams; and it was still in the balance early in the second half when Rob Andrew dropped for goal but missed to the right. Campese took the ball near his own dead-ball line, and the whole world expected him to touch down, with only Ieuan Evans and Scott Hastings following up – 'Just being a dutiful dog,' Ieuan said afterwards.

But instead Campese started running. As he crossed his own goal line and Evans approached him, Greg Martin, the full-back, crossed behind Campese. Martin probably had no idea that Campese was going to pass to him. Campese then fired out a bad pass behind Martin, it bounced, and Ieuan dived and scored.

It has probably gone down as one of the most horrendous defensive acts in Test history, and I am sure that it came about because of the pressure we had put on the Wallabies, restricting the ball to Campese so that when it did finally come to him, he felt he had to try to make something happen.

With more kicks from Gavin, we were leading by 19–12 and on our way out of sight. But even then, we couldn't break clear. We could not close it out. Lynagh brought it back to 19–18 with two penalties, but we carried on playing; our pack was still better. In the end, there was no late Aussie pressure – in the last six or eight minutes they couldn't get the ball out of their twenty-two. We missed a good scoring chance, but we had the clamps on them. They were going side to side, and our defence was tremendous.

The final whistle went. It was an extraordinary feeling. I felt that, as a group of people, we had come an incredibly long way. We went berserk in the dressing room, where Clive Rowlands was crying his eyes out. We had not been brilliant, backs-wise or team-wise; but, as the series went on, we had become formidable. We had stood up for ourselves, and I don't think you can say that about every Lions team. Rob Andrew said that it was a great pity we couldn't go on to New Zealand, because the lads felt it was all coming together.

In terms of style, we were saying that rugby could be played in more than one way, but this was where we were strong. If you could match us there, then we would have to go and play somewhere else. But if you couldn't match us there, this was what we would do. The Wallabies could not match us.

'Iron Mike' Teague was given the player of the series award, a tribute to a fantastic player. After the game, he came up to me. 'I can't believe it,' he said. 'No more training.' Dean Richards was instrumental, so was Rob Andrew when he came in, so was Robert Jones.

In the evening after the Third Test there was an official dinner at a big hotel in Kings Cross, where a large group of Lions supporters were staying. They had been fantastic all tour. As we walked into the foyer, we saw that they were lining the reception area, lining the escalators to the function floor. As we filed in, they applauded us all the way from the front door to the door of the function room. It was a moment when I thought: 'Wow! We really achieved something!'

Much later that night, Bob Weighill, the secretary of the Four Home Unions, and who was one of the main tour organisers, was being driven across Sydney Harbour Bridge by David Hands of *The Times*. They saw an odd sight. On the approach lanes to the Bridge, miles from the dinner, there was a figure weaving among the lanes of traffic, arms spread wide, doing aeroplane impressions. It was pouring with rain. They slowed down and suddenly realised that it was Brian Moore, who had no recollection of how he came to be there. Weighill dropped Moore safely at our hotel.

We finished the tour by beating New South Wales Country in Newcastle, 72–13, and the ANZAC team back at Ballymore, by 19–15. The attacks on the Lions started again after we departed, with Bob Dwyer leading the way.

Judy came to meet me at Heathrow and in the calm after the storm we took a caravan to Brittany; and there, with my family, either in the caravan or sitting outside in the sun, I wrote my Lions tour report, the final formality of any Lions tour. Lose, or win. Many Lions, players or coaches, have only one shot at history. If this was to be our only shot, we had made our history.

11

Nadi, and Leaving the Field

The hotel, and the world of business

Fiji. The Paradise Islands. The Fijian word *bula* (pronounced *mbula*) is their usual greeting. Significantly, it means both hello and welcome. Captain James Cook discovered the islands in 1779 and the McGeechan family– Judy, Robert, Heather and myself – discovered them 211 years later.

Parts of Fiji are idyllic, other parts very much Third World. Rugby in Fiji is incredible. They say that if there were as many rugby clubs in England per head of the population as there are in Fiji, then there would be twenty times the number of clubs. You see hundreds of youngsters playing barefoot as dusk falls. Their players are tough, wonderfully skilful and amazing handlers of the ball. They have been more famous in the past fifteen years for sevens, but they reached the quarter-final of the 2007 World Cup, a brilliant feat, and took South Africa, the eventual champions, all the way.

In 1990, Judy was left some money by her great aunt when she died. I was on tour that summer with Scotland, when we could and should have beaten the All Blacks. Derrick Grant and I agree that the period 1989–91, which included the 1990 Grand Slam, the New Zealand tour and the 1991 World Cup, saw probably the best rugby that Scotland had ever played.

The Second and final Test of that tour was in Auckland, and Judy decided to use the money to fly down with Robert and Heather, who were ten and six at the time. It was the first time either had ever flown, and here they were embarking on one of the longest flights of all, on Air New Zealand. Rugby's grapevine, and the essential generosity of the sport, had already been in action. Ian Robertson, who preceded me as Scotland's fly-half and who is the long-serving BBC Radio rugby correspondent and a superb commentator, knew someone very high up in Air New Zealand – no surprise really: there are very few companies in the world in which he doesn't know someone high up. We'd had dinner on the Wednesday in Auckland with the head of Air New Zealand. Robbo had told him that my wife and children were coming out for the last Test. When Judy checked in at Gatwick for the flight, the girl at the desk said that she and Robert and Heather were on the computer as VIPs. I had flown down with the Scotland squad weeks before for the tour in economy. Judy and family flew down business class, all the way. Heather loved the hot towels. At Auckland airport at dawn, an official of the Auckland Rugby Union was there to meet them. When they arrived, he picked them up, took them out, sorted the hotel for her and the family. Welcome.

When the tour was over we decided that there was one opportunity too good to miss. We elected to stop off in Fiji on the way home and had a blessed family holiday there, which we still reminisce over to this day. Then we stopped at Disneyland in Los Angeles on the next leg home. It was a trip, moreover, which set in train a sequence of events where, for the only time in my life, I earned my living in the business world in a way other than as a teacher or a professional rugby coach.

New experiences are the fuel of life. I have coached club teams, national teams, other representative teams and the Lions.

What I had never done, until I went to Fiji in 1990, was to coach a hotel.

When people are described as old school it is not always a compliment, but in some areas, notably education, it should be. By 1990 I had been teaching PE and geography for twenty-three years, almost all of them very happy ones at Fir Tree Middle School in Leeds. Fir Tree had very high standards and the school was well supported by the parents. We didn't compromise in standards of dress, work or behaviour. It was quality education. That's why we were there as members of staff. My two headmasters had been Ken Cobbett and Ken Wadkin, both outstanding men. Ken Wadkin provided another service for me as I used to buy his old cars from him, and so I had a succession of second-hand Ford Capris, which were brilliant cars, and I even snapped up a caravan from him.

As a Scotland player between 1972 and 1979, and when coaching various Scotland teams from the mid-1980s and becoming national coach from 1989 to 1993, I had to commute regularly from Leeds to Edinburgh and other parts of Scotland and I had to take time off school as big games approached. I have already touched on the generosity of the school during that period and the local authority was equally supportive. I always tried to make sure that I made up any ground lost in terms of teaching when I got back into the classroom and it is also true to say that parents sometimes sent their children to Fir Tree because I was there.

In 1989, however, a new headmaster arrived. He was younger, had different leanings and priorities. He had been marked down, apparently, as a high-flyer. But when the new man came in I sensed immediately that he was uncomfortable about me. The 1989 Lions had won the series against Australia with me as head coach and the 1990 Grand Slam thrust both Scottish rugby and myself into the spotlight. It is just possible that he was jealous of my profile. We took the cracking Scotland squad to New Zealand for the 1990 trip but, by that time, he had already acted. He stopped my pay and so I took that trip as unpaid leave. It was a fantastic tour but obviously the financial situation was poor and worrying, especially after twenty-three years of support and understanding from the school.

That was something to chew over as the tour ended and we prepared to stop over in Fiji, but when we landed we found that the rugby fraternity had got together again. John Hall is chairman of Gullivers Travel, the most famous of the rugby travel firms and which always brings thousands of fans to follow the Lions. John had been involved in one of the key matches of my career, as a second row alongside Roger Uttley in the North-East Counties team which lost narrowly to the All Blacks at Bradford in 1972. It was the game watched by Bill Dickinson, the Scotland coach, and it put me on the Scottish radar for the first time. John had organised a stay at the beachside Regent Hotel, along the coast from Nadi, and which was outstanding in every way. Its pool and bar area were lit after dark by flaming torches, and the sea lapped at the hotel beach just yards from the rooms.

Rugby in Fiji is based either on government teams, on army teams or on hotel teams and the Regent had its own team. Before long, the hotel management approached me. They had a big game coming up against a local club team. Would I coach them for the occasion? It meant extending the stay, but it was an easy decision to make. I rang the headmaster back in Leeds. I told him that I was staying longer to pursue a rugby opportunity but he didn't need to know what it was. He wasn't paying me anyway; he had brought in a supply teacher, so what could he say? He was not happy, but we stayed on and so I became coach of the Hotel XV.

It was a rare delight. They (or we, I should say) were a really good team. We had the remarkable centre, Noa Nadruku, the man who once created a key try for Fiji in the final of the Hong Kong Sevens with an astonishing pass between his legs, and who went on to a brilliant career in Australian rugby league with the Canberra Raiders.

We arranged to train at about four o'clock, and the manager

closed the seventeenth and eighteenth holes of the hotel's golf course for the session. We ran up and down the fairways (avoiding the bunkers, of course). Their skill levels and running ability were astonishing. The next night we trained at a village, on a field bare but for posts at each end. We had to clear the livestock first. Our captain was one of the elders of the village. He worked at the hotel bar and you could see the reverence in which he was held by the others.

We talked about mauling. I said to them: 'Look. I'm enjoying coaching you so much because you're just so skilful, you are natural runners. Why don't you maul on Saturday? Your opponents will never expect that. Who in Fiji mauls the ball?'

So we spent a bit of time mauling, just hiding the ball in the maul, practising little breakouts and then extending the breakouts into runs. That's all we did. While all this was happening, the family was being cared for royally. The women were fantastic with children. They loved Robert and Heather and fed them by the side of the field, cooking sweet corn on the touchline.

On game day we all climbed on to the backs of lorries and off we went to the match. We played so well. There we were, mauling and breaking out and bursting into runs. It was tremendously effective, and we built up a very healthy lead. At half-time, there was not much to say. I was pleased with them.

The second half was odd. In the end, we won the game by about 30–18, nothing like as convincing as it could have been, and the maul seemed to go to pot completely. It stopped working. But all the players seemed happy. We sat down together in a ring for the traditional prayers, alongside the opposition. Judy and the kids were there, too. Then we climbed back on the lorries and headed back towards the hotel.

As we rumbled along, the elder thanked me for my help. I told him it had been a fantastic experience for me. But something still mystified me. 'We'd played so well,' I said. 'But why in the middle of the second half did it start going wrong?'

The elder looked at me. 'Mr Ian. I have to apologise. Although

I work at the hotel and this is my team, a lot of my family live in the village. I knew we'd won, so I kept giving them the ball in the maul, to play a bit.' So he was handing them the ball so that they could have a crack, because he knew we were going to win!

On the Sunday morning, as a thank-you, they prepared a wonderful Fijian meal for us. This time we walked from the hotel, right along the beach to the village. They had been out fishing, they had killed some chickens and they baked the food in the ground. They dug a pit and filled it with hot stones, placed the food on top and covered the whole thing with palm leaves. One of the other hotel guests, familiar with the Fijian way of life, said: 'Do you realise that this is a tremendous honour they are doing you?' We did. We sat there on the beach, as a family, with our hosts, and had coconut milk, cooked fish and chicken, and vegetables. We just sat round and felt part-Fijian for the day.

We realised only later that day that our flight out was at two o'clock that morning, not the following one. We had gone to bed thinking we had more time on our hands than we actually did. It was a rush, but we made it, had our three days in Disneyland for the kids and reached home in time for a few weeks' teaching, before the summer holidays. Marvellous memories.

But towards the end of 1990, the headmaster approached me and said: 'Look, I think the children are getting short-changed and it is affecting the school. So really I think you've got to choose between your teaching here and coaching rugby.' In fact, he had expressed the view to the school council first without telling me and had also tried in vain to enlist the support of the staff. As far as I know, no parent or member of staff ever complained about me being away. But the headmaster was saying to the council that I was detrimental to the school.

So I had to decide whether I wanted to continue to teach at Fir Tree, or continue to coach Scotland. I think he got the shock of his life when I came back and told him that I was opting to coach Scotland and to give up teaching. I don't think he saw that reply coming at all. But I had been in the Scotland post only for a year, the Rugby World Cup was only a year in the future: it was a heady time to be the coach.

It was approaching Christmas 1990 when I left. At that point, professionalism in rugby union was still five years away and so I could not be officially paid for coaching rugby. Judy, who had done all kinds of jobs to bring in some money, was at college doing a full-time degree so she wasn't working either. The Scottish Rugby Union could not help because it was an amateur organisation itself. I was out of work.

Things moved quite quickly. The *Scotsman* ran a story that the coach of Scotland was having to give up his job in order to coach Scotland through till the World Cup. Within quite a short period, nine different companies approached me. One of those approaches was particularly touching. Mike Pearey, a former Royal Navy captain, was bursar at Christ's Hospital school, a famous boarding school, in the south of England. He said: 'Look, there's a job for you at our school, which will allow you to keep coaching Scotland.' This was a thoughtful gesture since, at the time, Mike was president of the Rugby Football Union at Twickenham and we had not long before beaten England in the 1990 Grand Slam match.

Most of the other jobs were in the public relations and marketing fields and one of the offers came from Scottish Life, the big insurance firm. I went to meet their chief executive, Malcolm Murray, a Scotsman himself, a man with steel-grey hair and who, at first sight, struck you as being rather terse, but who on closer examination turned out to be significantly warmer. It was the start of four happy years at Scottish Life, with freedom to carry on coaching. I am pleased to say that the friendship between Judy and me and Malcolm and his wife Muriel remains to this day, and that Malcolm was recently appointed captain of Muirfield Golf Club, one of the greatest honours the golf game can bestow on anyone.

Suddenly, from being out of work I was being paid more than I was as a teacher, I had a company car with a telephone in it, I had a pension, and I could hand down to Judy the latest in the line of Ken Wadkin's old Capris. She says that it was the first time she had ever had a car of her own.

At first, I was based in the company's Leeds office, working with the sales directors around the sales network, talking about communication, presentation, team building, rugby. It was enjoyable and challenging. But then the financial authorities declared that every company had to have a proper training scheme and Scottish Life did not have one. I did a report on the training which did exist within the company, with the help of Rob Wood and David Wood, two of the staff at Leeds with whom I struck up a close working relationship, and submitted it. Soon after the 1991 World Cup had ended, with Scotland finishing fourth, Malcolm asked me to become company training manager and to develop the training department.

It was an excellent opportunity but, significantly, it meant moving to head office, and taking the family to Edinburgh. Obviously, we had lived all our lives in Yorkshire. Judy loved our home, in which we had lived for eighteen years, and, like me, she loved Yorkshire. She had also graduated by now and qualified as a teacher. She had taught for only one year, and now faced leaving the job which she had worked so hard to secure, in the area she loved.

She also recalls that Edinburgh at the time was not that warm a place to be if you were English. It was the time of the introduction of the poll tax and huge resentment on the part of many Scots towards Margaret Thatcher, a time of a certain anti-English sentiment which some claimed spilled over into rugby in that 1990 Grand Slam game.

We made the move to Edinburgh nonetheless. But Judy never settled, Heather used to cry a lot and Robert, now at school in Scotland and the son of Ian McGeechan, was under pressure to start pulling out of a hat a string of international-class rugby performances. The family were just unhappy, so after a year they moved back to Leeds and I commuted, coming home at weekends. Malcolm was good enough to let me do the odd Friday out of Leeds as well.

Season 1992–93 was my last as Scotland's coach, but I kept contact with the players. While I was commuting on weekends between Edinburgh and Leeds, I was also flying down to Heathrow every Tuesday and Thursday afternoon to take evening sessions at London Scottish. Paul Burnell, the London Scottish prop, would pick me up at Heathrow to drive me to Richmond, where they played. And for a year I coached the team.

The post with Scottish Life had enabled me to keep coaching Scotland, which I did until the end of season 1992–93, and I was able to offer a thank-you of sorts to Malcolm Murray prior to leaving the company in 1994. On the 1993 Lions tour, Rory Underwood scored the try which sealed our victory in the Second Test in Wellington, one of the most satisfying matches of my career. Rory dived over in front of a banner advertisement for Scottish Life, which was situated near the corner flag. Every television replay and every still photograph showed the advertisement. Malcolm was delighted.

By 1994, coaches could be paid professionals and I heard that Northampton, a club probably quicker than any other to react to the impending arrival of the pro game in 1995, wanted me as their new director of rugby. Very flattering.

The process was rapid. I was on a train from Scotland to King's Cross. The Northampton contingent boarded at Stevenage. By the time we arrived at King's Cross, the deal was done. And the road led to the Midlands.

It was a way back into rugby. I was missing the environment and the Northampton job gave me something I had not had for years but which I loved – day-to-day involvement with good players, and not just players you saw every few months. I spoke to Malcolm Murray and I will always be very grateful to him. Thanks to him, we now had money in the bank for the first time ever. I enjoyed Scottish Life. They were good people. They gave me an opportunity to come out of teaching and look at things differently. I was in business, working with business people, working with sales people, I had targets. It was different and refreshing.

Making sure that I had completed all my assignments for Scottish Life, and finished the setting up of the training programmes, I went back to Leeds to sell the house I had always kept on, and we moved the family south to Northampton, to a new life, to the uncertainty of the fledgling professional era.

Suddenly, after twenty-three years in teaching and eighteen years in the same house in Leeds, everything had become fluid and unpredictable. Judy was far happier in Northampton that she had been in Edinburgh – although we were to find that she was allergic, almost literally, to the Midlands. For the moment, though, by way of Fiji and by way of the world of business, it was time to get back to rugby.

There was a final footnote to the family experiences in Fiji back in 1990. I heard that same summer that I had been awarded the OBE. As a family, we shared the investiture day at Buckingham Palace with Jimmy Saville, who was there for his knighthood, and was playing with our children. Bruce Oldfield, the designer, was next to me in the queue and it was all run with total precision. Her Majesty had to have just enough time to be briefed by a courtier whispering in her ear, so that she knew who you were when you arrived in front of her.

But in 1994, I was invited into the inner sanctum. I was asked to a small lunch party in the 1844 Room, which is in the Queen's private apartments. It was difficult to see what the qualification for the lunch was but I was mixing with industrialists and military men plus an actress. On my left was Helena Bonham Carter with the Duke of Edinburgh on her other side. On my right was one Sir Anthony Figgis, marshal of the diplomatic corps.

My career in the corridors of power had already begun, with a reception at Number 10 which I attended together with Finlay Calder, my first Lions captain. Mrs Thatcher said that she used to sit in the stands at rugby matches while everyone slagged off Denis, her husband, who was a referee. Cecil Parkinson approached me as well. He said: 'Can I shake your hand, you are my hero.' As far as I know, he was being serious.

12

Paying the Penalty

The 1993 Lions tour of New Zealand

During the second half of the First Test at Lancaster Park, Christchurch, on a bright winter's afternoon in 1993, I turned to Geoff Cooke, the tour manager. 'We have control of this,' I said. It was still very tight but our pre-match plans were working well and, indeed, we still led by a point at 18–17 inside the last three minutes.

We had already had to absorb a savage blow. We had conceded a very early try to the All Blacks when Brian Kinsey, the Australian referee, awarded a try to Frank Bunce, the New Zealand centre, that replays suggested should never have been allowed. Ieuan Evans took a high kick from Grant Fox, fell over our line in contact with Bunce and replays showed clearly that Evans had never let go of the ball. Kinsey, who looked neither the fittest nor fastest before the game, was a long way away when he awarded the try.

But we were almost there; we needed to be strong in defence for just a few more phases. Then Bunce made a lunge through the middle from around his halfway line, he was tackled by Rob Andrew and knocked off balance and then caught in a bear hug by Dean Richards, a past master at the all-embracing tackle.

'I enveloped him, turned him over, the ball was presented towards our side and our forwards began to ruck over it,' Dean says. 'Everything I did was legitimate [under the laws at the time]. Bunce was holding on to the ball after the tackle.'

With the nearest Lions demanding a penalty against Bunce, Kinsey came up and peered into the ruck. He blew his whistle and penalised the Lions. Dewi Morris, the Lions scrum-half, was in on the action. The expression of shock and bewilderment on his face was telling. And the whole thing still lives with Gavin Hastings, the tour captain. 'It was probably the most crushing moment of my career,' Gavin says. 'And I can still see the expression on Dewi's face to this day.' Up in the New Zealand TV commentary box even David Kirk, the former All Blacks captain, said: 'That was a really tough penalty against Dean Richards.'

From around 43 metres Grant Fox kicked the goal to win the Test. A Test that was there for the winning had been lost and we were faced with turning round a series from 0–1 down – and this was the first Lions tour of New Zealand to include only three Tests instead of the traditional four. It was a shattering blow, and has been described as 'the worst decision in the history of Lions tours'. And that takes in a few, I can tell you.

We were to recover brilliantly, but that first decision remained a millstone around our necks for the entire trip, and, as we were later to find, it was a curiously divided Lions party which took on the awesome challenge of trying to beat the All Blacks in their own country.

It was also a significant tour for another reason. Dr James Robson, then a young man helping at the Scottish Rugby Union, and vastly popular with the players, had already impressed me at home. His was an incredible story because he had begun his career as a physiotherapist, but had gone on to qualify as a doctor. One account of the 1993 tour concluded afterwards that 'McGeechan clearly trusted Robson to the ends of the earth'. That was putting it mildly. James already had an incredible knack

My father, seated with dog, with medical staff of the Argyll and Sutherland Highlanders, Geneifa, Egypt, 1941

With Hilda and Bob McGeechan, Mum and Dad, in my first year, 1947

Bad hair day at home

Classic street sports scene: sharpening the reactions with football on the cobbles near home in Kirkstall. Top left, the stable door, so often used for football target practice

With the family on a break in Bridlington

Best-dressed student on my first day at Carnegie College in 1965, with Dad, and jacket and tie

Captain of Carnegie College in 1968 with, far right, coach Bernard White, one of my most profound influences at college and club

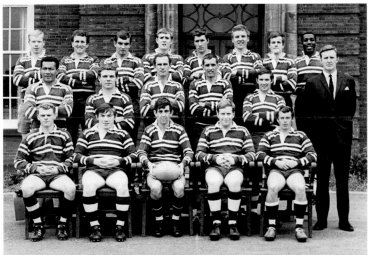

Action from Scotland–New Zealand 1972, my first cap for the country of my blood and an emotional day in more ways than one

Gareth Edwards deigns to take a pass from me as the Lions beat Northern Transvaal on the parched Loftus Versveld, 1974. Dick Milliken, centre partner and lifelong friend, in the background

The series is won, Willie-John McBride is lifted high and the Test team acknowledges the unity and support of the rest of the party, seated up in the stand. Boet Erasmus Stadium, Port Elizabeth

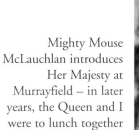

Robert and Heather, and Tara, on Loughrigg Fell, in our beloved Lake District, and with Lake Windermere in the background

Mighty Mouse McLauchlan introduces Her Majesty at Murrayfield – in later years, the Queen and I were to lunch together

In the jersey of my native county – evading Barrie Corless of North Midlands in the county championship semi-final, 1977

Winter man. Sidestepping on the 1977 Lions tour, a slog through mud and a Test series that was there for the taking, and which escaped

Clearing the lines for Scotland against England in 1979, with the great Jim Renwick preparing to chase

The fledgling Lion Coach. With Roger Uttley, Assistant Coach, and the ebullient Clive Rowlands, Manager, Australia 1989

Nick Farr-Jones was the key for Australia in 1989 and we wanted Robert Jones to upset him. He did

The wounded Wallaby. Farr-Jones after the Second Test

Possibly the best hotel team in the world. With the Hyatt team in Fiji, 1990

With Robert, Judy and Heather outside the Palace after the investiture ceremony, shared with Jimmy Saville

Will Carling with what was, frankly, a rare smile. He was one of many who found that Lions tours can be a harsh existence and 1993 in New Zealand was his first and last

With Geoff Cooke, Manager, and Dick Best, Assistant Coach, in New Zealand in 1993, with Best preparing an acid comment for the photographer

Great Scots. Derrick Grant, student of the history of the border raiders, and the parallels with life as Scotland Coach. And with Jim Telfer in the best days of our partnership, with the 1997 Lions in South Africa

The Test match animal. Jeremy Guscott, on his third Lions tour with me, drops the goal which won the Second Test and the series. The thunderous Scott Gibbs is first to congratulate

Keith Wood completes the short-back-and-sides he promised me if we won the 1997 series. Clearly, he had his done recently too

With the Calcutta Cup after one of Scotland's greatest wins, plotted in the week before and executed to perfection at a stormy Murrayfield in 2000

Lawrence Dallaglio of Wasps holds high the Heineken Cup after outsmarting Leicester in the 2007 final, and for me it was far better late than never

Danny Cipriani, one of the outstanding players from the Wasps system, breaking past two Llanelli defenders

Jamie Roberts offloading to Brian O'Driscoll in the First Test, with Stephen Jones in support. The combination of the massive Roberts and the brilliant O'Driscoll took the Boks apart in Durban

The sea of red. The whole of one side of Loftus Versveld was solid red for the Second Test. Our supporters were incredible and deserved better. Like the team

Rob Kearney stretches to score in the Second Test, with Tommy Bowe cheerleading. One of the chances that we did take in a period of dominance

Phil Vickery was under pressure in Durban. His greatness as a player and character saw a full-scale comeback in the Third Test at Ellis Park

A study in techniques as the coaches warm up before the final Test at Ellis Park. Peter de Villiers had a very tough week

Congratulating our towering captain at Ellis Park. Paul O'Connell was a true Lions giant throughout

of assessing players and getting them fit to play, way earlier than they should have been.

On that trip, such was the amateur nature that James had to go out to find sponsorship deals with medical companies so that he could tour armed with the medical kit that he needed. Dean Richards suffered a thigh injury which might well have ended his tour had not James brought along the correct treatment apparatus, essentially paid for out of his own pocket. He and Kevin Murphy, the hard-working physio, lost money in making the tour as they had to employ locums in their practices at home to cover for their absences.

Sixteen years after that 1993 tour, in South Africa with the most recent Lions, after James had been on every Lions tour in the intervening time, either with me or, after my strongest recommendation to the head coaches (Graham Henry in Australia in 2001 and Sir Clive Woodward in New Zealand in 2005) I was still enjoying his company, admiring his brilliance and still trusting him to the ends of the earth. He is as great a Lion as any player.

The post of head coach of the Lions was treated for a long time like that of Ryder Cup captain. You would have your turn and then someone else would take over. But that was merely a tradition, not a by-law, and I decided to put myself in the frame, together with some of the other national coaches at the time.

In the preparation and selection of the 1993 tour, we seemed to be back behind the doors of the East India Club in St James's, central London, once again. It was here that all the managements and all the selections for previous tours had been made, by committee men who may or may not have been in tune with modern thinking.

My experience in 1989 had been refreshing. Clive Rowlands had made his call to me offering me the job, without interview, and even though there were a small group of selectors, Rowlands was clever enough in the final analysis to ensure that I got the squad I wanted.

But by 1993 things appeared to have regressed and that will always remain a source of great regret to me because it hampered the tour's chances of success. There were interviews for the coaching position and I wrote down my views and presented them to the committee, with a blueprint on how I thought we could go to New Zealand and win. It was only a few days later that I received a telephone call telling me that I would become the first man ever to coach two Lions parties. It was a great moment.

Geoff Cooke, who I knew and respected from my days in Yorkshire rugby, was appointed tour manager. He always tells me that he taught me all I know about coaching and I have never completely worked out if he is being serious or not. He had done a superb job organising the England team from 1988, England had won a couple of Grand Slams and reached the World Cup Final under his tenure, all after decades of underachievement. Geoff was less emotional than Clive Rowlands had been in 1989 but he was very focused, he was tough on the players and he had the knack of assessing a problem and resolving it. He was a good manager. I was also happy that Dick Best had been appointed assistant coach. I got on extremely well with Dick and his rather acid tongue could be an asset now and again. Dick was good with the forwards. Technically, he was excellent. He can always produce a dose of heavy sarcasm but sometimes with the pack it was a good idea! He got the best out of the forwards on tour. We had a dinner the night before the Second Test and the tensions were running high. Geoff Cooke was there plus the medical lads and Judy had come down and she joined us, too. One of the good things about Dick was that he had started his working life as a chef, and quite a good one, so he knew his food and drink and he knew a good wine, so we usually had a decent bottle when he was around.

We had a little sweep on the result, and we all wrote our predictions down on a piece of paper. We looked at the predictions. There was 12–9 to the Lions, 18–10 to the Lions, and so on. When we opened Bestie's he had New Zealand to win. That's our forwards coach! Naturally, the players had to know about this disloyalty and that Dick had worked out that the way to make some money was to tip the All Blacks. He was fined an enormous amount by the players and it was a double whammy anyway, because we won the Test and he lost his money.

The big issue surrounded the tour captain, and the major contender in the eyes of many people was Will Carling, at that time England's captain and a man already on the way to widespread fame. But I had definite reservations. First, it was suggested to me that not everything in the England camp was quite right, but there was also the key point that Will had never before in his rugby career been to New Zealand.

For me, Gavin Hastings was far and away the outstanding candidate. He had won enormous respect in New Zealand, he had spent time there and he had played there in 1990 for Scotland when we should have beaten them. He had also impressed the Kiwis when he played in the third-place match against them in the 1991 World Cup.

New Zealand and England were slightly daggers drawn as rugby nations at the time, while New Zealand and Scotland had more of an affinity. I just felt that Carling's profile would have caused problems, even resentment, Down Under.

He had also had plenty to say for himself when wearing an England jersey, and it had not always been complimentary to anyone other than England. That was fair enough, and England had certainly put a fine team together at the start of the 1990s. But Will also liked to keep his own company, and I simply do not believe that a Lions captain can afford to be like that.

In the end, he rather struggled on tour. He did not appear to adapt to the whole Lions environment, he hated sharing rooms and he did not like the New Zealand media one bit. He was so unhappy that Ian Robertson of the BBC secretly brought Julia, then his partner, to New Zealand to try to settle him down.

Ultimately, I feel that Will was disappointed not to get the captaincy and I think that affected him deeply. I came to rely on a core of strong English characters on tour – the likes of Brian Moore, Dean Richards and Peter Winterbottom, a great player and a great character I had known through the Headingley club, and who I had coached since he was a small boy. These were the strong Test match candidates for whom I had an enormous respect.

There was also a stage on tour when Will was contributing so little that Geoff Cooke suggested that if he did not change his attitude he might as well not stay on the tour. We may even have bought him tickets home. The senior England players sat Will down and they told him that he had to change, and that his captaincy of England would be in doubt if he was seen to fail the Lions test. In fact, he pulled himself together in the last two weeks of the tour, and led the midweek team well. Whether that was because he was suddenly committed to the concept of the Lions or whether he saw his status, and even the England captaincy, slipping away is a question only he can answer. He never toured again with the Lions, and became, as I noted earlier, the only player in my experience to withdraw from consideration, which he did prior to the 1997 trip to South Africa.

But the biggest mistake of all in the '93 Lions tour was that the party was chosen by an enormous committee. There were about nine people on it altogether, including representatives from each country, and I realised en route to New Zealand that I had been persuaded to take players about whom I was not 100 per cent happy.

One of the major problems was that every position was just taken in isolation. There was no overview, no bigger picture of what the squad was going to look like, how it was going to mesh together as a group of characters. The selectors simply chose thirty players for thirty positions, but with no apparent consideration about achieving a balance or a mix.

The other error was that we met just two days after the last matches in the 1993 Five Nations Championship, with those final games too fresh in the memory. By 2009, I had asked for a much wider gap between the end of the internationals and the day the team was announced, because, in 1993, players were picked on the most recent form of the last two games, and others, who had played consistently well but been part of a struggling team right at the end, were left out.

It would have been interesting to have our time over again. Our pool of props did not impress out there and people like Jeff Probyn and Peter Clohessy missed out. They may well have proved to be good Lions. Paul Rendall, another prop, was probably a little old by then but he was the kind of player I always hankered after. On tour, we had to keep changing our pool of props because they were simply not good enough, and it was just as well that a truly great Lion such as Jason Leonard, who we switched from loose head to tight head, was able to paper over some of the cracks for us.

But as is well known in the game now, some of the players on that tour simply failed what you might call the character test. Especially after we had decided on the First Test team, some players lost concentration, even lost pride, and almost drifted off the tour. They were out drinking and womanising and, even though it was not easy to spot the signs at the time, there is absolutely no doubt that this caused problems on tour, killed some of the morale of the midweek team and reinforced yet again one of my key thoughts of any Lions tour – that at all costs the party must stick together.

The balance of the party was out of kilter because there were only two Irishmen in the original selection. This was to recur much later, in 2009, when, to my immense sadness, only two Scots made the original party. But again, in 1993 it was not a question of nationalities; it was the weakness of isolating every position so that you ended up with a compartmentalised squad.

It is also fair to say that some of the Scottish players on that tour should not have been there in the first place. There was considerable support for them from elsewhere on the selection committee, and, bizarrely, it was non-Scots who pushed in some of those

Scottish players. To their credit, and even though the 1993 tour was very far from their finest hour, they actually played quite well after they came back home. They obviously learned a hell of a lot, and they also found the home environment so much easier. A Lions tour should take you to a different level.

A significant number of our squad could not manage the pressure of life in New Zealand. It is not just Test matches that find you out. It is also the provincial games. Those teams are packed with players who are hard, who know about rugby. They may not be as good a rugby player as you are, but, boy, do they understand the game.

And the pressure comes on every time you go out. It is a pressure cooker; it is something that is massively intense. In international rugby at home, and in the Five Nations at the time, they were used to playing on the big occasions, to full houses. But in the evening, they would enjoy a convivial dinner and then go home. In New Zealand, players would go back to the hotel and were effectively returning to the same pressured environment.

That pressure is intensified by the New Zealand media, who are, to put it bluntly, graceless, and who target mercilessly whatever they believe to be Lions weaknesses. You have no family to support you, you have only a relatively small number of fans and the only thing on your side is the environment that you create as a group. Some of that 1993 team were in desperate need of a release valve, and they found it in socialising to a remarkable degree.

That annoyed me so much. It annoyed me that certain players could not be serious about it. The heavy defeats at the hands of Hawke's Bay and Waikato at the end of the tour in the final midweek games were an embarrassment. It is easy to say that the Test team was not involved but there was bound to be a knock-on effect in terms of morale and in terms of a dip in the unified mentality of the squad, as the midweek players were plainly just going through the motions, all the more so so that they could go home more quickly.

Yet again, I learned any number of lessons from that, which I carried over to the next Lions tour in 1997, and one of the main reasons why we were to be successful in 1997 was that we had a stronger calibre of player in terms of character, players who could take the pressure.

To his credit, Will Carling did stand up to be counted at the very end, and before the Waikato game, our last midweek fixture, on 29 June, he commendably took the players aside into a room, with no coaches present, to demand that they showed proper commitment. He himself played very well while others around him caved in. Perhaps he felt he was losing credibility with his own strongmen but he personally did well.

Part of the pressure in New Zealand comes from the attitude of the hosts. In 1993, and even if in my opinion we outplayed them in two of the three Tests, they were always graceless. 'That word again, but it is entirely appropriate. When we won, they simply complained that they had been lousy, rather than giving us any credit.

Laurie Mains, their coach, was described as 'stone-faced' by members of his own team. He gave us no credit at any stage of the tour, he complained after the Third Test that 'the Lions [had] been killing the ball throughout the series'. Afterwards, I remember reading the book *Inside the All Blacks* which dealt with that tour. Some of the things that the All Blacks said about great players like Dean Richards were quite out of order and completely disrespectful.

Mains had been there in 1992 when I helped coach the World XV for the New Zealand centenary. We beat the All Blacks in the First Test. That sent the New Zealand authorities into overdrive. They were so desperate to win the series, and not to have their party spoiled, that they would not let us pick the same team again. I admire them for always wanting the edge, but they find any way they can to keep that edge. At the dinner after the Third Test in 1993, Judy and I were on the same table as Mains and his wife. He did not appear to want to exchange more than a few words, and I felt that the New Zealanders showed a lack of respect for British and Irish rugby.

The other major story came at the time of the First Test, when Wade Dooley, one of my kingpins of 1989, heard that his father had died back at home in Lancashire, and Wade left for home. We replaced him with Martin Johnson, who was just starting his international career and, typically for a man I grew to admire enormously, Johnno arrived and soon played his way straight into the Test team. But there was a distressing aftermath, because, once Wade had attended his father's funeral and taken care of affairs, he wanted to rejoin the tour. The New Zealand Rugby Union, to their credit, were very happy for him to return. But in one of those rather typical four Home Unions strictures, we were told that there was some procedural rule which forbade Wade from coming back. It all left a sour taste.

Yet it would be incorrect to paint too downbeat a portrait of life among those Lions; it was a mighty challenge, there were experiences to savour and I would like to think that most of us understood New Zealand, ourselves and our sporting limitations and possibilities better by the time we came home.

We started with a week of training up in the Bay of Islands, and had a hotel overlooking the gorgeous bay at Paihia, near Waitangi, where, in 1840, the Treaty of Waitangi was signed. Under this, the Maoris conceded the sovereignty of the Land of the Long White Cloud to Queen Victoria. We trained at Kerikeri, and when we landed at Kerikeri's tiny airport we were met by local people with presents and gifts of fruit. This was still in the era when training sessions were open, when everyone could come along and watch, and I remember meaty old locals leaning on the fences and shaking their heads as we worked. It was also now that those Lions who had never before been to New Zealand were subjected to the full blast. They found that everyone from the waitress and chambermaids in the hotel to the bus drivers knew, understood and talked endlessly about rugby and its finer technical points. There was no escape from it and the best tourists were those who did not want to escape.

And at last the weather relented just a little, because for the first few days it seemed that the dreaded wet winter of 1977, when it poured for months, would be repeated. When we moved south from the Bay of Islands to Whangarei (pronounced Fong'ry) for our first game against North Auckland, it began to rain almost as soon as we left Paihia. That night there was a great storm. Our hotel actually had a corrugated roof and we listened to the rain hammering on it for hours. The electricity was cut off, and we spent two days in candlelight, awaiting the start of the tour.

If ever there was a bad omen, however, it was when Ian Hunter, of Northampton, was injured in the very first game and had to be replaced, but the truth is that we motored through the early games. North Auckland had the usual high number of Goings in the side but, by the end, they were Going, Going, gone, beaten 30–17.

On every Lions tour there always seems to be a match in which you are reminded of what might be called the physical challenge, a game whose violence jolts you into remembering that the touring party has to stick together. That game came early in 1993, in the second game of the tour, when we played North Harbour; there was violence during the match, there was a kick in the head from one of their forwards and a big altercation between Frank Bunce and Dean Richards. The refereeing was staggering, but we still won by 29–13, and we scored tries from Jeremy Guscott, Tony Clement, Tony Underwood and Scott Hastings, all backs. At this stage, I was concentrating on the loose play and on getting the backs operating at speed and we were effectively underprepared, so this was a satisfying result.

Rightly or wrongly, we did not complain in public about dirty play on that tour; we believed that it would only create further antagonism, which you didn't want the Lions to be involved in.

But I said to the players after the North Harbour game: 'No backward step.' I told them what had happened in 1989 with

Australia, and I said that if that was the way it was going to be, then we should make sure that our reaction was both concerted and physical. It was almost as though New Zealand wanted to kick us off the park, and many of the teams we played weren't trying to play that much rugby either.

Having said that, the New Zealand Maori game, next up, was incredible. It did show some of our weaknesses because we were 20–3 down at one stage, and some of our forwards were dire. The Maori coach said afterwards of Peter Wright, the Scotland prop, that he 'was short of a gallop'.

But gradually we started to come back. At the time, I was stressing phase play; I was talking about ninety-second rugby. If we could develop the game and take the ball through the phases, so that each play lasted more than ninety seconds, then there would be opportunities, there would be spaces in the defence or, at the very least, the opposition would concede penalties. We started this either from a set piece, or from attacks after regaining possession, and we were trying to keep the tempo up to make teams defend.

The Maori game showed that we could keep the ball on the field and play, and it gave us a great deal of confidence. We started attacking from deep, with Ieuan Evans making some great runs. Both Ieuan and Rory Underwood scored as we gradually came back into the game and Gavin Hastings triumphantly scored the winning try. It finished 24–20.

And we kept on playing that brand of rugby. We went to Canterbury next, always a difficult proposition, and even though the pitch was so wet that there were showers of spray after every tackle, we played really well. Ben Clarke and Dewi Morris were superb. Clarke was a huge feature of the tour; his ball carrying and physicality were superb. Against Canterbury, he played on the open side but he was one of the few who could also play in the other two back-row positions as well. Jeremy Guscott was outstanding that day too. Jerry and I were well-embarked on the second of the Lions tours where we worked together and by now, we had momentum. You could tell by the number of articles in

the New Zealand press claiming that parts of our game were illegal that we were beginning to worry them.

There is always one game on every tour, as we all know, where
the wheels fall off. We lost to Otago by 37–24 in the next game,
and it was at the wrong time, a week before the First Test. Otago
played high-tempo rugby with a young Josh Kronfeld on the flank
and we were chasing shadows. It was as if they were sending a message to New Zealand that we could not handle the Otago
fast-rucking style.

In fact, against Otago it was all bad news. The giant Martin
Bayfield was playing really well on that tour; he was feared in the
line-out by the All Blacks. He was flipped over when he was high
in the air at a line-out against Otago, and landed really heavily on
his shoulders and neck as he came down. Hand on heart, I could
not decide whether or not Martin was deliberately targeted but
Otago knew he was a threat and they were clearly having a go at
him. Martin was lying still on the ground for some time but recovered reasonably well. Scott Hastings was also injured in that game,
breaking his jaw and leaving the tour, another huge blow.

That match was also, probably, the one in which I decided that
if Stuart Barnes was a terrific player on the front foot he was not
quite so good under pressure, and that he did not have the kicking game to clear our lines when Otago put us under pressure. It
was probably that game which persuaded us that Rob Andrew was
the better player for the Test series and that Stuart would be a midweek player, even though he had begun the tour well. Rob sought
to give us what we were looking for.

We finally settled on the Test team – crunch time for the tour
and for the spirit of those who are not selected for it. We talked
about keeping the pace up, playing multiphases, working through
the back row. But we were also intent on running strike moves
from set piece, and we spent a fair bit of time on those as well.

By the time of the First Test, Wade Dooley had gone home and
Martin Johnson had not yet arrived, so, with Andy Reed and
Martin Bayfield in the second row, we were not fielding the ideal

combination. But we still reckoned that the All Blacks would give penalties away, because at the breakdown they overcompete. It is simply the New Zealand nature to do so, particularly for their back row, so we were going for a mixture of first-phase strike moves and then continuity.

But, as usual, there was the referee to consider before we could apply our own plans. His name was Brian Kinsey, an Australian. We spoke to him before the game for clarification, he told us how he would be reffing it but, of course, when it came to the game he did not do anything he said he was going to do. We tried to talk to him after the game, but he wouldn't speak to us.

So after a four-hour selection meeting, we unveiled the team to start the series. Rob Andrew, Will Carling and Jeremy Guscott formed an England midfield, and, although Scott Gibbs, the young Welsh centre, had already shown some electricity, he was battling with minor injuries in the early part of the tour. We chose Kenny Milne as hooker instead of Brian Moore and two other heroes of 1989, Mike Teague and Robert Jones, also failed to make the side. New Zealand had their famous front row of Craig Dowd, Sean Fitzpatrick and Olo Brown, the powerhouse Inga Tuigamala on the wing and Grant Fox, one of the best goalkickers of the era, at fly-half.

New Zealand scored their really dubious try early on when Ieuan Evans had his hands on the ball as the pair went over our line, but gradually we started to establish ourselves. We knew that if we retained ball we would at least draw penalties, and we did. Gavin kicked three penalties against two by Fox and we were only 11–9 down.

In fact, we kept our composure really well, and, as the match wore on, we were keeping the ball, worrying them; they were having difficulty handling us, and Gavin was still kicking the penalties. Our back row was superb and Bayfield was winging the lines out. Fox kicked two more penalties, Gavin kicked two more for us and, with only ten minutes left, Gavin put us into an 18–17 lead with a long kick against the wind and from a wide angle. We looked a very tidy side; we had never panicked despite that first unfortunate try and it was at this point that I turned to Geoff Cooke in the stand and told him that we had the match. The momentum was definitely going our way.

Then came the fateful penalty. People told me afterwards that they had been certain all along that Kinsey would give Fox the chance to win the game late on. Dewi Morris was distraught after the game. Dewi and Dean were going for the ball legally; Bunce would not release. The Lions on the field will go to their graves believing that the penalty should have been awarded their way, because Dewi Morris and Dean Richards tackled Bunce and turned him over, with Bunce still holding on to the ball.

After the game, Brian Kinsey refused to talk not only to us but to the media as well, although after he had gone back to Australia he tried to justify himself in an article which appeared in the *New Zealand Herald*.

There was a two-week gap between the Tests on that tour, which at least gave us a little breathing space. Martin Johnson had arrived by now, and he played in the next match, against Taranaki, and we won 49–25. It was never a big deal with Martin. He just arrived, got his head down and applied himself, and he knew New Zealand rugby because he had been there and played for New Zealand Under-21. He struck up a partnership with Martin Bayfield. I suppose the line-out in the game at the time suited his type of player. High leaping was not exactly on the agenda in the environment in New Zealand. I remember one photograph taken of the Taranaki game at a line-out, and it is total mayhem, not one 'jumper' actually leaves the ground amidst all the barging and obstruction.

Yet we also had this youngster, Gibbs, who was coming through strongly, who was both vocal and physical. The Second Test was, as it so often seemed to be, the life or death moment of the tour, and it was time for action. We dropped Carling for the Auckland game, which caused a lot of fuss and bother in the press but which was in rugby terms a fairly clear-cut decision.

It did not have the desired effect because we lost to Auckland, a team full of All Blacks, by 23–18, our scrum was not impressive and Gavin Hastings pulled a hamstring, an injury niggle which caused us no end of bother. Johnson, Moore and Evans improved matters but it was not enough.

And if we were looking for a lift from the midweek team we were to be bitterly disappointed; it was such a painful contrast to the 1989 midweek team's great win over Australian Capital Territory at Canberra, which was so important to our momentum. We were not at the time conscious that such a large group of players were losing concentration and socialising, and we were well in the lead, but as soon as Hawke's Bay got their teeth into the game we subsided. Perhaps only Stuart Barnes and one or two others played like true Lions and I told the media after the match that I had been upset that some players had not shown proper commitment. From then on it became a point of honour to keep the Test team divorced from the collapse of the midweek team. And of keeping the midweek team out of the bar.

Gavin's hamstring became a distraction in that key build-up week to the Second Test at Athletic Park in Wellington. Most people thought there was no way he could be fit, and Gavin was inclined to agree. But by this time James Robson, our tour doctor, was working hard on the injury and his overall influence was beginning to make itself felt. He worked quietly away at Gavin's hamstring.

That week saw the longest talk that I ever had with Gavin, and I enlisted Rob Andrew to talk to him as well. Then I detailed Jerry Guscott to bend the Hastings ear. 'You are so important to this team that you have to lead the team on. And it's what you do in the forty-eight hours before the game that we would also miss. Even if you last only five minutes, I want you to lead the team on to the field.'

It was a long process. He didn't train on Friday in Wellington. I was just walking alone with Gavin, miles from where the training was taking place. Finally, something clicked into place in his mind. 'Right. Fine. I'm playing.' And with that he jogged off. He joined Scott Gibbs in the team, and Jason Leonard, with a typical lack of fuss, switched to the tight-head side and took the place of Paul Burnell.

What else do I recall of that week? The pressure. We did a pretty physical session in Wellington; we planned to switch to taking the All Blacks pack up, but we also knew that if we controlled the ball then we had big runners – people like Ben Clarke, Scott Gibbs and Gavin were all powerful players. And we were telling ourselves that as soon as we got turnover ball or quick ball of any sort, we'd be away with it. We were not going to mess around.

And for the Test, we repeated that session we had held in 1989 where we almost literally walked every blade of grass on the field. In 1989 it had been just the two half-backs, Rob Andrew and Robert Jones, together with Roger Uttley and myself. In 1993 it was the whole squad. We looked at every decision to be made in every situation so that the forwards knew exactly what they were doing at the line-out, and what the move was going to be from every scrum. We would then make the call, jog through it. And just build the plays.

It was not that we did not trust individual players to make their own decisions. I just liked this one idea of bringing everybody together as a team, and that whether you were in the front row, the back three or wherever, you were becoming fully aware of all the possibilities.

Looking back, it was also evidence that the game was developing. In 1989 you could play a game that was fairly limited but by 1993 you were trying to take the ball through phases. Also, we were trying to force them into mistakes, an approach that demanded that we be in among them all the time.

The atmosphere was charged, the tension painful. At least Gavin was there to lead the team out. He was also there after a few seconds, standing under a high ball from Grant Fox on our own line. Gavin dropped it, Eroni Clarke dived on it and scored. It was a shattering start from any number of standpoints. We had decided to play into the wind and the sun in the first half as we hoped it would force us to play our game of keeping the ball in play.

And yet that day was to become one of the Lions' finest, one of the most satisfying results and performances, possibly in my top three of all time. Gavin dropped the first ball but he never dropped another and we began to find ourselves, to exert control and to play well into the wind. Rob Andrew took us round the field in masterly fashion, our line-out was superb and Martin Bayfield probably had the finest game of his career. We just controlled the set piece and we controlled the ball, we took it through phases. They made their mistakes, as we said they would, but we were actually going through phases as well. We got the penalties and by half-time we had cashed in. Gavin kicked two penalties and Rob dropped a goal and we led 9–7, a great result against the wind.

We kept playing. We forced another penalty, which Gavin put over, and then the crowning moment, something which probably summed up everything we were trying to do. The All Blacks were driving a maul but Sean Fitzpatrick dropped the ball in contact, under our pressure. We were geared to react immediately. We didn't just dive on the ball, we had it up and away. Dewi Morris attacked down the left and found Jeremy Guscott and Jeremy set off like a racing car. John Kirwan came across to shadow him with Rory outside, and yet Jerry just held it and held it. He said afterwards that he was waiting until Kirwan looked at him, and, the moment he did, Jerry fed Rory and Rory had the finishing burst for the left-hand corner.

At the time I was working for Scottish Life. Malcolm Murray, the chief executive of the company, was thrilled. The photograph of that try has a huge Scottish Life banner advertisement in the background as Rory dives in. I didn't pretend that it was all part of the plan.

It was one of two massive moments which won us the Test. The other, I felt, was a colossal tackle by Ben Clarke on their talisman,

John Kirwan. Kirwan came up the middle, Ben crunched up and drove him back probably as much as 10 yards. It was one of those psychologically massive moments.

Gavin kicked a final penalty, and that made it 20–7, an amazing win, and my favourite picture is that of Nick Popplewell, who had played well up front, beaming hugely as he left the field. Judy arrived just before the Test, with Robert and Heather. It was the first time any of them had ever seen the Lions live. Robert was in tears at the end of it. He couldn't believe it. He was only twelve and I wonder if he realised that in the Lions Test history it hadn't always been quite like this.

People always want to know what the night is like after a great win. I had a quiet dinner with the family, but I hear that the boys had a slightly noisier one.

Coincidentally, the great Brian Lochore was also in the same restaurant as us. He had been the manager of the World XV in the Centenary Tests, when I had coached with Bob Templeton. He was gracious. 'Congratulations. Big win. You played well.' He fished just a little for the secret of how we had done it, then went on his way. Everybody in the Lions camp felt good about himself. All that we had talked about and hoped for, but had not really achieved in the First Test, we had actually fulfilled in the Second. Unforgettable.

We then had a sharp reminder of how low the performances of the midweek team had sunk. Ideally, you need a vibrant performance in midweek to keep the momentum going but we were hammered by Waikato by 38–10, another embarrassment even though Waikato were a good side and had Warren Gatland at hooker, sixteen years before we were to be on the same side with the 2009 Lions in South Africa. It was the biggest of the six defeats we suffered on tour.

The build-up for the Third Test was incredibly tense and we knew that the All Blacks, with the way they understand the game, would be working furiously on countering us. They brought in

Andy Haden, the old lock, to help them in the line-out and they chose Lee Stensness in the centre to give themselves a bit more craft in midfield. The pressure on them was massive, no doubt about it.

And yet it all began so well. Gavin Hastings kicked a penalty and then, after we had pressured them in midfield, Scott Gibbs seized on a loose ball and scored and we were 10–0 up. But there were already bad signs. They nullified Martin Bayfield simply by jumping into him at the line-out, where the referee allowed complete mayhem to reign. We were not so sharp on their turnover ball either and we could not keep the ball long enough to wear them down or force penalties.

At the start, they had been nervous, and I felt they were there for the taking. They were pretty hyped up and that played to our advantage in the first fifteen minutes. But they came back. They had dropped Zinzan Brooke and brought in Arran Pene, who was good at close quarters, and just before half-time we made some bad errors – Frank Bunce and Sean Fitzpatrick both scored near half-time with spilled ball. Suddenly, we were going in 14–10 down.

In the second half the All Blacks were on top, Jon Preston scored a try from scrum-half, Fox kicked three penalties and they ran away to win 30–13. Psychologically, the Third Test is always so hard to win on any tour. You are on a plane two days later, it has invariably been a hard tour and a hard season, but we didn't really play in that last Test, and they produced by far their best performance of the series.

The party had a great opportunity to beat the All Blacks, just as the 1977 Lions did. It was thoroughly frustrating to come away having fallen short once again. It was vital to learn the lessons so that in the future at least the party would not be weakened before it even left Britain. The lessons were obvious to me and they all appeared in my tour report. The coach has to have the final say in selection. No committees. The coach has to be allowed to choose the party holistically, and in combinations, and by assessing characters. Selection cannot be influenced just by who you think might technically be the best players. Look at the chemistry and also find players who, whether they are picked for the Test match or not, will keep the whole thing on the rails between the Tests.

Before the First Test, everybody has to know he is in with a shout. But that First Test week is crunch time. It's when your strong characters say: 'Right, this is my role and responsibility now.' They support players and training and give a lead in the midweek game.

In all future tours I kept hammering home this philosophy. In 1993, players were going 'off tour' because they weren't picked. On tour in New Zealand or South Africa or Australia, even a united party will have its work cut out. In the final analysis, in some ways it was remarkable that in 1993, with all the division that existed, we came so close. The margins were tiny, and who can say if we were one dire decision by an Australia referee away from coming home victorious?

13

Northampton – Rugby's in Town

Reviving the old giant, and glory passed on

Compared with Edinburgh, Northampton is not much to look at. No castle or imposing buildings, unless you count the giant structure that one of the lift manufacturers put up for testing. No noon gun or internationally renowned festival or giant railway hotels or zoo or airport. We moved to Northampton in 1994 at a time when the fortunes of the rugby club were shaky, and the first sight of the unprepossessing town centre was not promising.

But I already suspected that something was happening below the surface in Northampton rugby. At heart, Northampton is a vibrant, teeming rugby town, where rugby players are recognised far more readily than footballers. The Saints are one of the great historical English rugby clubs and, even though the team itself was struggling when I arrived to become their director of rugby, I knew that they had real possibilities. They also had good people moving in to take charge and players of stature. It was a refreshing change to move from Edinburgh, where rugby was often lost in the landscape, to a place where it was a major activity, and where the atmosphere created by marvellous supporters added to the sense of occasion. I was to spend five happy seasons at the club. I should have stayed longer and regret not doing so. I was also robbed by bizarre fate of the ultimate reward that the club game in Europe can provide.

But they were exciting times, in every way. Hardly had I moved from Scotland and got my feet under the table and set about trying to transform the club on the field, than the sport itself changed under our feet, profoundly and totally. I arrived in 1994, just after season 1994–95 had started. Less than a year later, there was the mother of all upheavals because on 1 September 1995, in a hotel in Paris, the International Rugby Board announced that the game was to go open. In another word, professional.

In one sense it was not surprising because the abuses of the ama-teur era and the pressure on the amateur principle were causing severe problems. On the other hand, no one foresaw that the game would go professional overnight and it would be the exaggeration of all time to say that Northern Hemisphere rugby, and especially rugby in England, was at all ready for the new world – after all, in England and Scotland especially, the old guard had fought des-perately against the arrival of paid rugby for decades. Indeed, I am not entirely sure that everyone in Scottish rugby believes to this day that the game should have gone professional.

But Northampton coped with it all quite magnificently. It is no exaggeration to say that they managed the transition better than all the national Unions and better than the other English clubs. Deservedly, Northampton were the first club to make a profit from the professional era, this after years of losses throughout the game. They are still in the money.

They had the ideal benefactor. Keith Barwell, a highly success-ful local businessman and Saints lover, was waiting in the wings, and when the game went professional he stepped up and declared that he wanted to buy the club and to pilot it through the stormy seas ahead. We called a big meeting in a hotel in Northampton, the room was packed, the players were all there. Keith himself spoke, so did Tim Rodber and Gregor Townsend, the Scotland fly-half we had brought to the club, and myself. The vote was taken as to whether Keith would be allowed to buy the club – the price was £1 million – and whether we would go fully professional under his control. The vote was taken. It was, roughly, seven hundred to two in favour. The new era had dawned.

Northampton were very good to us. They soon had a house sorted and Keith Barwell, who was then in the background, made me extremely welcome. But it was not exactly a triumphant start. At the end of my first season, we were relegated and disappeared into Division Two. I had missed all the pre-season and, in fact, I did not join Northampton officially until October because I had insisted on finishing off my existing projects with Scottish Life. Northampton managed to lose all six of their opening games and it was clear that there was work to do. You only had to be there for a short time to sense that there had been factions and a lack of focus.

I made a point of going out to dinner to talk with some of the senior players, men like Tim Rodber, Matt Dawson, Paul Grayson and Brett Taylor, but what would have been even better in that difficult first season would have been if those top players had actually been able to play for the club more often. Jack Rowell was the England head coach at the time and, basically, Jack wanted his players to slash their commitments and almost intimidated them into not playing for their clubs. The message from England was that if the lads wanted to appear for their country, then there were certain weekends on which any appearance for their clubs would be frowned upon.

The players were very uncomfortable about this, and I was not prepared to see them caught in the middle. The upshot was that I would be up on the balcony watching us struggle in a key game at the bottom of the table, and up there with me, dressed in their day clothes, would be Rodber, Dawson, Grayson, Ian Hunter and Martin Bayfield. Some clubs simply insisted that their international players did appear for them. I remember being up on the balcony on one occasion surrounded by our England players, watching England's Dewi Morris inspire Sale to victory over us by one point. We won about half our games after our dire start but then came the final Saturday of the season, we had to win away at West Hartlepool and Harlequins had to lose away at Gloucester. We kept our part of the deal but Harlequins reneged on theirs and we had that sinking feeling.

That was that. It was time to act. Rugby was already in turmoil at the time, the sport was heading towards the 1995 World Cup in South Africa and everyone knew that the days of amateurism and also shamateurism were coming to an end. Interestingly, I was allowed to be a professional but only if I did not coach a team; just a group of individuals! Technically, the number had to be below fifteen, or above. I don't think anyone came to count. However, the big picture was not important in my list of priorities at Northampton. On the Monday morning after we were relegated I called all the players in for a meeting. I told them that nobody was leaving the club, and I told them that they would all be operating at a completely different level the next season.

Looking back, and even though it was all a painful experience at the time, it is also true that relegation shook up the club, allowed us to get rid of any factions and galvanised the whole operation. We began with the basic fitness sessions with Phil Pask, who was a former Saints flanker and a brilliant conditioner. Paskie was still working alongside me on the 2009 Lions tour recently. The idea was that when our England contingent rejoined us after the World Cup in South Africa, they should be intimidated by our levels of fitness. And they were. We were only preparing to play in Division 2 but I told the players that our standards, our fitness and our levels of play had to be as high as if we were competing in the top division, and the players said that they had never trained so hard before.

I also established a five-year plan, along with head coach Paul Larkin with whom I worked closely and whom I respected enormously. This was to take us up a few notches on and off the field and its ultimate goal was for us to win the European Cup within five years. As it turned out we did not stick to the plan – Northampton became European champions within four years.

There were advantages and disadvantages to the arrival of the professional era. In my first season we had still been training on Tuesday and Thursday evenings after the players had come home from work and rushed to the training fields. Now, gradually, as the players sorted themselves out and decided whether or not they would become full-time professionals, we were able to train during the day, and, for the first time in its history, rugby saw its players coming into work at the sport as if it was any other kind of job. Even now, nearly fifteen years on, it still resounds as a momentous change.

The Rugby Football Union had caused chaos with their last-ditch defence of amateurism and they added to the chaos greatly by declaring a moratorium. This was supposed to mean that the advent of professionalism would be put back one year while the RFU, which had made no plans whatsoever, tried to work out what to do. They were completely overwhelmed, as impotent as King Canute sitting before the waves; everyone just went on making his own arrangements and, if it was all haphazard and hairy, then it was also exciting.

We put our top international players on a salary band of £30,000. We also had other salary bands of £20,000, £15,000 and, for the younger players, £10,000. There was a downside. Now that clubs could pay players, it meant that they were inclined to pay for the best, not simply local boys who were not of the required standard. After a season of examination, we ourselves disposed of around eighteen players. I shudder as I recall the process. It was the hardest thing that I ever did in rugby, asking those young men into the office and telling them that they had no future in a professional existence at Northampton. Some were able to find other clubs, others just drifted out of the game; many left the office in tears. I hated it.

At the time, people with hard hearts simply saw rugby as a new business and no more than that. But Keith Barwell understood that, while sport was now indeed a business, it was also something else altogether. There was an emotional attachment to it which did not exist in other areas of working life. Keith had made a highly successful career buying businesses, reorganising them and sometimes closing them down. It was an environment in which you would drive somebody home, take his company car keys from him, drive his car back and have his desk cleared, and suddenly he was gone. I asked Keith to come and sit in on a few of the sessions when I dispensed with players, and he understood that you could put more of yourself into rugby and into sport, than you did into some businesses.

The major English clubs now formed a collective body, the forerunner to the powerful (and imperfect) PRL (Premier Rugby Ltd) body of today, and Keith and I were the Northampton representatives. It was here that I first came across Sir John Hall, the chairman of Newcastle United Football Club, whose company had bought Newcastle and intended to transform them into a major professional outfit. The club bought a whole group of experienced players led by Rob Andrew and Dean Ryan, and, to their credit, they won the first Premiership title – and the club is still in existence today, having done well to establish itself in an area where football tends to be more popular.

But Hall is long gone. At the very start, in all those meetings and in his public pronouncements, he clearly saw the whole thing as a rights issue for television. He owned United, was part of the dominant cabal of big football clubs and was used to dominating the situation so that the clubs received massive incomes from the television contracts. He did not understand the primacy of international rugby, or that the Rugby Football Union was not going to give up control of the game. Basically, he did not understand that rugby was not the same as football.

At one of the meetings I took issue with Sir John and explained to him that rugby had different values and standards, which were worth preserving even as we reaped the rewards and benefits of going professional. Next day, Keith took a call from Hall wanting to know who the little upstart was that he had brought along with him.

Keith and Northampton as a club were embroiled, along with the others, in years of fuss and bother. The clubs tried to assert their rights, but were greeted by suspicion at Twickenham – especially by a controversial and, in the opinion of most, impossible RFU chairman called Cliff Brittle who was doing his best to curb the growing power of the clubs. And even though Fran Cotton and myself had always got on well, even though we worked superbly together on the 1997 Lions tour in South Africa which he managed with distinction, we had endless arguments about the scene in England – Fran was suspicious of the clubs, and was a powerbroker inside the Union at a time when the RFU were not taking the game in the correct direction.

But writing at a time when we have a highly successful professional game in Europe, and especially a living, breathing professional club game in England, it is important to pay tribute to those who saved rugby – not the Rugby Football Union, who had no answers, but a bunch of good men who moved into the top clubs as benefactors – men like Chris Wright at Wasps, Nigel Wray at Saracens, Tom Walkinshaw at Gloucester, later Brian Kennedy at Sale, Keith at Northampton, and many others who formed the second wave of benefactors. What impresses me about them all was that they were all men with money but they were coming into rugby for all the right reasons. They have stayed the course superbly. Without them, there might be no pro club game in England and we could be stuck with silly franchises.

But one thing never changed. Rugby matches still had to be won, and Northampton were in the second strata. Not only did we set about raising standards, but we set about playing a brilliant brand of rugby and in 1995–96 we dominated the division. We scored nine hundred points and were promoted at the first attempt. Some of our rugby at the time was sensational, with the players challenging each other. I put a ban on kicking, and threatened to substitute players if they did kick. I was taking it to an extreme in an effort to convince them just what they could do, especially if they had the fitness to do it.

In my five seasons we never lost the edge that our fitness gave us. One example: a few seasons after I arrived we signed the great Argentine Puma hooker Federico Mendez, who had been unhappy at Bath. Freddie was brilliant at scrum time; he could tell when the other team was tiring and on the point of no longer being able to scrummage effectively. He would get messages to us – 'one more scrum and they've gone'. Or similar. We had the principle of integrating fitness with the intensity and the pace at which we played. In my last full season, we were so fit that we could play teams off the park, and frequently did.

And it was more than just fitness. It was at Northampton that I took my attacking ideas into different areas. I had been evolving my thoughts on the attacking shape of a team, and that came out as a cone! Wherever the ball carrier was, we demanded that there was a group of support players with him, making out the shape of a cone. The cone would stretch back around 10 to 15 metres away from where the ball was going into contact. Those nearer would be fairly narrow behind the carrier; those further away would be wider as they came into the cone. As the players in the cone were coming in behind the ball, their heads were up and they were sorting themselves out for their next task.

We didn't want all the support players to arrive at the same time. I wanted them to make decisions about whether they were first, second, third or fourth. If the ball carrier had been able to get free or made a half-break, the next man just played off him and carried on the move. The third man then had to follow him in, because if we broke through then there was going to be some kind of link pass to take – this all gave us the option of playing right through the contact area.

If the contact was not as advantageous, or, say, the carrier had been tackled, then the players arriving just changed their roles. If the ball was slow they didn't play through the contact; they formed a link group, or a wave support group. In the worst-case scenario, where the carrier had been tackled to the ground, they simply cleared out the ruck. We attacked our way out of Division 2, and we kept playing the same brand of rugby in the Premiership, especially when I convinced the players that they could do it. In one of the last games before I departed, we scored forty points against our deadly Midlands rivals, Leicester. They were confronted with so many cones that they must have felt sick . . .

Keith, myself and the entire administration were also aware that we were creating a professional rugby club in prototype. I told Keith he could make a start with the pitch, which had a reputation, fully deserved, of being marshland. As I said to Keith: 'It's no good us trying to play our style of rugby on a quagmire, because in the middle of winter we are going to lose the game simply because it is a mud heap.' And lo and behold, what appeared was nothing less than a billiard table. One summer, they took the top ten inches off the pitch, redid all the drainage and relaid the pitch. David Powell, the old England prop, still tends it lovingly, and you can still play billiards on it.

Then we moved on to the academy, and, once again, I think we were years ahead of the pack. Brett Taylor headed it, and it was full-time. The club had bought a house and it could take seven academy players. Brett would closely monitor the homes and the general behaviour and progress of all the players. Someone else went in and made three hot meals a week, the rest of the time the players cooked for themselves. But they had their own rooms, a shared lounge, a garden, a kitchen and an educational programme. Of the local lads who came through, there was a big wing called Ben Cohen, and a huge hooker called Steve Thompson. Both started for England in the 2003 World Cup final.

I was also keen for what we called 'the Northampton way' to be formalised, to spread throughout the club. Everyone, from Keith down, became really good friends. I still meet up with them at

Northampton even now. After matches, we would go out as a club coaching group, with our partners. There would be the first XV coaches, the under-21 and under-18 coaches. The Northampton way was back to core principles: this is what we want Northampton to look like. We want a Northampton player to understand that these are his roles, these are his responsibilities, this is how he behaves, and this is what we want Northampton rugby to look like. We did it in every team. If Brett Taylor was establishing the principles with a group of under-16s, I wanted those lads to be able to recognise them if they watched the first team, and they could see the same things applying. So everything we did went from the first team down.

Keith Barwell could be excitable, and impatient, but he was also excellent. There was a period when he was questioning some of the requests I was making and he called a lunch meeting. I needed some players and a few other resources and, at first, he was unwilling to let me have them. The club was trying to make a profit or to establish itself and to make it as a business going forward. At the lunch I said: 'Keith, you've got to back me on this. Trust me. If we do this, then we're going to kick forward.' It ended up almost a shouting match between us. Geoff Allen, the chief executive at the time, kept out of it. It was Keith and me going head-to-head. When I went home that night I said to Judy: 'Well, I might not have a job in the morning.'

Next morning Keith called. He said: 'I'll back you. You can have what you want.'

Eventually he laid plans for a total rebuild of Franklin's Gardens. It is now a fantastic stadium, it seats around 14,000 and it needs every seat it can get. It is sold out for almost every match. I had been involved in the plans and so, in 2001, I returned to Northampton at Keith's request to open the main stand. There is a plaque there which reads: 'Opened by Ian McGeechan'.

As season 1995–96 loomed, we gathered ourselves for a return to the Premiership. Tim Rodber was my captain, and very powerful character. Tim and I built up a fine rapport. He was a player I was anxious to take with the Lions two years later, in 1997. He was hurt by being sent off playing for England at Eastern Province in 1994 as a midweek player, and hurt that he was never chosen to captain England. But he was a magnificent player and leader and it was another barometer of Northampton's progress that we had to learn to play without him in his absences, just as Wasps had to learn in later seasons to play without Lawrence Dallaglio. Some people still see Tim as something of a military oddball; he was anything but, and working with him was very similar to working with Dallaglio at Wasps in later years. He was a hard man, he was clever and he was the perfect core of the club.

Around him the team grew. Dawson and Grayson bedded down, and then we saw the arrival of the likes of Nick Beal and Allan Clarke, who became an international hooker for Ireland, joining the giant figure of Martin Bayfield, a Northampton man from way back and who was always a brilliant line-out forward. Budge Pountney, whose origins were in the Channel Islands, making him available for Scotland – don't ask – arrived and I put him straight in at open-side flanker, despite reservations from Rodber. Budge became not only a brilliant open side for club and country, but one of the leading figures in Northampton rugby history.

Matt Dawson was and remains a controversial figure. It seems that he can rub people up the wrong way, and even now he provokes different responses as he develops his career in the media. I have worked with Matt since he was a cocky youngster; we talked a lot about his game, about the need to work on his service, and the need to wait for the correct moment before trying for the break. I also used him as a barometer for the whole team. I said that if Matt was shattered, we must be playing well. If he was tired, it meant that he would be getting to the breakdowns just as the ball was appearing, which meant that we were sending back quick ball and playing with the desired continuity. Matt and I never had a problem with each other; we signed him for Wasps towards the end of his career and he was excellent, and it was an outstanding moment when he became a world champion in 2003.

The Northampton situation replicated that which eventually developed in my time at Wasps. When I arrived at Northampton, we had a few international players. As the team developed, more and more of our squad began to represent their country. That was the original mixed blessing. Then, as the seasons passed, it was time to strengthen even more. I brought in Garry Pagel, the South African loose-head prop, who was a sensation. He is the best loose head I have ever seen, and he was a brilliant signing for us. I could never believe that South Africa had let him go because he was big and fierce and inspirational. A lovely man off the field, but ruthless on it.

As well as Mendez, the Argentine hooker, we also brought in, in latter years, Allan Bateman, the Welsh centre who had gone to rugby league, and the great Pat Lam. Pat was a wonderful warrior. He reversed the trend of great Samoan players who left their country to play for the All Blacks, where the money and profile were so much bigger. He was not very big at all, but he was indomitable, and a volcanic leader. We kept in touch after I left the Saints. I brought Pat into the Scotland set-up when I took over the coaching of the national team a few years later and we caught up with each other on the 2005 Lions tour, when he coached Auckland against the Lions' midweek team, a match in which we maintained our unbeaten midweek record. Northampton became full of class players and fantastic characters.

We safely negotiated our return to the top division in 1996–97. A company produced a video of our season in two parts and it shows some great attacking rugby. We were far from the finished article but we were dangerous. And we took six Northampton players with the Lions in 1997 – Rodber, who was incredible, plus Dawson, Grayson, Beal, Bateman and Townsend. I was criticised for taking so many from my own club, but they all played well, and I knew first hand who I could trust. We finished eighth in

'97–98, which was the first season of the Premiership itself, and at the end of the second year of my five-year plan we were well on target.

Yet the season after, 1998–99, with Pagel and Rodber by now giving us a fantastic foundation, and with the team realising that we could still play fast and inventive rugby in the top division, we finished second in the table, with only Leicester ahead of us. There was now another team on the radar in Europe. It was probably the best season the club had ever had. We produced a burst of eleven consecutive wins in mid-season, and the crowds, which had started to come back during the end of our promotion run, began to grow commensurately. Throughout the Premiership, and especially at Franklin's Gardens, architects were being called in to expand the arenas.

At the end of season 1998–99 we were exactly where we wanted to be. We had finished the season by putting fifty points on Newcastle and forty on Bath and we had beaten Wasps away from home. After the Newcastle match, Rob Andrew said: 'Well, if Northampton decide that they want to win, then there is nothing anybody else can do about it.' After the same game, Inga Tuigamala of the Falcons commented: 'It looked as though we were playing twenty players out there.' The atmosphere and sense of occasion at Franklin's Gardens was amazing. With the ground sold out almost every week, the home crowd was a wonderful bunch to play in front of. I would not have swapped those people for anything. For the first time in my career, as a player or coach, I was living in an area and a city where rugby was king, where people would stop you in the streets and approach you in restaurants to wish you well. It was a great feeling, and one I missed an awful lot when I left.

It was at this stage, however, that a cloud appeared on the horizon. Judy started feeling unwell. She suddenly began having physical reactions whereby her body looked as if it was blistered all over, and this upset her. She would have bursts of ill health as her allergies grew and she became uncomfortable and unhappy. Obviously, she had various tests, and they came up with any number of theories. The first year we lived in Northampton she had three separate chest infections. One theory was that she was allergic to the rapeseed which was grown extensively around Northampton. Another was that Northampton was one of the areas affected by radon gas. Then there was the theory that she was allergic to bread or wine or yeast. At one stage, when she had a very severe attack, she was covered in large red patches and, as she recalls, she looked like Herman Munster. Her head was swollen and her eyes mere slits. It was very distressing and annoying because, but for that not inconsiderable concern, she had been very happy in the area.

However, Judy's problems happened to coincide with an approach to me from Jim Telfer and the Scottish Rugby Union. Jim told me that he wanted to give up the job as Scotland coach and wondered if I would consider replacing him. I was loving my time at Northampton, but the idea of being part of the international scene again was attractive, and a growing belief that something in the local environment was affecting Judy was a major consideration as well. As it turned out, that belief was spot-on. When we left Northampton so that I could take up the Scotland post once again, first as assistant to Jim then as head coach, Judy's problems abruptly disappeared.

I left in the September, at the start of season 1999–2000, with the players already bursting for action. The team had kicked on again, were playing explosively well, and they started by taking Leicester apart by an enormous margin. Paul Larkin had worked closely with me over the years, he and I were on the same wavelength and he understood how we had reached such a point. He carried the torch under the new director, John Steele. The team kept up the momentum: they were at the top of the league, they reached the Tetley's Bitter Cup final, and they fought their way through to the Heineken European Cup final.

By this time Pat Lam was captain, and the warrior had already become one of the favourite players in Northampton's history. But the team began to lose momentum as the really massive matches arrived, possibly because of a fixture backlog which drained them, and also because they may have lost just a little of their impetus, inspiration and optimism. They were denied in the chase for the Premiership title, they were beaten in the domestic cup final and they staggered towards the European Cup final against Munster at Twickenham, wounded in body and mind. Incredibly, they pulled themselves together, and won 9–8. Pat had been suffering from a shoulder injury and it was suspected that he was not really fit to play. But he caught the ball at kick-off, ran straight back at the Munster forwards and smashed into them with his injured shoulder, as a gesture of defiance.

That day I watched the club that I had enjoyed so much, and the team that I had put together, win the European Cup, one year early in my five-year plan. I watched as Rodber, Dawson, Grayson, Bateman, Pagel, Mendez, Pountney and Lam went up to get their medals. Shortly after the trophy had been presented my mobile rang. It was Pat. 'It's there! We've done it!' he said. It was one of the real bittersweet moments of my career.

To leave Northampton was the one decision that I have regretted. It was a joint decision, though, looking back, Judy suggests that we might simply have tried to move away from Northampton town itself, way out into the country. In hindsight, I should have just stayed put. The atmosphere at the club, with the crowd, the players and the coaches, was brilliant. Keith Barwell was a terrific owner, he and Maggie remain friends. The old Northampton people were excellent and great to talk to. I also regret that because the Scotland call came late in the day, I didn't say goodbye properly to the fans. Northampton diehards still tell me that they were the golden years.

Judy always felt bad about it, but for no justifiable reason. There was no way I could have gone on with her in her condition. Seven years later, however, it had all ceased to rankle. By then I was director of rugby at Wasps, and revelling in the scenes at Twickenham as Lawrence Dallaglio lifted the Heineken Cup above his head after our win over Leicester in the European final. Seven years on, I had made it.

Judy was the most joyful person in the stadium on that wonderful day. 'This marks the end of a seven-year guilt trip,' she said.

14

Murrayfield

The Milkman and I, in the SRU 2003–05

The basis of rugby, the introduction, the classroom of our sport, is seen to be mini-rugby, played at thousands of clubs and schools across Britain and Ireland by youngsters as young as five. It is massive. And where would we be without it? That is a very good question, and the answer could be that we might be in a better place.

In 2003, after a disappointing end to my second stint as coach of Scotland, when we lost in the quarter-final of the World Cup to Australia by 33–16 in Brisbane, I effectively took off the tracksuit, donned a suit and became the Scottish Rugby Union's director of rugby. The Australian Matt Williams succeeded me as national coach and for the first time for a long time I had a job which gave me no day-to-day contact with players. It was a wrench. I did not realise at the time just how big a wrench.

But back to the minis. I was already rather suspicious of mini-rugby. I admired the commitment of those who organised it but part of it was misguided. One of my targets in my new job was to change the emphasis so that Scottish youngsters had a far more rounded sporting upbringing, and played *less* rugby so that, in fact, in the future they would play more if they so chose, and would play it far better.

So often parents of toddlers come up to me and tell me, in excited tones, that because their son or daughter is about to reach the age of five or six it means that they can go to mini-rugby next season. They are often far too excited about this prospect for me even to begin to commiserate with them, but I have long felt that mini-rugby is far from the best basis on which to introduce young-sters. Sometimes, you come across youngsters only in their mid-teens who have already played mini-rugby for eight or nine years. They are tired of it, and they do not want to do it any more. A pupil of mine at Fir Tree Middle School in Leeds had been play-ing mini-rugby since the age of six and I spent ages trying to get him to switch to football and cricket.

Simply, I just want our young people to play sport. My back-ground, as I have already explained, was very much based on the classic street sports environment. I feel I was incredibly lucky. I was brought up on street games, and it was quite simply the finest programme you could imagine for developing core sporting skills. I am chairman of Sports Coach UK, and have discussed the street game approach in our meetings.

The idea is a simple one. You just give the kids a ball or some other piece of sporting equipment, find them an area to play in, and you let them play. Gradually, they introduce their own rules, and it evolves. You put a different ball in, and they will play a dif-ferent game. If you give them a different space, they will adapt the shape of the game to suit. If the surface is hard or soft, they will adapt. Naturally, I do not expect children to replicate all my expe-riences, playing ball sports on cobbles, or kicking a football through the open upper door of a stable.

But there is a principle here which is important, and one that I tried to instil and push forward at the Scottish Rugby Union. All I wanted the young people of Scotland to do was not to specialise too early. My ideal was that the major sports organisations would band together, so that the programme between the ages of six and twelve was multi-sport – you would have football teams and rugby clubs running multi-sport leagues, with a spread of football, rugby, cricket, indoor cricket, tennis, basketball, or whatever. The football authorities were the most resistant. I formulated an eight-week programme aimed at primary school teachers on how to introduce skills, of which rugby eventually became a part.

What I tried to do in Scotland, within the schools and the age-grade arenas, was to establish a multi-sport league, which started and finished with rugby in the best months, but in the dark days of Scottish winters the youngsters were inside playing basketball or indoor cricket.

Rugby needs to be even more alert than the more simple sports. Rugby in concept is completely different from the others. In my view, you cannot play rugby properly, you cannot grasp its concept, until you are around the ages of twelve to fourteen. You can only play by numbers. Rugby is, in a sense, a three-dimensional sport, and children do not become conceptual thinkers until they are at least eleven. In rugby, you have to pass the ball backwards and run forwards. You have to try to get the ball into space. But the public school or preparatory school teacher, and others involved in teaching rugby to youngsters, do it by numbers. He tells them where to stand, and what to do, and when. They react accordingly, and, at the end of a season, they have no idea what the game and its decision-making process actually is.

A rugby player can be like a fighter pilot who arrives at the key point at the key time. The best rugby teams get their player arriving at the right angle, deliver the ball to him at the right angle and the right time, and then he causes the defence a problem. Then, unless he scores, the game continues with a similar exercise, all in three dimensions. There are skills to help develop players towards this ideal, and by no means all of them can be picked up and learned on a rugby field. Research carried out in Australia concluded that all the key decision makers in all the key team sports had multi-sports backgrounds.

It was an initiative I was not able to pursue for very long and, regretfully, I had to abandon it, although I still strongly espouse the cause of non-specialisation. Why did I have to abandon it? It was not mini-rugby I came to be suspicious of in my career as director of rugby at the Scottish Rugby Union. It was the Scottish Rugby Union themselves. Of them I grew extremely suspicious.

To be appointed Scotland's director of rugby was momentous, even though the challenge was enormous, and even though I found that to plot the course for the game at all levels, especially the professional game, was something like three jobs in one. The SRU were always the biggest sticklers for amateurism, and so it followed that they were the slowest to embrace the new professional era. Ever since the game had gone professional eight years before I took up my new post, there had been endless debates, bickering, investigations, steering committees and reports on the shape of the game, the governance of the Union and the future of the professional arm. All factions of the game had their say.

Furthermore, there was another pressure group which hampered change, in the shape of the Scotland clubs. The clubs and the Union had been at war since the game had gone professional, chiefly because the clubs felt that they should become the professional arm of the game, and all they wanted was finance from the SRU. The SRU, and especially Jim Telfer when he was director of rugby, saw the future in the hands of newly created professional teams representing the major areas of Scotland. Those soon shook down into four teams, then three – Edinburgh, Glasgow and the Borders – and by 2007 had shrunk, on the grounds of cost, to just two.

Back in the fledgling years it was true that some of the clubs demanding their own professional future had a distinguished past. But why would you give funding to Melrose and not to Hawick? Or to Hawick and not to Gala? It was also important to remember that the clubs with the bigger names were generally situated in the Borders, an area which still had a solid game in the schools, but was actually in decline in terms of economy and population.

Border rugby and the Border economy was, in a sense, on the way out; the population in the Borders had diminished to around only 100,000, and yet people were demanding that, with that tiny population base, and with little commercial activity, the SRU should establish at least two professional clubs. The numbers simply did not work. Nor did a suggestion by David Johnson, the former Scotland centre, that Scotland should simply have a semi-professional game. He justified this partly on the basis, if I read him correctly, that the game would be so insignificant on the European stage that Scotland's rivals in the Six Nations would be unable to assess our players, and therefore would be taken completely by surprise by them. Talk about things not adding up.

Jim Telfer fell out on these issues with Melrose, the club he had served for so long and with such distinction, but he was clever enough to know that more and more Scottish players were now coming from the north and midlands of Scotland, from areas like Dundee, so there was an argument that, instead of giving a professional team to the Borders you would give it to the north and midlands – Glasgow and Edinburgh, obviously, were musts. The debate rages on and I am not sure that it is over yet.

But in my time at Murrayfield the absolute key was to reform the Scottish Rugby Union itself. Until then, it had been dominated by the old and populous amateur committee, overseen by a president who may or may not have had any involvement in the game at the top level. The president tended to be chosen from within a small circle, and the SRU moved at a funereal pace. It was a system which had been set up when the game was amateur, to deal specifically with an amateur game, and the fact that it was still in place utterly failed to recognise that rugby was now changing massively, and by the week.

It was also patently obvious that, while it did not work for the professional game, then the game in other rugby nations was striding way, way out in front of Scotland – and Scotland had the results to prove it.

And at first hand I experienced the level of self-interest, self-serving, the lack of professionalism and the lack of action from the SRU committee. Not to mention the crooked aspects. Notoriously, one SRU committee member was alleged to have said: 'I am a milkman. I milk Scottish rugby for everything I can get out of it.'

We did have a chance to transform the Scottish game, and to avoid the kind of pit into which it appears to have fallen since. David Mackay, a decent man whom I greatly admired, had become chairman of the SRU, with a mission to drag the organisation into something resembling the modern era. He was clever, intelligent and driven. And yet, instead of being allowed to drive the game towards new standards of professionalism, marketing and income, Mackay was duly ousted by the old committee. He was ejected in a vote of no confidence on what many saw as spurious grounds; he and other members of his executive departed. 'Blazers battle against the suits' was one newspaper headline. Another opinion column expressed it perfectly: 'Some of the old guard have seized the opportunity to return to the forefront of the game'. I felt so sorry for Gordon Dixon, the president for 2004–05, who had to try to sort out a shambles that was not of his making.

From my position on the inside I saw the anxiety of the old committee. Some were fine men, but others saw their old privileges being eroded, their currency of international tickets, for example. There was misuse of funds, some committee men allegedly ran up massive unpaid bills for the international tickets they had requested, some of which, presumably, went towards entertaining their business contacts.

I am proud of the fact that, during my time with the SRU, I took part in a committee on governance, which, when followed through, changed the structure and the way the president was selected, and put in place a controlling group along the lines of a council, which, in some ways, has become far more effective. Prior to that the presidents tended to be appointed on the basis of longevity of service, and the process under which they were voted in seemed a little cloudy. They seemed to fall into place, rather than being elected. The new system allowed Andy Irvine to become president, and to restore some dignity to proceedings.

As it turned out, however, I rapidly became disappointed and disillusioned with a number of people around me, people who were weak, people who were self-serving, people who were dangerous. I worked endless hours, did my best to advise Fred MacLeod, an old committee man who had been appointed as acting chairman in the wake of David Mackay's departure, and who did his best. But the organisation was suspicious and moribund.

It was also, financially, a disaster area. Gordon McKie, a businessman and financier, arrived as chief executive but what was uncovered was, according to one SRU member, 'nobody's business'. At the time, the International Rugby Board (IRB) were very anxious that the SRU was simply going to go under and that Scotland rugby, one of the pillars of the game in Europe, would cease to be as a professional concern.

However, the SRU in recent years, battling against a horrendous financial position caused by the years of mismanagement, has lost sight of the rugby. As I write, there is no director of rugby in place, and it seems that the financiers heading up the union, who no doubt have done wonders in reducing the debt, are now making rugby decisions which they have no background or ability to make. The problem is that in the professional era you need a strong and integrated system that takes the most promising players from school to club to academy to professional team to the national team. Every successful rugby nation has that system. The English system is excellent, backing up the professional clubs. Ireland have it all sorted – school, academy, province, country. Wales have invested massively in the same kind of system, and the best players are moving up.

In Scotland, this sort of system has never been accepted. Too many people in the Union were uncomfortable with the idea of professionalism anyway, and too many of the top clubs have failed to grasp that they cannot hold on to their young and thrusting players, they cannot deny them a professional career and an international jersey. They do not understand the benefits of the years ahead, when the players could come back, either to play for the club or to use their experience and influence for the good.

Richie Dixon and myself formulated a graduated development system for Scottish rugby; we presented it to the IRB, who welcomed it and told us that it was the best integrated work of its type they had seen. They planned to give the SRU a huge grant to breathe life into it. It all fell into abeyance when I left the Union and only now have the plans for the system been revived, based on some of the principles we formulated in 2004.

Some people are pessimistic about Scotland's future. We may never have dominated the rugby world but at least up until the last three or four seasons, we have usually been competitive, and sometimes we could be a nightmare to play against. Recently, we have been alarmingly easy to beat. Results have been very disappointing, and people seem to have lost the habit of coming to Murrayfield to support the team. Frank Hadden recently joined the list of coaches who were ejected for poor results, Matt Williams had an unhappy tenure and is long gone, and Andy Robinson, with whom I have worked and whom I admire, is the latest to be given the task of building bricks without straw, of putting together a competitive international team on the basis of years of distrust, self-interest, financial problems and the lack of a proper professional structure.

Everyone will wish Andy well. People may be too pessimistic, notably those who were almost suicidal when Scotland had only three representatives in the original party which toured South Africa in 2009. In a sense, that is being too gloomy. There are only two professional teams in Scotland these days, so for them to produce two Lions is, pro rata, not too much of a disaster. But until Scotland really picks up the pace, until there is a strong rugby element restored to the union, there may be more gloomy times ahead.

In the end, I was worn down and disillusioned by Murrayfield and by some of the people there. I yearned to discard the suit and to return to the tracksuit. After the demise of David Mackay, I was working thirteen- and fourteen-hour days, and way outside my original terms of reference. Judy had become disillusioned, too, and unhappy with life in Scotland, and at the antics of some in the SRU. When I was once asked what specific reasons I had for leaving the SRU, Judy said, quick as a flash: 'Why would you want one?'

Well, I had one anyway. Wasps had recently lost Warren Gatland, their director of rugby, who was returning to his native New Zealand after transforming the club, winning trophies and leading them, above all, to the Heineken European Cup. I spoke to David Davies, the chief executive, and Chris Wright, the owner. There was a focus there which appealed strongly after what I had just been through. I also realised that, compared to some of my other destinations and teams, the Wasps challenge would put me under a new kind of pressure. They were already successful, and demanded nothing less than continued success.

When I left the SRU, less than two years after taking up the reins, I reflected in a newspaper article about the whole bad experience and also about how excited I was to be returning to the tracksuit to take up the post as director of rugby at Wasps: 'I'm going back to coaching because the closer you get to a rugby field, the more honest people are.'

15

Drop of History

The 1997 Lions tour of South Africa

'There are days like this that many rugby players never experience. It is special. Jim and I have been involved in rugby for a very long time. I can tell you that these are the days that you never believe will come again. This one has. I can tell you that I have given a lot of things up. I love my rugby. I love my family. But when you come to a day like this, you know why you do it all. You know why you have been involved.

It has been a privilege. It is a privilege, because we are something special. You will meet each other on a street in thirty years' time and there will just be a look, and you will know just how special some days in your life are. We have proved that the Lion has claws and has teeth. We have wounded the Springbok. But when an animal is wounded it returns in frenzy. It doesn't think, it fights for its very existence. The Lion waits, and at the right point it goes for the jugular. The life disappears. Today every second of that game, we've talked about what they are going to do. We will go for the jugular. Every tackle, every pass and every kick is saying to the ******* Springbok, you are dying. Your hopes of living in this Test series are going. On that field sometimes today all that will be between you

*is a look, no words, just a look. It will say everything. The biggest
thing it will say is, you are special, you are very, very special.*

*It has been and is a privilege. Go out, enjoy it, remember how
you have got here and why, and finish it off. And be special for the
rest of your lives . . .'*

Ian McGeechan, Lions team room, 28 June 1997,

Durban, two hours before the Second Test

How much more momentous could it be? The Lions of 1997
toured the Rainbow Nation of South Africa just a few years after
the African National Congress had come to power in the post-
apartheid elections, and two years after South Africa had won the
1995 Rugby World Cup, on that fantastic day when Nelson
Mandela danced on the podium as he presented Francois Pienaar,
the captain, with the Webb Ellis Trophy.

The tour also took place less than two years after the sport of
rugby union had declared itself open, tearing up the ancient code
of amateurism and taking steps into the unknown. The 1997
Lions were the first professional Lions, the first tour under signed
contracts. The old days of the tour allowances, the few pennies a
day to be used for making telephone calls home, and the rest of
the paraphernalia of amateurism all disappeared.

It was to be the first Lions tour to South Africa for seventeen
years, and for South African rugby fans familiar with the great
traditions of the Lions a painfully long gap. The sense of expectation and intensity may not have been better encapsulated than on
the front page of a local paper in East London, the second stop on
the tour, where the Lions squeezed past Border on a muddy pitch
after a few days of rain. The paper's preview edition had a front-
page headline of significant size. 'Muddy field awaits Lions' it said.
Lower down the page, almost tucked away, was the second item.
'Assassination plot against Mandela uncovered'. If you are to tour
successfully with the Lions, you have to absorb this kind of intensity, this powerful adherence to rugby. You have to make it work
in your favour; you have to show equal intensity.

There is no doubt that the 1997 Lions tour is my favourite experience as coach. To win in South Africa is always such a colossal achievement. Do not forget that in more than a century of trying, on tours that were long and regular, the All Blacks have won just one Test series in South Africa. It was in 1997 that we got closest to the style of rugby that I have always wanted a team to play. We probably reached the highest level of my Lions tours. The key was that we surprised them with the style and quality of the rugby we played in the provincial games, and the knock-on effect was that we took the attitude and confidence engendered into the Test matches.

In fact, I think we surprised South African rugby in every way. The 1997 Five Nations tournament had been poor, and accounts of some of the games were really scathing. The South Africans felt that British and Irish rugby was not constructive, not dangerous in an attacking sense. They felt that we were not particularly heavy and powerful defenders, and that Northern Hemisphere rugby in general was stereotypical and limited.

This was all to our advantage, and we planned to move their big men around, to set great store on really quick ball and support play, on moving the target and attacking them. Obviously, everything we planned depended on gaining parity in the set pieces. It was not a question of looking for some massive advantage, but just taking away one of their big areas of strength, and breaking them up with continuity and a skilful game.

In terms of the tour selection, I was intent on putting players together who I really wanted to work with, people who could play differently, people who could play head up and be prepared to take risks. We had to be incredibly strong mentally because a huge amount of physicality was needed, and we had to play our game boldly throughout, never retreating from it.

It was the third time that someone had been generous enough to ask me to take the Lions' reins as head coach and the third time that I was excited enough to accept, but there was no rigmarole of interviews this time and no need for me to go to Belgravia to address the old-school officials. Looking back, the 1997 Lions could so easily have lost their tour coach in that room as I told the four Home Unions, with absolute frankness, that the tour would be done my way, with me, the coach, having the final say in selection, otherwise I'd pack up and take my ball home with me.

Fran Cotton, the great old Lion of 1974 and 1977, had been appointed manager. Fran rang me early in 1996 and asked me if I was of a mind to coach the Lions again. I went up to Manchester to meet him at his office at Cotton Traders, the sports and leisurewear firm he had built along with Steve Smith, the former England scrum-half. We talked through the challenge and my philosophy, we spoke about what would be needed to win in South Africa, and the deal was done pretty much there and then. The challenge was massive, but my decision, frankly, was simple. So was the choice of my assistant coach – Jim Telfer. There was no better man.

There were some changes, however. This time, we left far less to chance than on so many previous Lions tours. I went to South Africa that summer, nearly a year before the tour, to check out facilities and to see what lay in wait. The All Blacks were in town at the time. They were playing their 1996 series, the one in which they were to become the first-ever All Blacks team to win a series in South Africa, so was there any more awesome indication of the measure of our task a year later? I met up with John Hart, the coach, and Sean Fitzpatrick, the captain, and they were open and businesslike.

The All Blacks were pushing the boundaries. They were touring with a squad of thirty-five instead of the usual thirty. Previously, with thirty players, it meant that the specialists – the scrum-halves and hookers – were on duty for every match, either in the team or on the bench. The bigger squad allowed for an extra hooker and scrum-half, giving the specialists a down day, and also gave them scope for resting the odd key player, so that for some games they did not even have to get changed. Another wise tip from John Hart was that we should be self-sufficient, that we should have our own scrummaging machine, tackle shields and padding, drinks bottles, training aids, the whole lot. So, well before the tour, our kit set out for South Africa by container ship, and, on arrival, chugged around the country by road to be ready at each training venue. Hart and I were on the same wavelength as to the calibre of player we needed – mentally strong, tough and resilient, unfazed by setback, and able to make decisions on the field.

Yet with the game two years into professionalism, another of the more modern Lions problems reared its head. The domestic season was by now far longer, and those clubs and provinces and national unions which employed the players were no longer willing to let them rest when they were selected for the Lions. In 1977, for example, some of the Welsh players chosen for the Lions, whose clubs reached the Welsh Cup final, actually missed the final so that they would be rested.

By 1997 that was a thing of the past, and one of the biggest problems we had was that some players were in action right up until the weekend we first met. Leicester had a strong contingent in the party, and they were only just finishing an incredibly difficult season, and their players were clearly still tired when they joined us. It was going to be a question of care and recovery rather than flat-out training.

We also needed to do something quick and clever to bring the players together. Fran and I decided that we did not want to rely on players bonding in their rooms, and nor did we want flip charts. We wanted practical exercises which would show the boys how important it was to bond, to support what we were going to do as a team. We therefore brought in a company called Impact, whom we chose from three or four companies which tendered a bid. I wanted nothing that was wordy, I wanted nothing in classrooms; I wanted physical exercises so that the players understood support, teamwork, and that you could never achieve anything on your own.

Impact came to work with us at our headquarters at the Oatlands Park hotel, Weybridge. They devised all these little exercises. One involved climbing on beer crates. Once you stood on one crate, another was passed to you and you had to place that on your growing stack, and keep climbing as the stack of crates grew higher and higher. As your stack grew taller and became a little more unstable, your safety rested in the hands of your team-mates, who were holding the ropes attached to your harness.

Eventually, those players who really piled up their stacks had to be handed the extra crates on the end of a long pole. Tom Smith, the prop, managed a stack of thirty-five crates before his tower collapsed. He did really well, balancing with his feet on the outside of one crate, grabbing the next, lifting his foot and replacing it to secure the next crate. It was an exercise in which you put yourself entirely in the hands of your supporting friends. Jim Telfer admitted that he was scared stiff, because he hates heights. But with this and the many other exercises that we did, and with the natural ebullience and friendship which comes to exist in a group of players – even those who have been sporting enemies for most of their lives – you could feel the team coming together, becoming one. At the end, the mantra was: 'Right person, right place, right time, and this is how we are going to exist throughout the tour.'

Looking back on the trip, and at the influence and aura of Martin Johnson, you might have considered that he was an obvious choice as captain, even though his experience in that role in his career to date had been limited. He was the obvious choice to me, but I had to work hard initially to persuade Fran and Jim. Will Carling had already ruled himself out of the tour, but there were other candidates beside Johnson – Ieuan Evans was an influential figure with Wales at the time, and we also discussed the possibility of Jason Leonard taking the role. We passed Jason over in the end, but he played a mighty role on tour and I shall always regard him as one of the greatest Lions, one of those who understood deep down what the Lions are.

But Johnson, I always believed, was something else. I was coaching at Northampton at the time and Leicester were our big rivals. Games between the two were always massive. So I saw first hand the impact Johnson had on his own team and the impact he had on the opposition. I spoke to Dean Richards, my old confidant, about him. Dean simply nodded: 'He will be fine.' After Martin was chosen, he even went off to do some public relations and media training, although the essential gift he brought on the pitch and into the team environment was to be the man himself. It was also the first time I really became set on having a physically imposing figure leading the Lions. I felt that psychologically it would unnerve the opposition captain to arrive for the toss under the stands before the game, and to see a giant of a man waiting for him, beetle-browed and scowling, rather than some weedy back!

The 1997 tour is also remembered for its prodigals, for the gang of former rugby union players who had gone over to rugby league in union's amateur era, but who had returned to their original code now that the game had gone professional. We chose six for the tour – Scott Gibbs (Swansea and Wales), Scott Quinnell (Richmond and Wales), David Young (Cardiff and Wales) and Allan Bateman (Richmond and Wales), all of whom had been cruelly missed by their country; John Bentley (Newcastle and England), a Yorkshireman with a huge personality and ability which appealed to me – indeed, Bentos was to become a signature player on the tour; and Alan Tait (Newcastle and Scotland), the centre, originally from a rugby league family, whose departure had thinned his country's ranks after he had gone north. Or, in his case, south.

But now they were all back, and they gave us huge value. Professionalism in rugby union had not yet been bedded in, and here was a sextet of players who had come back from rugby league and who understood about life as a professional sportsman. They were all characters, and they set a standard. They also helped with our defence because defending had moved on rapidly and become far more sophisticated. The speed of the line coming up in defence became vital, so too the importance of the inside man, the player immediately inside you as you came up who was ensuring that no one stepped inside.

And in terms of the players we took, in terms of the decision makers and their stature, it was an extraordinary group. It probably had more hard men and more inspirational leaders than any other Lions tour. They were quite incredible, and it was a comforting feeling to look around the dressing room and to be aware of the steel that existed there.

In the selection of any large group, there are invariably choices which turn out to be mistakes. But Jim and I could put our hands on hearts to this day and say that there was not one individual we would change if we had our time all over again. People like Jason Leonard, to name but one, were quite unbelievable at creating the right atmosphere and setting high standards. He had already won all the caps, he had played in Tests in 1993 in New Zealand, but he did not make the First Test in 1997. Yet he was superb in the support he gave to Tom Smith and Paul Wallace, who did make the team. That sort of behaviour and professionalism sets the tone for the whole tour.

Some players who toured did not get quite the same publicity as others. Rob Wainwright was well known to us through Scotland, and perhaps because of his being a slightly reserved character he was not initially considered one of the core Lions on tour. But that would be wrong. Rob had a terrific tour, he led well in the midweek games and he had an absolutely superb match when he went on for the Third Test in Johannesburg. Barry Williams, the Welsh hooker, was the wild card. He was nowhere near the Welsh team at the time, but we watched him playing for Wales A and he was one of those we felt could make a difference, could play rugby as well as doing his job in the tight.

The key decision probably revolved around fly-half. Gregor Townsend was not a shoo-in as the Test fly-half at the start, and the fact that he was not a front-line goalkicker caused us problems. But he was an attacking threat, he played flat and was difficult to defend against. Yet if we played Gregor it meant that we had to choose a goalkicker in another position. Neil Jenkins, who kicked magnificently for us throughout the tour and brought us back into the Second Test with his kicking, was therefore chosen at full-back in the Tests. This was a trade-off, something of a compromise, because Jenks gave us guaranteed points but did not offer a threat from full-back in attack.

But we had such power elsewhere. Scott Gibbs is regarded as the signature player of the tour and he was an incredible force but also in the centre we had Will Greenwood, Tait and Bateman, and Bateman especially was a very fine player, really unlucky not to start a Test.

We also had none other than Jeremy Guscott, who was by then making his third tour with me, and who was to have another superb series. He was much tougher than people think, he was a Test match animal, and I was always confident that, under pressure, he would do the right thing. At that time, England were not even picking him in the centre; they had chosen Phil de Glanville as captain alongside Carling, and it seemed to some that Jack Rowell, the head coach, was unwilling to take the major step of dropping Carling, in order to play Jeremy. But once I ascertained that he was still hungry and that his passion for the Lions remained strong, he was an easy and obvious choice. Jeremy was influential throughout the tour, and there are few people with any knowledge of Lions history who do not recall with affection an incident towards the end of the Second Test in which he was heavily involved!

But we had strength elsewhere. We had a choice between Richard Hill and Neil Back on the open side; we had no fewer than three Test match animals contending at number eight in Scott Quinnell (sadly invalided home), Eric Miller and Tim Rodber. We had, too, a choice between Wainwright and Lawrence Dallaglio on the blind side. These were riches indeed and vital to combat the supreme physicality of the Springboks.

It was probably Rodber who had most to prove. People felt that, for all his size, power and ability, he was not always the most consistent of performers. Jim for one felt that Tim was a little bit too much army officer in bearing and character (and he wasn't far off: Tim *was* an army officer at the time, and his standing to attention for the National Anthem at Twickenham was a sight to see). Jim somehow felt that Tim might not buckle down when the pressure was on. Others were more ambivalent about him.

In fact, Tim was colossal. I knew from Northampton that he was a hard man, and a superb player. One account of the 1997 tour stated that 'Rodber terrorised Gary Teichmann, his opposite number' and that was not far from the truth. Tim had a brash confidence about him, a little like an older Lawrence Dallaglio, and at that stage of their careers both the young Dallaglio and Hill needed a man like that between them. They formed one of the greatest back rows I have worked with.

The tour also probably represented the finest hour in harness for Jim and myself. By that time we knew each other's every move and thought and, as ever, we appreciated each other's honesty. Jim was a massive figure. We probably dovetailed better than ever, and from the start Jim knew that he had to produce a forward pack that would stand up for itself against the heavy Boks.

There are more ways than one of taking on a monster pack, however. Perhaps our key selection on tour, and perhaps of any tour, was the front row for the First Test, when we went for Smith and Wallace, who were our smallest props, to take on Os du Randt, the huge Bok prop and talisman, and his friends. We could easily have chosen Jason or David Young, who were both worthy contenders, and the selection looked more than a little shaky after the first scrum of the First Test, when we were taken apart. Keith Wood, the Irish hooker, thought: 'Christ! What the hell are we doing here?'

But all that happened was that in that one scrum we had gone in too high. Afterwards, for the rest of that match and for the series, we reaped the benefits of scrummaging nine inches lower than the Springbok front row, and all the anxiety as to whether we had done the right thing gradually dissipated. In an article written after the tour, Kitch Christie, the coach of the South Africans at the 1995 World Cup, said that our effectiveness in the scrum was a key factor in the Test series win. I have never been afraid of change if I have the gut feeling that the change will be positive and beneficial, and that selection is often held up as one of our boldest. You would be dishonest if you denied that such choices kept you awake the night before the game, however.

It was also a wonderfully high-profile tour. Sales of the Lions replica jersey back in Britain and Ireland were huge, and it was the first time that travelling Lions support from Britain and Ireland was numbered in the tens of thousands. The advantage we gained from seeing walls of red in huge areas of the stadiums in which we played was immeasurable.

The tour also became an age thing. It seemed that the 1997 Lions in particular and rugby in general were catching on with younger people. It was labelled the 'rock and roll tour' in one paper, and the tour anthem was unquestionably 'Wonderwall', by Oasis. It was sung in the stadiums by the fans, it was sung in team rooms by the players and, by the end of the tour, even Jim Telfer and myself knew most of the words.

There was also, for the first time, a documentary team with us, and I mean *everywhere* with us. It was a major departure from previous tours, one that many felt would detract from the mystique of the Lions. Yet when *Living with Lions* came out, it went down a storm, it helped the Lions legend to grow and non-rugby people caught on to it massively; it was so successful that a sequel eventually appeared. There was the usual on-tour material, with Judge Wood presiding over a hilarious court session, but *Living with Lions* also showed the emotions, the pain and the rugby. There were the moments when both Doddie Weir and Rob Howley realised that their tours were over, with Dr James Robson breaking the news to them; the moment when John Bentley, after an all-night vigil of hope, finally opened the envelope pushed under his door and discovered that he had not been chosen for the First Test.

There were also the (uncensored) pre-match speeches in the team rooms and the last frantic moments in the dressing room, with some impassioned talking from Fran Cotton, Jim Telfer, Martin Johnson, Jason Leonard, Keith Wood and others. People who have seen the DVD of *Living with Lions*, even a decade and more after the tour, always say that, had they been in those charged and intense rooms listening to the speeches, they too could have gone out and played for the Lions. The swear box would have been full to the brim, and Jim Telfer said that his mother always found her son's colourful language hard to take. My speech before the Second Test seems to have been held up as a model of carefully prepared motivational speaking, but there was nothing written down, just thoughts that came to mind at the time. I was just being honest with the players about what they would face, and the effect it would have on so much of their lives. Before any Test, home or away, I have always taken time out to walk by myself in the morning, just to clear my head and focus on my final words to the team. It was the same in South Africa, and, whatever I said, for good or ill, came out spontaneously.

It was a relentless, vivid, striking, eventful, high-profile experience capturing the imagination of people from way outside rugby, and other sports tapped into what a build-up for such a massive occasion entailed. It was in many ways one of *the* sporting events, one of *the* sporting crusades of the era. It still remains real and vivid in my mind.

In any new team it is often hard for the coaches and players to know how the team is shaping, and what sort of team it is. Everyone has his head down, working furiously, and sometimes you need a perspective, another angle.

As the First Test approached, I was very conscious that the team needed to know how we looked, what sort of team we were. One of the defining moments of the tour was the production of a twelve-minute video. I was using Keith Lyons, a Welshman based in Cardiff at the Centre for Notational Analysis, for video analysis and, sometime before the First Test, I asked him to send me something on what he thought we looked like from where he was sitting.

When the video arrived, it was staggering. Keith had done a great job because his film encapsulated everything that we were trying to do, as well as the way we wanted to be perceived.

The first six minutes of the video were all shots of us defending. Keith wrote: 'What is hitting me from this distance is how good you are when you don't have the ball, the support you create for each other, the tackles you make. The way you have played when not in possession is, to me, defining this group.'

And the second six minutes were all about the way we were trying to play with the ball in hand – the continuity, the little offloads, the changing, the offsetting. At the team meeting on the Friday night before the First Test, I produced the video. I said to the players: 'We have to determine what the 1997 Lions are about, and what we are going to look like. I have asked someone who is six thousand miles away to put together a tape, so that we can recognise what we are taking into the Test match.' I put on the video and sat down.

There wasn't a sound. When the video ended, there was still not a sound. Keith had captured all thirty-five squad players in action. It was a quite brilliant twelve minutes. When I stood up I said: 'That is what we are about. Don't change anything. If you believe that there is something on, just do it 100 per cent, because you will get support from everyone else.' I left it at that and walked out of the room. The players stayed and watched it again, and during that night they must have watched it every ten minutes for the next three hours. It was absolutely superb, and keynote, and after watching it we knew far more about ourselves.

What about the opposition? Perhaps the greatest fallacy about the tour is the idea that it was a good time to play the Springboks.

That theory was based on the fact that they had just lost their coach, André Markgraaff, who resigned after he was taped making racist comments, and he had been succeeded by Carel du Plessis, who was far less experienced and who had coached his country just once before, in a game against Tonga. The idea seemed to gain credence that, under du Plessis, the Boks were weak. But you only had to look at their team. They had there some of the Springbok all-time greats – du Randt, Kruger, van der Westhuizen, Andrews, Joubert. And others. They were a huge, passionate and physical side and it is interesting that, not long after the Lions tour, they beat Australia by sixty points.

Our planning to beat them centred around our identification of a small group of players on whom they based their game, and who they always played through. Once we had picked out those play-ers, we got to know every millimetre of their games – they were Henry Honiball, the fly-half, Andre Joubert, at full-back, Joost van der Westhuizen at scrum-half, Mark Andrews, who was a class lock, and Gary Teichmann, the captain. We worked hard on nul-lifying them – and Honiball was a particular target. We set up defensive systems that took Honiball into areas where he didn't want to be; when we achieved that we were on the front foot men-tally as well as physically. As Fran Cotton said after the series: 'We had Honiball worked out to a T.'

The art of subduing van der Westhuizen was along the same lines as Doug Morgan aggravating Gareth Edwards at Murrayfield in the seventies, and Robert Jones winding up Nick Farr-Jones on the Lions tour in 1989. Matt Dawson was charged with marking Joost after Rob Howley had to leave the tour before the Test after dislocating a shoulder against Natal. Marking him in the literal sense? Possibly.

But Dawson stepped up. He had been a controversial choice in some quarters but again, when I looked at him at Northampton up close, I saw a Test match animal growing. I told Matt to sit on Joost, to harry him, and if Joost did not make a break all game then Matt had done his stuff. But Dawson struck back with a break of his own, scoring a sensational try which turned the First Test. That doubled the challenge. I knew that Joost would feel his pride had been hurt and that he would be desperate to make individual breaks and search for his own glory, to challenge Matt. I told Dawson that the more Joost saw it as a man-to-man confrontation with him, the more that would take him away from his team. He did score a superb try in the Third Test, but by then the series was won and we had kept him very quiet.

Whether or not our plans would work, how good the Springboks were, how good the Lions were – all that was in the future as we started off at Port Elizabeth against Eastern Province and we laid down a marker with a 39–11 win, with Jeremy Guscott playing brilliantly, following people through half-gaps and accelerating on to the ball. But it was not until after the game that we knew how well we had played. Johan Klutz, the Eastern Province coach, told the media that we would lose the series 3–0. We took it as an affirmation of what we had achieved.

The intensity of the training and the competition for places was shown by a bust-up in a training session between Barry Williams and Mark Regan, and, while Jim stepped in to cool things down, I don't think any of the coaches were surprised or particularly concerned. But we did not play well in the second game, against Border, and it took a late try by Rob Wainwright, driving over from close range, to secure an 18–14 win.

Our scrummaging was poor against the powerful Western Province next up, on 31 May, but we played some rugby which suggested to me that the boys were taking things on board, and we pulled clear at the end, when a brilliant long run by Rob Howley made a try for Ieuan Evans. Martin Johnson had problems with a shoulder joint from the previous season, problems which we played down, and he made his first appearance of the tour in this match. It was at this stage that recognition first began to dawn on South Africa that these Lions might be a surprise package. Two days after that game, James Small, the ever-controversial Springbok wing who had clashed with John Bentley during the game, accused Bentley of eye-gouging him – an accusation we treated with the contempt it deserved.

The poor scrummaging was bad news for the forwards, however. We moved on to Pretoria, where we were to be based to play Mpumalanga and Northern Transvaal, and, on one of the back pitches at Newlands, Jim Telfer took what has become one of the most famous training sessions in Lions history, immortalised in the media, who were all watching, and in *Living with Lions*.

It was the most sustained and ferocious scrum session, mostly against a hydraulic machine with huge blue pads, which Jim cranked up to full power. He circled round behind the pack as they tried to dig in against the machine, roaring: 'Hold the world! Hold the world!' Such were the weights being applied that every time the scrum broke up the front-row players had to be dragged backwards out of the pads, into which they had become embedded. The commitment the players showed was exemplary.

Not only did we scrummage well against Mpumalanga, we also played superb rugby against a team which clearly fancied its chances and which had beaten Wales just before. Dawson made his first start and looked needle-sharp, and we again played fine attacking rugby. Yet the match is best remembered for a sickening foul, one of the worst I have ever seen. Doddie Weir, the Scotland lock, was standing on the fringes of a ruck when Marius Bosman, the home lock, who had a history behind him, kicked out with studs upraised, for absolutely no reason, and caught Doddie on the knee. It was a shocking act that severed the medial ligament of Doddie's knee and he had to go home for an operation. Bosman was fined a derisory amount and then only because the South African Union was shamed into taking some sort of action. Doddie left for home, which was a crying shame as his parents were already on their way out on a package tour to see him play.

At this time, England were touring in Argentina, and we made ourselves just a little unpopular with Jack Rowell, in charge of

the England trip, by asking for Mike Catt as replacement for
Paul Grayson, who had to leave the tour with a thigh injury, and
then Nigel Redman, for Doddie. Rowell at first refused to release
Catt and took him on an unnecessary journey upcountry to
Mendoza while the issue was settled, but our stance was firm.
The Lions come first and when that changes the Lions die. Mike
arrived and played well. Nigel was something else. He is an ami-
able and engaging man, and is perhaps never mentioned when
the subject of great locks is being debated. He regaled us all with
the story of him and Jack Rowell discussing his Lions call-up in
Argentina.

'Jack told me that I was going to South Africa. I said: "Jack, I
don't believe it." He looked at me. "Neither do I," he said.'

All good stuff, but Nigel Redman was superb when he arrived,
we were soon awarding him the captaincy of the Lions for a midweek game, and he proved to be every inch the real thing.

The traditional match on every tour which sees the wheels
falling off duly arrived in the next game. We lost 35–30 to a fired-
up Northern Transvaal at Loftus Versveld; we were far too loose in
the first half, when we gave them an eleven-point start, and generally played like a team that was too confident after the early
sparkle. We told the boys at half-time that they were starting to
believe their own publicity too much. Jeremy Guscott and Gregor
Townsend conjured up two brilliant tries, but we gave ourselves
too much to do and Northern Transvaal deserved their victory.
Scott Gibbs was cited for throwing a punch, and banned for a
match; far more seriously, Scott Quinnell injured a shoulder and
he soon became the next Lion to be forced to go home.

The following game was against Gauteng Lions (formerly Transvaal). It was so important for us to win, to recover our momentum.
Redman, just arrived, had his hands full. He was marking the massive Kobus Wiese, one of the most popular hard men and crowd
favourites in the country. He had stated in the press that he was
going to give us all the trouble in the world.

The portents may have been gloomy, but it turned into one of the great Lions days. We were 9–3 down at half-time against a very good side. But we kept playing, kept our shape in attack and defence and took control. We also scored one of my all-time favourite Lions tries. John Bentley had not been at his best, was sensitive to such matters beneath his bluff northern exterior and desperate to contribute. After we had scored a brilliant team try, touched down by Austin Healey, Bentley fielded a kick ahead only 12 metres outside his own twenty-two, and with every other Lion bar one upfield from him.

He set off first down the right and cleverly outflanked two defenders. Then he veered inwards, stepping off his right foot, beating more defenders, at one time running almost flat. Then he veered again off his left foot, set course for the posts, beat off two desperate tackles and scored. It was a glorious individual try and a classic moment, and some outstanding kicking by Neil Jenkins took us home. The players who had been in the stands rushed to the dressing room to acclaim the heroes who had put the tour back on track and we witnessed one of those wonderful dressing-room atmospheres which only a winning Lions team can produce.

Kobus Wiese is around six foot eight and at that time he weighed in at around twenty-one stone. He sported a brutally cropped haircut, so you could not miss him. It was also his night, as he was contending for a place in the First Test and he had told us in the press just how good he was going to be. Yet that evening at Ellis Park we never saw him. Nigel Redman, genial fellow that he is, did a spectacular number on him, playing wonderfully well. We won 20–14, and South Africa, by now, really was beginning to open its eyes.

We thrashed Natal, one of the best teams in the country, by 42–12 the Saturday before the First Test, helped, as usual, by excellent insight from Andy Keast, our on-tour analyst, who had once worked for Natal, and we established our game on the back of a dominating scrum – even though the euphoria was somewhat diminished when James Robson diagnosed that Rob Howley had dislocated his shoulder. Rob had been on brilliant form and it was a shocking experience for him to have to depart for home just as the Tests were approaching. He was to tour again with the Lions as a player (in 2001) and coach (in 2009) but he may well have missed a career height in 1997.

The chief off-field interest of the Test week was the fact that Eric Miller's father, seeing his son struggling with cold and flu symptoms, had bought him an over-the-counter preparation to help his recovery. Unfortunately, as James Robson quickly grasped, the medicine contained a banned substance, one which might have made Eric liable to a one-year ban had he played and been tested positive for it. James had to read the riot act, in his traditionally gentle fashion, so that the other players were far more careful.

The week also saw the momentum maintained. We beat the Emerging Springboks in Wellington, with the team safe under the leadership of Jason Leonard and with Nick Beal scoring a hat-trick of tries.

The team for the First Test was chosen by a panel of Fran, Jim, Martin and myself, and there was some sharp discussion but, in the end, no vote. We opted for our two smaller props, for Jeremy Davidson in the middle of the line-out above Simon Shaw; Richard Hill shaded it over Neil Back at open side, with Jim pushing the Back case, and we opted for the supreme kicking ability of Neil Jenkins at full-back; we chose Tait instead of Bentley or Tony Underwood on the wing, and, as Cape Town filled up with rugby fans, as the major tour groups hit town, the sense of expectation grew – in particular, the expectation in South Africa that the Lions would be thrashed.

'They do not respect us here,' Jim told the forwards at a meeting two hours before the Test. 'They do not rate us. They expect to bully us. The easy bit is past,' he told them. 'You now have an awesome responsibility. This is your Everest, boys. Very few ever have the chance in rugby terms to get to the top of Everest. You have the chance today. Being picked is the easy bit. To win for the Lions in a Test match is the ultimate.'

In the end, we did not give the ultimate performance, on an atmospheric, nerve-shredding evening at Newlands, in front of bank upon bank of noisy, red-clad Brits and Irish. What we did do was play well, with enormous courage. We played smart, stuck to our plan, and we won – and gave British and Irish rugby history another glory day. And we won going away, against a team and a country that we had forced to pay attention to us, to respect us and, who knows, even to fear us.

It began with big forward drives from us, and two penalties from Neil Jenkins. The Springbok forwards drove Os du Randt over for a try from a line-out in the first half, and, although Jenkins put us 9–8 ahead at half-time, there was no doubt that we were under pressure from the intensity of the Springboks. However, after our first scrum had been shattered when we scrummaged too high, we had settled down, were looking increasingly comfortable up front, and Jeremy Davidson was winning ball in the line-out. Martin Johnson was clever enough to use Davidson as a banker and to keep calling ball to him.

The Springboks attacked down the left wing, and they kept on coming. It must have seemed to many then that we would be swept away, but we had told ourselves before each Test match of that series that, if we were in touch with twenty minutes to go, it was our game. We may not have had the best of it but we were down only by 16–15 with barely ten minutes left.

Then we forced an attacking scrum near their line, and we went forward just a touch on the right-hand side. Matt Dawson picked up, burst rapidly outside Ruben Kruger, the Springbok flanker, and set off. Gary Teichmann came across to cut him off so Dawson transferred the ball to his right hand and held it aloft as if he was going to flip a high pass inside. Teichmann checked, Dawson kept on going and scored. 'Impish genius' said one newspaper. For a young man in his first Lions Test, with most of his career triumphs still well in the future, and for a player who might not even have played had not Rob Howley been injured a week earlier, it was stunning stuff.

The crowd no doubt expected an all-out assault for the rest of the game, and it duly came. From the Lions. We kept up the pace, and, towards the end, Scott Gibbs made a thundering charge up the middle, we recycled and some superb handling by Tim Rodber allowed Neil Jenkins to put Alan Tait over in the corner. Tait touched down and ran a big semi-circle in triumph, gesturing with his two index fingers as if they were pistols. It was 25–16 at the end, as the celebrations began.

As we had hoped, the First Test not only caused a sensation among our supporters in South Africa and an absolute avalanche of calls and faxes from Britain and Ireland; it also caused a storm of protest in South Africa, with all kinds of attacks being made on Carel du Plessis, the coach, and some of the players. However, we also knew that in the end it might have a knock-on effect with us because, as the week went on, we could sense their squad and the entire country declaring that such a defeat must never happen again. It was a monumental challenge for us as coaches to get the team back up for the challenge of the Second Test, which we knew was going to be far more intense than the First Test.

All in all, it was a nerve-wracking but wonderful week, and once again in the charmed life of this tour it was the midweek team which gave us the boost precisely when we needed it, and they did so by playing what may possibly have been the best rugby in any match of my whole career as coach of the Lions. But before discussing the game, there was a worrying and jarring note when Will Greenwood, then in his infancy as an international player, took a very heavy knock and had to be carried from the field, obviously in distress.

In fact, Will had swallowed his tongue and, but for the rapid reaction of James Robson and the medical people at Bloemfontein, Will's life would have been in danger. There was a time when, after swallowing his tongue, there was no reaction from his pupils for long minutes and James was preparing to make an emergency incision to open an airway for Will to save his life. In the end, the belief was that he had been saved by his gum shield. His teeth were clamped together but the shield allowed a small amount of air to pass through. Will's mother, understandably distraught, arrived on the scene to check on her son, adding to the drama, and it was wonderful news when we heard that he had come round and when we saw him up and about soon afterwards, even though he was shaken for some time.

For the Orange Free State game, we gave the captaincy to none other than Nigel Redman, and this time, for the only occasion on tour, the party was split. I stayed with members of the likely Test team in Durban and Jim and the rest flew on a charter up to Bloemfontein. 'We've worked like beasts,' Jim said before the match, urging the lads into a response and ensuring that the momentum was maintained.

It was, and with a vengeance. We played some absolutely brilliant rugby, keeping the ball moving, keeping the pace up, with backs and forwards. We did allow the Free State in for three tries, but we scored seven of our own, with Bentley scoring a hat-trick, and there were tries apiece for Tim Stimpson, Allan Bateman, Neil Jenkins and Tony Underwood, another player in such good form that he would without question have played a Test in a party of less depth. The 52–30 victory was received warmly back in Durban, and the players there insisted on staying up to greet the midweek team later that night, after their charter had landed and they arrived back at our Durban headquarters. 'This was one of the greatest Lions performances in history,' said Fran Cotton afterwards. 'To have come up to altitude just for the day, to have played such fast-moving and attractive rugby against one of South Africa's top Super-12 provinces was just incredible.'

We knew that we had to be clever for the Second Test; we knew that the ploy of playing our smaller props and scrummaging low would no longer be a surprise; we knew that Jeremy Davidson would be targeted as a danger man in the line-out, so Martin Johnson had to call the ball to himself far more often.

And we knew that we would have to defend for our sporting lives. Jim took an intense contact session in Durban on the Wednesday, but then we backed right off. One of the lessons I had learned from Syd Millar on the 1974 tour was that it was counter-productive to beast the players almost up until kick-off, so on the Friday we simply gave them the day off. We had done the same in Cape Town, and the only joint activity was that the Test twenty-two had met for a cup of tea together in the late afternoon, at the botanical gardens near Table Mountain. It is true: prior to meeting the fearsome Springboks, we had had a cup of tea and some scones. In Durban, again with the match twenty-two, we walked together to the snake park on the seafront, and, with the waves crashing outside, we once again had our tea and scones.

It was part of the spirit of the tour that we never ignored those players not involved in the Test series. On the morning of the Second Test, with the hotels and the entire promenade on the seafront seemingly packed and bursting with excitement and tension, we took the non-Test players for a training session, away from the crowds. It was one of our best sessions.

And then it came to the immediate pre-match, and those speeches which seem to have gone down in history, and not only for the rather questionable language. Just as at home in the build-up to any Test or any big game, I went for a walk. The dogs were not there to accompany me, but I walked for an hour on my own, tried to settle my head and get my thoughts together. By now I had a great deal of experience at the sharpest end of a Test series. All I tried to do was to put in front of the players the true situation, the almost frightening intensity of what they were about to go through, and to get it across to them how it would feel.

First, we got the entire touring party together in our team room. Fran said something to the whole group, then he left and took with him the non-Test players, the medical staff and everyone else. That left Jim and me and the twenty-two. That was when I gave the talk; that was when I asked the team to go out and finish the job, and to make their history. And to be special for the rest of their lives.

I am not trying to be clever when I say that everything in terms of the brutal intensity of the South African team turned out exactly as I had predicted. They just came at us in wave after wave so that there was hardly a chance for us to establish our game; all we could do was try to absorb, try to hit back in any way that we could. Yet we were still causing them grief in the scrums and here and there around the field, and with Jenks kicking two penalties before half-time we actually led by 6–5 at the break, staying ahead of a try by Joost van der Westhuizen, although we could tell in the dressing room that the Springbok pressure had had an effect.

It was typical of that squad of Lions that they were simply thinking their way around while riding out the storm. At half-time, Jeremy Guscott, who tended not to say very much in team meetings, gave the team a tongue lashing. He said that we were too sketchy, that we needed to build some attacks to establish momentum of our own and to get the Boks on to the back foot. 'Let's play some ******* rugby,' he shouted with anger in his voice.

But in the third quarter we conceded two awful tries, to Andre Joubert and Percy Montgomery, the first when Bentley badly missed a tackle and another when Tait coughed up the ball under pressure. They did not create an awful lot, and we still had Henry Honiball and van der Westhuizen under lock and key. But by this time we were 15–6 down, and I suppose a try then would have killed us off and sent us to Johannesburg for the final Test at 1–1.

And then we were lifted again by another of those seminal Lions moments. Gibbs was magnificent all day, and in one of his runs he saw that the massive Os du Randt was in his path to make the tackle. Gibbs simply blasted straight through du Randt, leaving the giant reeling. At the next break in play, with du Randt still groggy on the ground, Gibbs ran past him and gave him an earful.

Gradually, with Jenks kicking beautifully, even though his all-round game was struggling just a little, we dragged ourselves, run by run, back to 15–15, and a little of the steam had gone out of the South Africans. They were to miss six kicks at goal in all, and people said that that made us a lucky side. Not a bit of it. We had given our strategy a huge amount of thought, we had chosen a brilliant kicker in Jenkins, and we reaped the rewards.

Then came a passage of play which I will always rank along with that brilliant series with which England took the ball into range for Jonny Wilkinson to drop the winning goal in the final of the 2003 World Cup. That was world-class rugby, with people making good decisions, and with which all rugby fans will be familiar. If the Lions of 1997 were not quite so clinical, perhaps it was because by this stage the match was a maelstrom. But Jeremy Guscott had helped to turn the ball over after Tait had lifted a siege and then, when the ball came back, Keith Wood improvised with a chip and chase. We felt afterwards that Woody, though inspirational, had perhaps allowed the tension and atmosphere to get to him rather too much, so that he had not always made the best decisions. But his chip and the pace of his chase were perfect; he forced South Africa to concede a line-out and suddenly you could feel the unrest around King's Park.

We won the line-out, drove the ball on powerfully and then, more improvisation, with Gregor Townsend taking the ball flat and making a run into the heart of the Springbok defence of which any forward would have been proud. We piled in again, Dawson fed Guscott, and there was Guscott as cool under pressure as Wilkinson in 2003, putting over a drop kick from short range which would have been almost ridiculously easy in training but which was profoundly difficult in the circumstances of the match. The players ran back in sheer delight, but still with a huge job to do. It was one of the most famous kicks ever struck in rugby, and Guscott had once again taken the stage at the glamour moment, and executed perfectly.

It would be silly to pretend that the dying moments were not some kind of nightmare, but our defence somehow held up. Neil Back at one point won a priceless turnover, and then Jenks went scuttling back to shepherd the ball away for a drop-out after

Honiball had chipped the ball into our in-goal and the backs chased it.

Jenks then came up to take the drop-out, and he horrified Jim and myself up in the stand by dropping it out of play, and suddenly we saw the future – a Springbok scrum in midfield, and, at best, a kick which would tie the match. But Jenks knew better: the referee had told him that the next stoppage would be the end of the game. And so it was.

The whistle went. Of all my rugby moments, the sound of that final whistle in Durban in 1997 was probably the sweetest, perhaps even shading the Scotland Grand Slam in 1990. It was the complete feeling, too, because, although the Boks had had around 70 per cent of the game, so much had gone well for us. When we dissected the game afterwards in preparation for what we hoped would be the whitewashing of the Springboks in the final Test, we found that, in truth, we had not played at all well, we had not set up our game and we had, on occasions, been bullied. But we had stayed the course quite magnificently; we had won the series in the face of a predictably relentless South African onslaught. For most of the match, the hostility of the crowd seemed to be willing us to lose the game by a wide margin.

But we didn't. I went on to the field at the end as the players and the followers were united in scenes of incredible joyfulness. I ran into John Bentley, one of the most emotional players of all. 'They will never be able to take this moment away from us,' he shouted. He was dead right. Twelve years later, at a dinner in London, I met Bentos again. 'Thank you, Geech, for giving me that opportunity,' he said.

That night the Lions enjoyed one of their greatest celebrations. Next morning, they were all packed, some of them rather tardily, because we were moving on to Vanderbijlpark, where we were to be based for the final week, to play the last midweek game against Northern Free State, and to prepare for the final Test. Keith Wood was asked how well he had slept. 'I did not sleep at all,' he said. 'I was worried that if I went to sleep, I would never wake up again.'

That may have been a comment on the celebrations, but it was also recognition of what the players had put themselves through to become all-time greats.

We left the Durban hotel on the Sunday morning to board our coach. Every vantage point and every step was lined with Lions supporters, although the hotel staff bravely came out to perform a Zulu dance in our honour. Individually, and bleary-eyed, the players were applauded all the way to the coach.

When we got to Vanderbijlpark, we found it to be a terrible place, full of chemical fumes belching from nearby factories. The hotel was probably the worst we had stayed in on the entire tour. There was little to do.

We wondered, in our hour of victory, where they would have stuck us if we had lost.

Martin Johnson stood up in front of the team that Monday and asked for a commitment for the rest of the week. We labelled the final week 'whitewash week'; we were anxious to whitewash South Africa, both because it had never happened to them before and also because any consolation victory might have prompted them to suggest that they had been the better side all along.

We beat Northern Free State 67–39, annoying ourselves by conceding soft tries to them, but playing some tremendous rugby, with Tony Underwood and Tim Stimpson leading the try scoring. Then the selection committee had a no-holds-barred session in preparation for the Third Test, in which we were honest enough to admit that we had hardly played our game in the Second Test, that we had won by existing through the hard times, absorbing the disappointment of conceding soft tries, and coming strong at the very end.

We intended to make changes, perhaps even moving Jeremy Guscott to the wing to bring Allan Bateman into the centre, and threw in as an option moving Neil Jenkins to fly-half instead of Gregor Townsend. We also decided to give Neil Back the Third Test at open side. But the tour had taken its toll. Keith Wood, Tim

Rodber and Ieuan Evans all had to miss the Test, others were hobbling and, although we did bring in Backy, we kept other changes to a minimum, otherwise we would have changed two-thirds of the team. Rodber was the only player to miss the match because of a stomach bug which went through the entire party, but others were weakened by it and we patched ourselves up and went for the whitewash.

But in the end, it never looked on. We went 13–0 down. The Boks scored tries by Percy Montgomery and Joost van der Westhuizen, practically the only time he had escaped on the whole series. We climbed back to 13–9 with three penalties by Jenkins, two of which were awarded when the Boks killed the ball to stop us attacking, and some of our play was remarkably good. We came back again to 23–16 when Matt Dawson orchestrated a series of drives and managed to score himself, but at the end, when we were running on empty, Pieter Rossouw and Andre Snyman, the wing, scored a try each and the final score was 35–16, an unsatisfactory end for us. Or maybe not. At the end, we were presented with the trophy for winning the Test series.

The South Africans pointed to their feat of scoring nine tries against our three in the Test series. I pointed to their own World Cup triumph of 1995, which was defined largely by a reliance on fine kickers. After the tour, Kitch Christie singled out three areas. First, our scrum, which he said gave us the platform, instead 'of [it] being an area of weakness and concern'. Second, he pointed to our defence, which, especially in the Tests, he thought had been 'magnificent'. Third, he said that we held the edge in the tactical battle, that we seemed to know from the outset that Henry Honiball was not a natural fly-half so we targeted him, forcing him to move deeper and negating him. Frankly, as a tour summary, I felt that Kitch was on the button.

It was the second time we had won a series in South Africa. We were history men, it seemed, and the feel-good factor from the tour lasted a long time, through the long flight home and well into the future. I feel, too, that the experience gained on that tour by the England players gave them the core of their world champions team of 2003, with the likes of Johnson, Hill, Dallaglio, Back, Catt, Dawson, Greenwood, Leonard and Bracken coming to the fore in the six years between the two events. I felt that it showed that British and Irish players would no longer be pushed around, but also that we could play outstanding attacking rugby, contrary to the image that people had of us. I also felt that we had spanned the eras triumphantly, and that now, in the professional era, the Lions were bigger than ever.

Let's go back to 28 June 1997. As the Second Test reached a climax, and as the Lions drew level and came surging up the field in search of the winning score, one of Jeremy Guscott's close friends was apparently watching with a group of pals in a Bath sitting room, just as millions of people were watching in sitting rooms, bars and clubs all over Britain and Ireland. He knew Guscott's ability to come up with that theatrical, match-winning moment of skill, and knew that the bigger the stage the better Guscott responded, as the Test match animal in him revealed itself.

'I'll bet that so-and-so drops a goal to win it,' Jeremy's friend said. Less than a minute later, he did. To win the Test, and everything.

16

Travelling in the Dark

The 2005 Lions tour of New Zealand

Was the verdict of *The History of the British and Irish Lions*, described by one review as 'the consummate Lions book', harsh or was it accurate? It described the tour as 'a calamitous circus'.

Certainly, from many standpoints, it was the worst ever. The Test series was lost by a margin of 3–0, by 107 points to 40 and by twelve tries to three and, frankly, we were humiliated. We had not made ourselves very popular in New Zealand either so the edge on the New Zealand celebrations was marked. The Second Test, a 48–18 defeat at the hands of the All Blacks in Wellington, was probably one of the lowest points in Lions history. It was very difficult to take.

Sir Clive Woodward was appointed head coach of the 2005 Lions tour to New Zealand after the remarkable England triumph in the 2003 World Cup in which he had revolutionised the way in which Test teams were prepared, introducing meticulous planning and organisation and, clearly and understandably, Clive saw the Lions as his next great challenge in rugby. It was quite correct that he was appointed to see what he could do. I was flattered when he asked me to join his management team and I was interested to see what his approach would be and what I could learn. The answer is that I learned an awful lot.

Clive saw the challenge as finding a way to bring the Lions into a different and new age. He is famous for his attention to detail and for pulling the strings of a large, specialist and committed operation. His problem was to apply all that inside a remarkably short period of time, because there were only eleven matches on the itinerary on tour, together with a unique home match against Argentina at the Millennium Stadium, Cardiff, which was staged in part to raise money for what Sir Clive saw as a large and expensive operation.

But Clive had been a Lion himself and was keen to retain some of the old elements of the tour and, to his credit, when he could easily have demanded simply a few Saturday games plus three Saturday Tests he decided to retain the midweek games.

Obviously, this immediately created difficulties because he did not want his Test players travelling all over the country in midweek. So his answer was bold. He effectively created two Lions parties, with the players dividing up every week, one group staying in situ for the weekend game while the other travelled off to fulfil the midweek fixture. Altogether, there were fifty-one Lions who played on the tour and two enormous management teams, which replicated each other and numbered, at their peak, forty-four. One newspaper remarked that whatever problems the Lions faced on their tour, loneliness would not be one of them.

In theory, it sounded good but where it missed the boat was that, while it would have been fantastic for a four-year build-up to a World Cup, it was far too cumbersome for a five-week build-up to a Test series. It was all too unwieldy. Paul O'Connell has said that the players never really got to know each other properly, because they were always being split up and going their separate ways. He and other players have also remarked that they were never sure about who was who and who did what among the management team.

The chemistry of Lions tours is based on players getting to

know each other and becoming relaxed and easy in each other's company. But, as the tour went on, we split into two groups with separate training and travelling and separate games. There must have been some Lions who hardly saw each other and others who hardly played.

The outcome was disastrous – a kind of Test series that we had never seen before. Even on Lions tours that were unsuccessful, the Test series had invariably been incredibly tight, with a bounce of the ball here, a refereeing decision there or a controversial penalty, such as the one given against Dean Richards and Dewi Morris in New Zealand in 1993, being the difference between success and failure. In 2005, however, it was one-way traffic.

It was bitterly disappointing, because, while the All Blacks were good, with Dan Carter pulling the strings to great effect, they were not as good as we made them look and certainly British and Irish rugby at the time was not so bad that we could not even mount a proper challenge.

Sir Clive deserved every chance to impose his philosophy on a Lions tour. He was the only European coach ever to win the World Cup and his amazing record when in charge of England, when his teams dominated the Southern Hemisphere between 2000 and 2003, has yet to be equalled and may never be. He beat those giants consistently and was unbeaten against Southern Hemisphere teams for three years. But even Clive has admitted that 2005 was not his finest hour.

When he asked me to take part in the tour, I was pleased to do so and I have no regrets. I was keen to learn from Clive by observing him at close quarters and it was also rewarding to work with the other coaches and to sit down with players like Jonny Wilkinson, who has always impressed me, even though I had only observed him from a distance.

Jonny was fascinating to talk to on tour and, by the end, I felt I knew him quite well. Was he as great a player as everyone said? Yes, he was, if not on that tour. He was always incredibly brave, but he was also clever under pressure. He had what I always saw as world-class basics. He won Test matches because he possessed an animal instinct for survival but also because he could employ those basics at crucial moments, and do the right things. Under pressure, it is not a question of big and fancy game plans in which you are making sweeping attacks. It is simply doing the right things. I believe that under pressure Jonny did things better than I have ever seen them done by a number ten. The sadness in 2005 was that he was only just back after a long injury lay-off and was never at his best. The real Jonny Wilkinson never appeared.

Indeed, selection was something which Clive kept very close to his chest before the tour and most of us had no real inkling as to what the squad would be until it was announced in a fanfare of trumpets – in fact to the backdrop of loud rock music – in a hotel near Heathrow. Clive, perhaps understandably bearing in mind the short time frame, decided to stick with players he knew well, players who had made a great impact under him around 2003. They were tried and tested.

However, by no means all of them were on their best form by 2005. Lawrence Dallaglio was involved and he had had an excellent season for Wasps. But he was injured, cruelly, in the first match of the New Zealand tour at Bay of Plenty and played no further part. Players like Jason Robinson, Ben Kay, Richard Hill, Will Greenwood, Danny Grewcock and Neil Back had done wonders for Clive, but, by 2005, some of them were simply not the same players. Same thing with Jonny Wilkinson. He had missed so much time with his sad run of injuries and, by 2005, we were setting too much store by him. It would also be true to say that some highly rated forwards on tour did not produce their best, as many have themselves admitted.

The 2005 Six Nations had been dominated by Wales, who won the Grand Slam, as it turned out, Clive went for the men with whom he was comfortable. While there were ten Welsh players in the original squad, there were twenty-one English players.

There were some successes. Ryan Jones, the Welsh number eight, came down as replacement, immediately made a huge impression when he arrived during the Otago match and was soon in the Test team. Players like Shane Williams, Geordan Murphy, Graham Rowntree and Donncha O'Callaghan were with me a good deal of the time and we built up some understanding.

Simon Shaw came down as replacement, too, and played just as he can. But I couldn't get Shaw into the Test team. The top team coaches had this idea that he couldn't jump because he was too heavy, and they saw other drawbacks. I said: 'You are crazy. He's a big man, he's a good ball handler and he's great for mauling if the ball's off the ground. And he's very, very clever.' In the Manawatu game he ran about 80 metres and was only pulled down three metres short of the line.

But the problems caused by the huge squad and the shortness of the tour were exemplified by the fate of Matt Dawson. Daws was extremely loyal to the party, he did his very best to be a leader and to back up Dwayne Peel, who was the starting Test scrum-half, and tried his hardest under difficult circumstances. But he did not actually start a game as a 2005 Lion until the very last week, against Auckland on 5 July. Clive, with his philosophy of maintaining two separate teams, did not want Matt to be tired in case he was needed to come off the bench as a back-up in the Test. In the end, I persuaded Clive to allow Matt a start against Auckland, which is something that should have happened in week one.

Clive decided that the coaching squad for the top team would comprise Andy Robinson and Phil Larder, his old England lieu-tenants, and Eddie O'Sullivan of Ireland. I had no input into the top team and so stayed very focused with the midweek team. My goal was to give everyone in the midweek team the very best chance and to make Clive's life extremely difficult in terms of selection.

Indeed, I was determined to keep the midweek team competi-tive and I got tremendous satisfaction from the fact that the team went through the tour unbeaten and won 17–13 against Auckland in the last week of the tour in a match which I and others came to regard as the unofficial Fourth Test. The attitude of the players that day was fantastic and, in terms of the goals of myself, Gareth Jenkins, Mike Ford and the other midweek coaches, we were pleased at the end to do our maths and discover that eleven players who had begun in our midweek group had played in the Test series.

Yet the odd thing was that we'd never really set down a tour policy, which meant that there were differences in the way the weekend and midweek teams were coached and the way they played, making it extremely difficult for players moving from one team to the other.

Before and during the tour, we went through a number of management strategies, team stuff and flip-chart exercises. Cards kept arriving in the post to motivate us – 'They'll be ready, will you?' – and all the other motivational messages. It all helped to build up the excitement, but what I always longed for was the equivalent of the boot-room chat, the invaluable times I had had in all the coaching groups in which I played a part.

In fact, I kept asking Clive when we were going to talk rugby, when we were going to sit down to say: 'This is how we are going to beat the All Blacks.' My view was that we should be presenting that view to the players early on and then we would incorporate it into everything we did, no matter which team we were preparing. But on tour we never had that continuity and I feel that was a major drawback.

Clive admitted that he was not comfortable speaking to the players. He was always splendidly efficient and clever, but perhaps not as emotional as some of us. When he announced the team, he would put it up on a flip chart, which was fine for the announcement itself, but he seldom explained to players why they had not been picked so as to alleviate their disappointment to some degree. He lacked the personal touch. As a management team I don't think we considered properly the importance of developing relationships with players. Perhaps my tendency is more towards the emotional side as well as the methodical. But we became something that we were not; something that the Lions were not. I was very uncomfortable with the way we were being portrayed.

Perhaps we did ourselves few favours with our public face. We took along a former referee, Dave McHugh, and the theory was that he would help us with interpretations, that he would smooth over the relationship between the team and the referees so as to clear up any areas of doubt. But in the end he was getting referees' backs up because it seemed as if he was challenging them and assessing them. That may have caused ill feeling.

Sir Clive also wanted a major presence in terms of public relations and the media and, in a typically bold move which even he would agree became notorious, he picked as the tour communications manager the former Labour spin doctor Alastair Campbell. On paper it looked good, but, in terms of chemistry, in terms of the way that we were perceived by New Zealand rugby and by the New Zealand nation, it came across as confrontational, even paranoid.

On the Lions tours where I was head coach, including the tour to South Africa in 2009, I think we had a good relationship with the media because we kept it on a human level and we maintained contact with the media and with the home country. That relationship was missing in New Zealand in 2005 and we came across as arrogant, we were unpopular and it made the All Blacks and the country desperate for us to get beaten.

Alastair Campbell was very good at his job in politics, but in his new role he overstepped the mark. When Brian O'Driscoll, the tour captain, was injured and invalided home with a cruel shoulder injury in the opening stages of the First Test, Campbell ran a vigorous campaign hinting that the injury had been deliberately inflicted by an illegal double tackle by Tana Umaga and Keven Mealamu. That may or may not have been true, but we seemed to lose the moral high ground in the dispute when Campbell came out with a stream of statements and interviews so that, very soon, everyone was fed up with the whole issue.

He would also put in front of me pieces of paper, saying, effectively, that if you are asked question A, this is the answer that you will give and this is the response that you will receive from that answer. I refused to play along with that. I said that I would answer as a rugby person whatever I had been asked and that I was not prepared to follow a predetermined line set by someone who had no experience of talking about rugby to the rugby press.

But, again, I have no regrets. It was fascinating to experience some of Clive's thinking and especially to absorb the way he planned things. He had a superb organiser in Louise Ramsay, with whom he had worked in the World Cup and who I was delighted to be able to use on the 2009 tour. She was and is an absolute master at organising and in taking the team around the host country.

The attention to detail was meticulous. The planning and quality of hotels and facilities, the employment of a chef, the organisation of the flying schedules so that we would fly when we wanted to fly and not when a timetable dictated: all top-notch. It was how the Lions should always travel. There was plenty to learn in terms of all that background stuff and there were things that I integrated into my own future planning.

Clive was open to new ideas, too, which was refreshing. England had always used the ProZone analysis system but I preferred the Sportscode system, which I was used to, which was cheaper. Both systems are effectively computerised tracking systems which you can use to assess individual performance and team and unit performance throughout every phase of the game. But Sportscode was better and far more coach-friendly and has since swept the coaching world. He agreed that I should use it for the midweek games, became interested in the system, and, to his credit, we adopted Sportscode universally throughout the tour. He was never complacent about his work.

Yet, while Clive was making a brave attempt to update the Lions, to bring them into line with modern-day workings and

with his own philosophy, and while I respected his boldness, I
suppose that some aspects of 2005 reinforced my own beliefs of
the principle of a Lions tour. In 2009, for example, we abandoned
the 2005 strategy of all the players having their own rooms and we
went back to sharing. We went back to keeping things tight, being
open with each other and the media, and being very selective in
terms of developing the team and the tactics, because we simply
did not have time to be comprehensive.

The other thing that we missed out in 2005 was moving round
as a group and actually going into the places where we were to
play, meeting the local people and giving them the feeling that
something special was coming to town. The main team had three
main centres – Auckland, Wellington and Christchurch. It was all
a bit clinical, even antiseptic, on both sides; we never really
absorbed the culture, and readers will by now be aware of just how
important I consider this to be.

In the eyes of some of the players, we might have been touring
anywhere in the world.

When, in the second half of 2008, I was interviewed for the job
of the 2009 head coach, I told the panel what I believed a Lions
tour was all about, what a Lions tour should look like and that, if
they disagreed, they should not appoint me because I was not
going to change for anyone. Gerald Davies, who had already been
appointed manager, agreed with my philosophy and he and I
became stronger and stronger as the months passed.

Sir Clive had Bill Beaumont as his tour manager. Bill was a
great Lion himself and, in 2005, he and I spent hours in each
other's company talking about rugby. He may have been uncomfortable with the razzmatazz and Clive probably now regrets not
tapping Bill's knowledge a little more. Bill knows his stuff. He was
indeed from another era, but a successful Lions tour depends to a
great extent on the past as well as the present. Bill had great experience but that was never really called upon. By the end, I feel that
Bill may have been a little disillusioned.

On the way round New Zealand, I tried to take every

opportunity to introduce some of the Lions traditions. The mid-week coaches were asked to coach the team for the Otago game in Dunedin, which turned out to be one of our most impressive performances and brought us a 30–19 victory. After the game, I took the players out on the town for drinks, just so as to have a proper social evening. The city of Dunedin was well set up, the streets were blocked off for the thousands of supporters and we had a good night out. All I did was to remind the players that we had a community engagement at the Carisbrook ground on the Sunday morning at ten o'clock, that they should have a good drink but that absolutely everyone had to be on parade at ten on the dot. To a man, they were there; they mixed with around five hundred children, they signed all their autographs and they seemed to enjoy themselves.

Clive also became a little too anxious, concerned perhaps that New Zealand had inside information or at least that they were desperately trying to pick up secrets from the camp. He convinced himself, too, that the All Blacks had tapped into our line-out signals, so we changed them all the week before the First Test. At half-time players were still asking themselves where they had to stand for certain calls.

Most probably, we also overreacted to our only defeat in a provincial game, which came 19–13 against the Maori, who were a very good and committed side. In fact, considering it was only the fourth game of the tour, we did not play at all badly, but that one defeat cost too many players their Test places.

We had opened with a 25–25 draw in Cardiff against Argentina, in a packed Millennium Stadium, which illustrated that the love for the Lions among the public in Britain and Ireland was as strong as ever – as did the fact that replica jerseys sold at an incredible rate and that the iconic jersey became the biggest seller in European sport, bigger even than the jersey of Real Madrid.

We set off in New Zealand beating Bay of Plenty, Taranaki, Wellington, Otago and Southland as well as losing to the

Maori, and the atmosphere at the midweek games was excellent. But we had never set the tour alight and, on a horrible day of driving and icy rain in Christchurch, when many supporters of the British and Irish Lions were desperately hoping that we had all kinds of tricks up our sleeve, we were hammered 21–3 in the First Test. Ali Williams and Sitiveni Sivivatu scored tries for them and all we managed was a penalty by Jonny, who was chosen as a centre and played outside Stephen Jones. It was also the day that we lost Brian O'Driscoll with his dislocated shoulder. He was the tour captain, he was respected by all the players and feared by the All Blacks and he was a man of stature. To lose both O'Driscoll and Lawrence Dallaglio so early was a disaster.

We did put 100 points past Manawatu, scoring seventeen tries, with five from Shane Williams, but the Second Test was an embarrassment, a 48–18 defeat, with Dan Carter running wild; we actually scored first, through Gareth Thomas, but we were mercilessly picked off and we had very little to offer. Carter scored two tries and thirty-three points in all with an incredible display of kicking, and Tana Umaga, Richie McCaw and Sivivatu also scored. Simon Easterby scored for the Lions in the second half but we were left with a horrible feeling as the host nation celebrated.

We did win our 'Fourth Test' when the midweek team beat Auckland. Martyn Williams scored our try, and the players were delighted to have won such a big game, in front of more than 47,000 at Eden Park. In the dressing room afterwards, as Clive and some of the Test players filed in, it felt like a real Lions day, as if we were a united party at last.

And yet there was to be no consolation in the final Test at Auckland, which we lost 38–19. Umaga scored two tries, and Ali Williams, Rico Gear and Conrad Smith one each. Lewis Moody scored for us, but, apart from keeping the margin lower than it had been for the Second Test, there was nothing to celebrate.

It was probably on the journey home that I realised that the Lions had substantial ground to cover in order to become respected again, and to be treasured. And that in some important aspects, in order to secure the future we had to delve into the past.

17

Highest Wycombe

Top of my game in the Wasps years

There was no one at home. Leon Holden, the talented New Zealander who was a member of our coaching team at Wasps, was analysing Leicester in preparation for our forthcoming match at Welford Road. It was to be the last match of the regular 2006/07 season.

Leicester were the best team in England that season, and they would win the Guinness Premiership final against Gloucester a fortnight after we played them, by the dominating margin of 44–16, and the power of Alesana Tuilagi and Seru Rabeni, their wings, appeared to some to be almost unstoppable.

We were to finish fifth in the regular season, not good by Wasps' standards, but we did have one shot at glory because Leicester and Wasps had reached the final of the Heineken European Cup, which was looming large as a magnificent occasion in front of a world record crowd for a club match. It was important to me personally then, too. In 2000, the Northampton team I had helped put together had won the Heineken Cup just after I had left. It was wonderful to see a team and squad that I had put together beat Munster in the final, but the fact was that I was not involved in it. Now I had another chance.

Leon's analysis revealed something interesting. There was plenty to be impressed about as he combed the DVDs about Leicester to see what they did, who they played through. But he noticed that on the opposition throw to the line-out, their defending in the five-metre channel down the touchline, usually defended by the hooker or possibly the scrum-half, was almost non-existent. They often put their hooker in the line-out to give them an extra lifter and the idea that someone might attack them down that undefended channel was, they seemed to think, a risk worth taking.

Leicester were too good for us in that final Premiership game. They beat us 40–26 and went on to beat Bristol in the play-offs and to blitz Gloucester in the final, played one week before the Heineken game. At one stage of the game, we were considering throwing in the moves that we had formulated to try to take advantage of Leicester's defending at the line-out. But we quickly decided against it, and sent word on to the field that we should keep the moves under wraps. Who knows, we might need them another day, and the match was already lost anyway. But one matter was not in doubt, I now knew how to beat Leicester.

When you enter the Wasps club you are immediately struck by the complete absence of airs and graces. You know when you come through the gates that you just have to knuckle down and get on with it. If you forget that aspect of life at Wasps, there is always someone like Lawrence Dallaglio, Simon Shaw or, latterly, Raphael Ibanez to remind you forcibly. I first went through the gates in the close season of 2005. The offices and training headquarters in Acton were anything but palatial, and the industrial-size gym was fairly pungent. But in a way it was also a blast of fresh air. I had done my penance at the SRU, and was thrilled to be away from that dire committee and to be back among players as the director of rugby. It was to be the start of four happy seasons.

Wasps are an amazing institution. We never had any of the advantages of the big city clubs like Leicester and Gloucester, situated in the middle of their supporters and in the heart of the city, with all the attendant advantages. In my four seasons at Wasps, an appointment which ended in May 2009, we trained in Acton, a rather anonymous suburb of west London, and we played our games up in High Wycombe, in Buckinghamshire, about thirty miles west of London off the M40.

There had always been quite an enclave of Wasps supporters out there and Adams Park, while too small for the needs of a progressive club, has always been good to the players and to me. Our support base grew from the start of the professional era so that, for some of our biggest games, we could sell out the stadium.

But also in my time there were issues about the way that the club was being marketed and promoted and some of the players, Lawrence included, went on record after our big cup final victories, demanding that the pace of the club off the field begin to match the achievements of the team on the field. We were rarely allowed to spend up to the salary cap limit, and we often had to scurry round trying to sign players after injury.

The club was its players, full stop. They were and are a truculent, experienced, talented, grafting bunch, great to work with. On the coaching staff we had at first Craig Dowd, the former All Black, who was excellent, Leon Holden, and obviously Shaun Edwards, the great Wigan rugby league man who has proved himself so well in rugby union. It was always lively; with people like Lawrence and Josh Lewsey around, yes men were in very short supply. Judy and I were happy in our home in Penn (still are), there was a good atmosphere around the place and Chris Wright, the club owner until recently, rarely interfered. He was very supportive of the rugby.

Alex King was vastly influential, not only as a marvellous controlling fly-half on the field, but as a wise man in the team room. His knees were shot and he played through a lot of pain, we didn't train him all the time and we had to manage him quite carefully. Player management was something which began with my predecessor, Warren Gatland, who did so well as Wasps' director of rugby. It continued in my time, because we knew that we had to get the best out of people like King and the medical team we had in my time at Wasps was second to none.

It was management of this sort that prolonged the career of Phil Vickery. Phil was having his problems at Gloucester, always his spiritual home, and the list of serious injuries he has had over the years would be enough to send lesser men into retirement, good and proper. But at the end of my first season at Wasps, and as a long-time admirer of Phil from afar, I asked him up to see us. We had lunch at Marlow; he joined us with Kate, his wife.

Unsurprisingly, he was carrying an injury at the time. I said he should come to us, even if he was not fit until well into the season. I promised that we would give him the best treatment, that we would not overplay him, that we wanted him to make a difference for us in the big games. The result? Phil has come up trumps in every way. He has been outstanding as a player and a character; he is one of those players who can be injured and not play for six weeks, then come on and be outstanding. In my opinion, and Phil has expressed it too, Wasps have prolonged his career. We were able to keep him going strong so that he captained England in a World Cup final and he also had what he himself said was the time of his life with us with the Lions in 2009. We have given him three years, and everyone at Wasps can be proud of that.

The challenges are always there. Danny Cipriani and James Haskell made frequent appearances in the gossip columns in my time at Wasps and, as I write, and despite their brilliant talents, they are both totally out of the England set-up. James has departed to play for Stade Français in Paris, a move which upset me at the time. Danny is still with Wasps, and is happy there, but there are many issues surrounding him and the perception in which he is held – not least by Martin Johnson and the England hierarchy, because in something like fifteen months he appears to have sunk from number one to number six in the England fly-half standings.

Players have to make money; they will be a long time retired. But you cannot compromise on your rugby. I feel that James has been badly advised, particularly in the idea that was being put around when he was negotiating with several clubs, that there was such a thing as Brand Haskell. There is James Haskell the rugby player, who ought still to be a Wasps player and an England player because, at his best, he is outstanding. The brands are Wasps and England, not James Haskell. The players burnish the brands by dint of their characters and abilities but as soon as you think that you are bigger than the team or the club, then you are heading for a fall. James has lost his way a bit. I was disappointed when he went to Stade because, like Danny and many others, he has been a beneficiary of the outstanding Wasps academy system. He promised that if certain things were put in place or guaranteed by Wasps, then he would stay. In the end, he did not. He asked for equality with certain other players but ultimately that was not enough.

Danny Cipriani faces the challenge of being the best rugby player he can be, and putting everything else to one side. He is seen in some areas as a playboy, but that would be unfair, because he is supremely dedicated when he has his rugby head on. He is a good man; he is good to talk to. As I have said, Shaun Edwards and I spent a lot of time with him, and I hope that from now on he can get things back on track. England need that talent.

Raphael Ibanez was another massive influence. French he may be but he became a really powerful character at the club till he retired at the end of the 2008–09 season. We have never been able to rely on local players at any point in our existence; we have always relied on outsiders coming in and adopting the ethos and work ethic of the club. Raph appreciated what he was getting from us, the rugby he was playing and how he was managed. He is such a fantastic person off the field, but what he delivered on the field was incredible.

In my opinion, the reason we won trophies at Wasps in my four seasons was because Lawrence was captain and Raphael Ibanez was hooker. He was so powerful up front, psychologically so dominant at taking on the other front rows. He was such a good scrummager, such a focused player and his ball play was excellent. When you saw Raph and his family around the club, you might assume that he had always been Wasps through and through.

Another good example of an outsider becoming a true Wasp was Eoin Reddan, whom we signed as a young scrum-half from Ireland and who advanced so emphatically with us that he became one of our key players. He did lose a little momentum last season. I had spoken to Declan Kidney, the Ireland coach, and it was obvious that if Eoin wanted to play for Ireland, he was going to have to go back home to play, so he signed for Leinster.

Perhaps it was a slightly short-sighted view because I don't think anyone could deny what we had done for his career with Wasps. But he became influential for us as well and, even though he had a year left on his contract, I told him that I would never stand in his way when an international career was at stake. Essentially, he did not want to go, he was brilliant for us in the way he played and the way he understood the game, and he was another player who came in who really bought into the whole Wasps thing. In the dressing room after the final game of last season, he was in tears as he said his goodbyes.

When I arrived, I felt there were a few people who did not fit in. All of them were on the periphery, and they soon departed. But the club was also packed with great men and great players. Just consider the characters: Simon Shaw, the giant who has played more Premiership games in history than any other player and who, in 2009, at thirty-five, may well have been the best lock in the world; Josh Lewsey, for whom the word 'singular' does no justice, and who retired at the end of season 2008–09 and is now preparing to climb Everest. Only Josh could do that. And Fraser Waters, now in Italy and who worked with Shaun Edwards on our famous blitz defence; the massive Joe Worsley, recently a Lions Test player; and Tom Rees, the most dedicated and promising of the younger Wasps.

Yet to single out individuals is unfair. Wasps may have struggled a little last season and we did not win a trophy, which was a disaster for us, but the ethic at the club is still very powerful and the essence is a collective one in which no one is allowed to single himself out. Once a Wasp, always a Wasp. It is the mantra that has sustained them since they were founded. I will always be a Wasp and trust that Steve Hayes, the new owner, will invest in the club and push ahead with growing it. There were some of us who, like Lawrence, were disappointed that we did not cash in and become bigger after winning so many trophies.

One of the major pressures of joining Wasps when I did was that they were already incredibly successful. Under Warren Gatland they had dominated the Premiership and won the Heineken Cup, with an absolutely brilliant run which may never have been bettered in the history of English rugby, winning away in an electrifying match in Perpignan in their pool, and then beating Munster in Dublin in what is still widely seen as the greatest non-international match every played. They went on to beat Toulouse at Twickenham in the Heineken Cup final, the zenith of Warren's career at Wasps. It was in some ways a rare treat to be taking on a team that was not struggling, to be working with players who expected to win and who had a powerful pack of forwards. The need for the traditional Border scavengers' approach was far less when you looked around the dressing room and saw Dallaglio, Shaw and all the others. I relished the challenge.

The Heineken Cup was massive. I had put together a team which went on to win it at Northampton but, although we had won the Anglo-Welsh Cup in my first season at Wasps, that was not enough for the club at the time, because we were accustomed to more. We did finish fourth in the Premiership, but lost to a good Sale Sharks side by 22–12 at Stockport in the play-off.

We had a very tough pool in Europe; we beat Castres only narrowly at home and then we lost 19–12 away in Perpignan, which is an incredibly hostile place to play. We beat Treviso heavily home and away and then we beat Perpignan at home by a margin of eight points – which meant that, while we had taken a bonus point down there, we denied one to them at Adams Park and so we had to win away in Castres to go through to the quarter-finals.

We did, and it was one of those days when it was more than just a victory because Raph and Phil and the senior players all saw that as the making of us as a team. We went 13–3 up, Alex King played well that day and Joe Worsley had an incredible day with his defending; he was in the mid-twenties with his tackle count and, indeed, one paper described his as the greatest defensive display of recent seasons, by anyone. Castres came back strongly but we held on to win, and it was one of those times when in the dressing room that evening over a beer, and on the flight back, you could sense that the team had advanced and was bonding together even more strongly.

We then had Leinster at home in the quarter-final. They had all their stars, with Brian O'Driscoll and a host of internationals. For a time, they were quite dangerous and in the last two or three minutes of the first half they were inches from our line following a long series of attacks and it looked as though they would have to score. But again, we found that Lawrence was clever. He ended up on their side, where the ball was, it was never going to emerge and he took the yellow card and three points, rather than seven points.

And then we came out and dominated the second half; psychologically, we made a virtue out of starting the half with only fourteen men with Lawrence in the sinbin. And we started scoring. They had a big, heavy pack but in the end we broke them. The bad news was that Tim Payne and Alex King were injured; we lost Tim for the rest of the season and Alex came back only for the final, where he did his best to hide the fact that he was hobbling. But by beating Leinster 35–13 in what had originally been a tight game, we showed that we were back among the elite.

We showed something a bit different in the semi-final against Northampton on neutral territory in Coventry. At one stage, we were 13–0 down. We took time to get the basics right and we had to subdue a feeling of invincibility because we had played them in the league the week before and we had won comfortably. But we were always stuffing them in the scrum, and we just kept playing. We dropped Josh Lewsey for that game because he hadn't been playing that well and, to say the least, Josh was annoyed. But he came on in the second half to prove a point, and, as usual with Josh, he did just that. Paul Sackey was just coming of age at that time as a top international player, and he finished off two movements to score twice, Josh scored as well and we scored thirty unanswered points. There was a nice atmosphere in the Ricoh Arena, and all roads then led to Twickenham, where we were to meet none other than Leicester.

We had to manage the rest of the season very carefully, because the fact was that we had not qualified for the knock-out stages of the Guinness Premiership, so, once we had finished our regular season programme, we had no one else to play for a few weeks. There was evidence of a lack of integrity at the end of that competition with teams putting out reserve outfits, which affected those who reached the play-offs. That annoyed me, because the PRL are always talking about the integrity of the competition. But with Leicester waiting, it became a priority to keep our players match hardened. We gave them some time off, and when we came back we had a full-on black v. gold game, which was effectively the first against the second team at Henley. It was a terrific game. Craig Dowd and I coached the second team and Shaun and Leon Holden coached the first. Wayne Barnes refereed. Psychologically, I wanted to give the first team a rocket so when the second team took the lead just after the halfway stage in the second half, I got the message on for the final whistle to be blown. Suddenly, what the top players had felt to be a walkover had become a defeat.

But there was food for thought afterwards in another of our problem areas. Tim Payne would miss the final and Alistair McKenzie, who should have propped in the black v. gold game, was caught in traffic on the M25. So we put Tom French in, and from the sidelines it looked as if it had gone very well. Indeed, when we spoke to Raph and Vicks afterwards, they both remarked how well Frenchie had done.

After that, we all went out for a meal in Henley, we had a good night in a pub and then we were back concentrating on the final. We had it all to do, because, on the previous Saturday, Leicester had smashed Gloucester in the Premiership final and they had taken all their big players off at the end to rest them.

Lawrence was always brilliant in a week like that, talking up the fact that everyone had made Leicester favourites, that they had hammered Gloucester and so no one thought we stood much of a chance. He was really good at bringing the team to its peak, just by what he said and by his presence alone. Even when past his best, he created winning environments. We also announced a team which, as Leicester expected, had Vicks at loose head, essentially out of position, and Peter Bracken at tight head. But in private we had no such intentions and my argument was that Vicks was the best tight head in the world, and we should play him in his best position. We only announced that Tom French would play in the match just before kick-off. Richard Cockerill, the Leicester forwards coach, apparently went nuts in the tunnel when he heard, because all their plans had been laid for Julian White to take care of Vicks in the scrum. But now Vicks was still on the other side.

In the first scrum, Tom French was really solid and, if anything, we went forward. Josh brought off a fantastic tackle in the first minute, typical of him and a great psychological blow. Then we produced another one of the elements of the game plan we had decided on before the game. Because Leicester liked to play off the first breakdown, we had decided not to compete very often in their line-out. So we sent three in at the first breakdown, we smashed them as they tried to set up the play, we turned it over and Alex King dropped it into their corner. Then they gave away a penalty, Alex kicked the goal and it was the perfect start. Everything that Leicester had expected to happen, did not.

There was also another very important game played before the final. This was the game at which Leon Holden and the analysts had noticed the open five-metre channel at line-out. Going into the final we were pleased that we had decided not to use our moves, that we had decided to save them for the final; it was one of the best decisions we ever made because, on the day, Leicester paid for their defensive alignment in spades.

It began when we had a line-out on the left-hand side of the field. They left Julian White near the tram lines and Raph held the ball up to throw it in. We called a move in which our line-out retreats, and the replay shows Leicester moving back with us as Raph prepares to throw. Suddenly, as everyone moves back, Eoin Reddan, who was in the normal place at scrum-half, simply moved into the space, Raph threw it to him underarm and Eoin set off. That was all it was; it was so simple and blindingly effective and, as someone said afterwards, it was the ultimate sucker punch.

Nearer to half-time we had another line-out, this time on the right-hand side of the field. Again, the tram lines were empty. George Chuter was at the back of the line-out to give them an extra lifting pod. This time, Raph threw it straight to Simon Shaw at the front of the line-out, again Leicester were fatally slow to cotton on, Shaw ran round the front of the line-out and passed it back outside to Raph. Raph ran on to score, and the replay shows Lawrence happily waving to his friends in a section of the Leicester crowd as the Wasps players celebrated. After the game, I gave credit to Leon for his work in putting together those little moves. The satisfaction you get as a coach from bringing off something like that to such good effect is impossible to quantify.

The final score was 25–9. Alex King kicked four penalties and a drop goal to add to our two tries, we shut them down completely and we were European champions. It was a lovely day, played in front of a world record crowd, and the coaches walked round the ground behind the players on the lap of honour. It was a massive win. For me it was up there with the Grand Slam game in 1990 and the Tests with the Lions in 1997. Judy was the most joyful person in the stadium on that wonderful day. 'This marks the end of a seven-year guilt trip,' she said.

By 2007–08, it was obvious that Lawrence was coming to the end, and he had not been starting for England in the World Cup.

He is an incredibly proud man, and would never admit that he was anything other than in his prime, but he was slowing down a little and, with players like James Haskell coming through strongly, there were opinions being offered around the club that we should phase him out.

To me, Lawrence was still the core of the club, and it was essential to have him there for the build-up to the big games, to have him in the dressing room and to have him influencing events on the field, and so the season became a balancing act, as I did my best to manage him. He was not so effective over the whole eighty minutes any longer. But I wanted him out there and the way I was able to manage Lawrence in his final season gave me great satisfaction.

It was a tough season, and an especially tough start, because we had our international contingent away at the World Cup. Among the most ridiculous ideas that the PRL have had is that the money from the Rugby Football Union which goes to the clubs as a reward for producing English-qualified players is actually put into a pool and shared twelve ways, rather than going to the clubs who actually produce the players. We reckoned that this cost us £750,000 per year, and it meant that we fell well behind at the start of season 2007–08 when the World Cup was on.

Another incredible aspect of that season was our reward in terms of seeding for finishing as champions of Europe. We were put straight into the Pool of Death for the new season, alongside Munster and Clermont-Auvergne.

Annoyingly, we often played fabulous rugby in Europe, as the players came back from the World Cup. We scored three brilliant tries at home against Clermont, and we could have won there because we were leading at the end, and then we gave away a try in the last move which stopped us getting the bonus point. And, back at home after dominating them in the first half and scoring those three tries, we could not score again so missed out on another bonus point. We could easily have been clear and qualified before the last game, but we lost to Munster in a day of appalling weather in Limerick, and so it was time to concentrate on domestic matters.

We came from way back that season. We had also had two games called off during the campaign, one because of frost at Adams Park and the other because of strong winds at Newcastle. So it meant that, from eight or nine games out, in a fixture pile-up and having to manage a squad which was smaller than most, we had to make the best of our resources and we had to win every game in order to make the play-offs. We did, and I was very proud of the achievement, even if the cliffhanger was bad for the heart. We picked up bonus points against Saracens, Worcester and Newcastle, and we finished second in the table at the end of the regular season.

At some stages, Lawrence was clearly not quite his old self, notably when Bath started off at 100mph in the play-off semi-final. They went 10–0 up and we also had to absorb the blow of Danny Cipriani, who had been playing so well, suffering his horribly complicated ankle injury. We also lost Tom Voyce with a dislocated shoulder.

But we were so bloody-minded as a team. We went straight back and scored through Fraser Waters, we came through and won the game and it meant that Lawrence, who was retiring at the end of the season, had a potential dream farewell in the Guinness Premiership final, before another monster crowd at Twickenham, and against a familiar enemy – Leicester.

The final was another incredible day. Riki Flutey had to play at fly-half in Danny's absence, but we prepared as best we could, planned to get the ball behind Leicester with kicks, or to keep the ball and to keep Leicester in their own half. We planned to make their heavy forwards work really hard, and when the ball was in the spaces to attack their line. Lawrence was immense before the game; he and Josh became quite emotional.

And again, we dominated. Tom Rees scored after a superb pick-and-go move involving backs and forwards and a break by Eoin Reddan, and this was a blow at the heart of the Leicester team which always prided itself in its power up front. And later in the first half we put in a whole series of phases after a turnover caused by Lawrence and Simon Shaw. We ran their front five around, Tom Palmer drove the ball on and we went wide to Josh. Josh put in a great finish and scored at the posts. Mark van Gisbergen kicked stupendously that day, played brilliantly around the field in fact, and even though they came back and scored two tries we won 26–16. Cue cup wielded by Lawrence, and another lap of Twickers. The first half had been flawless rugby.

Leon Holden said afterwards that it was only when he looked at the video of the match that he saw how our game had evolved over the three years. It was also the time when I felt that the years of experience had all come together. I never felt that, as director, I had to have the last word or the credit. Shaun was a great talker, and I was always willing to let him or Leon have their say.

Lawrence departed on the hour, to be replaced by James Haskell. He received an incredible ovation as he left the field for the last time, and it was good to see large sections of the Leicester supporters stand to applaud him as well. He deserved it. There would be no thanks from Lawrence for our skills in managing him so well, simply because his pride and self-belief would never allow him to admit that he was anything other than on top form for every game and, secretly, he would probably pick himself for England today. He quickly moved on to the board at Wasps and yet he went out with the trophy, and it was another great feeling.

By this time, the Lions tour of 2009 was looming and eventually, in discussion with the Lions and with Judy, I decided to throw my hat in the ring and I was appointed as head coach of the Lions for the fourth time. These days, it is just impossible to hold down another job as well as doing all the research and player analysis and the mountain of planning for the Lions. What I should have said was that I would take a sabbatical from Wasps.

However, it turned into a mishmash. What happened was that the Lions paid my entire salary for the whole season, while Wasps kept things going such as my pension. But, basically, Wasps had a very cheap year and I agreed to be around for 30 per cent of the time – that amounted really to one day a week and also the game day. I wanted to be involved still because it was important to be coaching under the experimental law changes but I also wanted to keep my hand in and keep the contact.

It did not work. I found that I was far more heavily involved than was planned, had a season when I sometimes felt torn, but also found that, until they took on Tony Hanks, late in the autumn, Wasps did not bring in anyone to fill the gaps and basically seemed to be saving the money and leaving the coaching staff a man down. I was not able to put in the analysis, I was thinking Lions first.

The Lions commitments built and built, and there were Wasps games which I simply missed because I was away, either assessing players or holding planning meetings. Our results were not good; in fact, at some stages we were very low in the table. We still played with great courage in Europe, beating Leinster 19–12 at Twickenham to give ourselves a chance of qualifying, but then we lost 21–15 to Castres on the following weekend, and we were out.

We finished only seventh in the regular season table, and so there was to be no silverware. It was a poor way to bid farewell to Josh Lewsey, who was retiring, but as the season was coming to an end I simply became annoyed with the way things were going. We seemed to be playing by numbers behind the scrum, we were playing with no width and I told the players so. I was quite unceremonious at the end. I told the players we had gone backwards, but at least we had an uplifting end to the season, with a thumping wins over Bristol and Gloucester, with the old width and sweep returning, after which the crowd could wave farewell to the likes of Josh, Raph and Eoin.

By this time, a new Wasps board had come in, who wanted to plan for a long-term future. I had not intended to go on beyond the end of season 2009–10 but we decided on a parting of the ways a season early to assist the Wasps planning. I regret how we all handled that last season but I left with nothing but the best wishes for the players and the club and the supporters, who created such a friendly atmosphere.

It will be fascinating to follow the fortunes of Wasps. The period of transition caused by the retirement of Lawrence will need careful management. But the Wasps years will always remain close to my heart, not only for the trophies and the final ascent in Europe, but for the background and the characters and the aura of an amazing institution.

18

Pennyhill Park

The 2009 Lions and the gathering storm

Waiheke Island is around forty minutes by ferry from Auckland harbour. Bill Beaumont and I were on Waiheke during the 2005 Lions tour, talking about that ill-fated venture in which we were competitive in none of the Test matches, and it was obvious, as we talked, that the Lions as a concept might be in jeopardy unless the next tour, to South Africa in 2009, was done properly. It was a matter of urgency. Sir Clive Woodward, head coach in 2005, was as upset as anyone at the way it had turned out.

Bill was manager of that tour and one of the matters we discussed was the manager/coach relationship, because Clive had taken complete control of the tour – as was his right – leaving Bill rather sidelined. As we sipped our coffee, we discussed whether I would put myself forward for 2009 as manager. It was not ideal. I was desperate for the Lions to get back on track and desperate for the generation of top players who would come to a peak in 2009 to have the best opportunity to become Lions, to become *winning* Lions, and to experience the magnificence of the whole event. But there seemed to be too much administration and too much ceremonial, and too little contact with players in the office of manager.

In any case, Gerald Davies, the brilliant Welsh wing and a Lion himself in 1968 and 1971, had put his name in the frame to be manager and I immediately realised that he would be a good choice. I told Bill and others that, if Gerald was up for it, fine, move on.

But towards the end of 2007, Andy Irvine, my old colleague in the Scotland team in the 1970s and by now chairman of the Lions Board, called me. They had obviously been assessing contending coaches and, during the call, he asked me if I had considered becoming Lions head coach again. I had done three as head coach. Surely I couldn't do it again. Could I?

It would be twelve years after the 1997 tour, my last as head coach, and Andy's question was not one to be taken lightly. Even as long ago as 1989, the task of head coach was incredibly difficult, but now, with all the new ultra-professional preparation culture, at which the Lions were to be at the cutting edge, with all the pressure, the challenge and the media, it was a responsibility of forbidding proportions.

It was not yet an approach from the Lions. I spoke to Judy about the 2009 tour and, as ever, she cut to the chase. 'If you really want to go for it, then go for it.' I would never have gone ahead if Judy had been unhappy or wavered, but in the end I had another light-bulb moment. I was really enjoying my coaching at Wasps at the time, I still felt that I was thinking clearly about rugby at the sharp end, and I felt that I should have one more crack – but only if the Lions allowed me to do it exactly as I felt it should be done.

So I stood in front of the Lions board in early May 2008. 'I think there are certain principles that you have to work to as a Lions coach,' I told the board. 'If you don't agree with them, then please don't appoint me, because I am not going to change my values.' I meant all kinds of things, and in many ways it meant improving the future by using the best of the past – things like players sharing rooms, hanging out together, travelling together, really getting to know one another. It did not mean staying in one big centre in the country, flying in and out and never coming into contact with the country or its people. I wanted the players to go to every town and city in which they would play, and to understand their environment. I also wanted them to understand the rugby – with one coaching team, one medical team, one strong management team that set an example to the players, and a party that contained character. In every way it was a blueprint which I put together from all my tours and all my experiences, good and bad.

It seemed that that was what they wanted to hear, and Andy Irvine rang me to tell me that the position of head coach of the 2009 British and Irish Lions in South Africa was mine. The old feeling of the world lurching round me was as powerful as ever. It would be my seventh Lions tour, either as coach, head coach or player. People asked me how I felt about this appointment in comparison with those of 1989, 1993 and 1997. The truth was that I was probably more excited than ever, and that only became more intense as time passed. I was still anxious. In the saner moments you realise, with something of a shock, the responsibility you are taking on for rugby and for players in four countries. It is still the toughest thing in rugby coaching, anywhere in the world.

Luckily, too, I found that Gerald Davies and I were entirely in agreement in terms of values. Gerald was anxious to protect the Lions' heritage but the great thing about him, as he demonstrated on tour, was that he appreciated that he was not part of the professional game and all its advances, and was determined that he would manage the tour and look at all aspects outside it, leaving me with the responsibility of looking at all the internal problems. That was exactly how I wanted to work.

There was a certain serendipity about the way things began to come together after that, because I managed to put together my first-choice medical and coaching team. That was a wonderful start. Dr James Robson, who I had taken on the 1993 tour and who had made every Lions tour since, was immediately tasked with putting together his own medical team. Warren Gatland had been hooker in the Waikato team that had thrashed the midweek Lions in 1993. In defeat, that was a match which reinforced many of my ideas being formed at the time, that the absolute key to success was in retaining harmony throughout the squad, and that the strength of a Lions squad would be defined by the unity and loyalty of those who did not make the Test team.

I had followed Warren at Wasps; we had kept in touch as he began his career as coach of Wales, winning a Grand Slam in his first season. Warren and I were on the same wavelength, which was important. I had so far been lucky with the coaches I worked alongside – Jim Telfer and Derrick Grant, for example – and, as it turned out, I was lucky with Warren, too. He could be caustic, but he understood the shape of the game; he understood, too, about building up cumulative attacks, he got on well with players and when he spoke he was effective but never too intense. He agreed to join the group as well. Shaun Edwards was desperate to make the tour, and was an obvious choice; I also went for Rob Howley as my backs coach. Rob had begun his coaching career really impressively with Wales and he was clearly a man on his way up, and Graham Rowntree is a man I like as a character and as a forwards coach.

In terms of selection, we were looking for characters, and footballers. In my so-called sabbatical from Wasps, I watched an awful lot of rugby. But after the autumn internationals of 2008, I was concerned. I had asked Jim Telfer to keep an eye on the Scottish players, and I was frequently in touch with the three other national supremos, Declan Kidney of Ireland, Martin Johnson of England and Frank Hadden of Scotland. They were all superb, very supportive and they made excellent comments. They offered some pointers, especially in terms of looking for character in adversity, character in training and character under pressure.

At no stage were we under any illusions about the challenge ahead of us, and I was aware that this might turn out to be my toughest Lions tours yet. I had no doubt either that South Africa were far stronger than they had been in 1997. They had a superb captain in John Smit, a line-out champion in Victor Matfield, a world-class scrum-half in Fourie du Preez, good wins, massive physicality. And they were steaming for revenge for 1997. *Steaming.* Compared to 1997, they had better players, more world-class players, they had more depth, a better structure and they were better coached. Some of the rugby they had played in November, especially against England at Twickenham, had been exceptional and I was certain that they were developing into a better team than they had been when they won the World Cup in 2007 in France.

By contrast, the home teams' development was patchy. Wales seemed pretty settled in terms of personnel and were playing intelligent rugby under Warren, but Ireland were beaten very easily in the autumn by New Zealand and England, and, full of new players, were very much finding their feet. They were short of experience, and there was a mental frailty and a naivety about the way they had played against South Africa in the autumn internationals of 2008.

Things improved a little during the Six Nations Championship. England became significantly better, while Ireland stepped forward conclusively, so when the Lions selectors met during the Six Nations we were a little happier. I wanted to wait at least three weeks after the end of the championship, so that we did not make snap decisions on the last games, and I also wanted time to consider players appearing in the final stages of the various domestic leagues and, obviously, the Heineken Cup.

On previous tours, I had not selected those players whose character I did not trust. This time, no one missed out for that reason. One advantage of the professional game is that the top players look after themselves – they genuinely keep the balance and if they go out for a drink they know when they have had enough. I was happy with the character of the squad we eventually chose, and not a single individual gave us cause to regret our decision.

As usual, the issue of who would captain the Lions on tour was an enormous one. Now that the 2009 tour is over, I can genuinely say that I have never made a wrong choice on all my Lions tours. The three I looked at carefully for 2009 were Brian O'Driscoll, Phil Vickery and Paul O'Connell. I have made my feelings about

Phil perfectly clear, and, to be honest, I cannot understand why he was not retained as England captain after the 2007 World Cup.

Brian had been back to his best in the Irish Grand Slam, but eventually I decided to go for Paul. With Warren as forwards coach, I felt that it was good to have the captain in the forwards, and, as I said earlier, I felt it important to have a figure with a towering physical presence to lead the team. Paul O'Connell fitted the bill. Apart from Paul, I rang one other player before the squad was announced – Brian. I felt he deserved that call, particularly after 2005 and what had happened to him. 'In the end, I have decided to go with Paul as captain,' I told him.

Brian was philosophical. 'Look, I'm disappointed, but Paul will get my full support. He has always given me his when I have captained Ireland, and I will reciprocate.' Brian asked me if he could ring Paul, and I told him that I would be delighted if he would. He did just that.

It might seem remarkable, given the bristly personalities involved, that we did not need a deciding vote to come up with the thirty-seven players we ultimately chose as the 2009 British and Irish Lions. We might have wished that a few players we selected had been on better form, among them Shane Williams, who we saw as a match winner, but we still thought he was worth going with and the evidence of the tour was to prove us correct.

Perhaps the omission of Tom Croft received the most adverse publicity, especially when we chose Alan Quinlan, the Munster flanker, instead. There were several reasons for this. At Leicester, Croft had the luxury of being able to play in a certain way. Often he would stay out on the wing and not be involved in three or four successive breakdowns. We could not afford that style of player in a Lions context. When, however, Quinlan was suspended for eye-gouging in the Heineken Cup semi-final, he was banned from the tour and Croft came in. I took him to one side, explained that I wanted him in on the midweek matches and wanted him using his pace, but that he had to graft. He did; he adapted superbly and he looked like a player with huge talent.

Opting for Quinlan was probably a nod to the importance of leadership in the midweek team. We needed someone like Donal Lenihan, so effective in 1989, someone who would be really focused, good off the field and a focal point for some of the younger players. Fate then took a hand and Quinlan missed out.

And so the Lions selection die was cast. We knew that British and Irish rugby was not on an all-time high and we knew that we faced world champions who had improved since winning the title. But we were happy. It seemed that we had a good balance, and we had options up front. For example, we knew that we would be able to choose between the incredible industry of Gethin Jenkins or the awesome power of Andrew Sheridan; we knew that we had riches at blind side, where Stephen Ferris, Joe Worsley and Croft would be contending. People said that the party contained no X factor, no James Hook – who was to join us later anyway – and no Danny Cipriani. But we chose two fly-halves in Stephen Jones and Ronan O'Gara quite deliberately. They would be the people who set the tactical tone and controlled matters, and we felt it was a good idea that one or the other of them would be starting every game.

Elsewhere, it seemed that we had plenty of attacking options, and plenty of potential. Mike Phillips had impressed us as a scrum-half and, while we were in no way pre-judging any of the selections, there was also a certain something about the prospect of Brian O'Driscoll teaming up in the midfield with big Jamie Roberts. Roberts is still pursuing a medical career, and anyone who can fit two professional careers into one life deserves the utmost respect.

Famously, one writer decades earlier compared a Lions tour to a Sunday School outing and there were moments as we gathered at Pennyhill Park hotel in deepest Surrey when you understood exactly what he meant. Players were arriving in dribs and drabs, dressed in their ordinary clothes, sometimes with their fathers driving them, almost as if they were dropping them off at a school match.

Players meeting in the corridors of the hotel experienced a strange feeling. Simon Shaw recalled: 'I was walking down the corridor and Paul O'Connell was coming the other way. I was just about to give him the glare, as usual, but I realised that, actually, he was now my mate.' It had something of the beginning of term about it, albeit a new term at a very hard and serious school. Remember that the Heineken Cup final was still to be played in six days' time, and, in fact, Leinster didn't want their players gathering with us at all. In the end, both the Leinster and Leicester players did join us, and it was only Northampton who let us down – at the last minute, we heard that they were not going to release Euan Murray. We only wanted the Leinster, Leicester and Northampton players for the one day before we released them back to their clubs, and I found it extraordinary that Northampton, who had not even played for a couple of weeks, would not let Euan be there for the tour photograph, for all the distribution of kit and orientation and for all the excitement.

We also had commercial matters and sponsorship requirements to attend to. I had stipulated that on that first day any commercial obligations should be done and dusted. So we called it 'Messy Monday' – it would have everything in it but after that every other day of the week, until we left, would be devoted to rugby. So we met. We had lunch. Everybody was getting their kit. Tons of it. It was all excitement. We were all chatting and there was a real good buzz. Then we had a meeting after lunch in the big room. Gerald spoke first. I spoke last. I spoke about what I thought of the tour, what we were trying to do.

I spoke openly. 'Look,' I said, 'my intention is that you will all get an opportunity to go for a Test place and we won't pick the Test team until the Test week . . . *but* we will all be planning to beat South Africa from tomorrow. The first time we go on to the rugby field, the tactics we start to introduce then are the tactics which will build towards the Test.' In that sense, I was not too bothered about the style of the opposition in the provincial games. But we had to get ourselves right, because they were credible opponents. I said there wouldn't be a huge number of meetings or analysis. I noted a few smiles as I said that.

Eventually, with all the details covered, we boarded our bus at Pennyhill Park for Heathrow, and for Johannesburg. Once there, we drove out to Sandton, in the safer northern suburbs of the city, and we checked into the Sandton Sun hotel, a vast place with a central atrium the size of several aircraft hangars. The kit came rumbling in on lorries, the team room was set up, the gyms were located, players consulted their tour diaries to see where to go next and what to wear; those with niggling injuries checked out the sports physio, those with adventurous spirits took in their surroundings, sized up their rivals for the Test match, tried hard to impress in the early sessions at St David's School in Sandton. The media conference began, for a media group which was to number over 300 by Test time. And the peculiar rhythm of a Lions tour started to build up.

The coaching set-up was easy to fix, once I had the people I wanted with me. Rob Howley was in charge of the backs, and I oversaw the back play with him. Warren Gatland was overseeing the forwards, but Graham Rowntree was doing contact as well, plus looking after the scrum. Shaun Edwards was in charge of the defence. I didn't need to run everything myself. All I wanted was for the coaching unit to be effective, and for the players to be getting a clear message.

The training was structured entirely towards taking on South Africa in the Test series. We took every provincial game seriously, but we never really analysed the provincial teams. Our game plan in those games was to play it as we wanted to play against South Africa. We knew that the physical confrontation at the contact would be massive. But we wanted to move their front five around and make them work. We wanted to attack, to try to get mismatches, our backs against their tiring forwards. And offsetting was still important. We knew that with South Africa running straight at us, to smash us, if we could change the point of attack really late we could get in behind them.

As the tour progressed, we set up a traffic lights system. If we were happy with the phase of play we were practising, we called it green. If things were okay but we probably needed more time on it, we gave it an amber. And if we were undercooked or it was simply not working, we gave it a red.

Obviously, there were problems with the time frame. We had so little coaching lead-in time before the tour, and we had only six days in South Africa before the first match. As it turned out, the players were fantastic. We simply could not do everything that we wanted before the matches started. Before the opening game in Phokeng, we spent hardly any time on the restarts. Nor could we say that we were going to run five or six kick-off options. The time we had was spent on set piece, breakdown, contact and regrouping after the contact. In a way, we used the fact that we were underprepared to test our reactions on the hoof.

One of the core principles we tried to instil in the players was the importance of becoming part of South Africa, a personal mantra with which readers will now be familiar. We wanted players to understand the country, its different regions and races, the areas in which they would be playing; they had to understand the place of rugby in South Africa and the way in which the Lions were regarded in the country. It is important to try to absorb the culture; once you start to shy away from it, or complain about it, however harsh life becomes, you are in trouble. We played twice a week, we travelled twice a week, but I felt that it was so important that we stuck together, and that we understood where we were.

With all this in mind, we moved to Phokeng for the first game, against the Royal XV, drawn from some of the smaller provincial teams but in a rugby heartland. We stayed in a colonial hotel, and the conditioners were brilliant. Paul Stridgeon and Craig White set up all the equipment outside, so here we were on the highveld, absorbing the glare of the sunshine and the heat, in what amounted to an outdoor gym.

Ugo Monye was appointed as our travel guide. It was his job to research every town we were to visit. He had to report back to the whole squad what was important about the town, what there was to see, what each place and the region was renowned for. He took it seriously, and he added immeasurably to our insight.

It was the players who appointed him, and what was fantastic was that they took charge of their own tour. To have small groups of players arranging the rooming lists and discipline and social matters, even the tour music, might strike you as vaguely old school, but I thought it was terrific.

Nathan Hines was in charge of allocating rooming lists. He and his group did it in all sorts of non-scientific ways. Players were paired up at various locations through bingo calls on the bus, or names pulled out of a hat, or even by the position of darts on a dartboard.

The senior players' group consisted of Paul O'Connell, Phil Vickery, Stephen Jones, Brian O'Driscoll, Martyn Williams and Ronan O'Gara. The bus announcers, the players with responsibility for communicating any changes or announcements during the day, any departures from timetable, were Andy Powell and Donncha O'Callaghan. The entertainment committee, which would liaise with our hosts to organise shark fishing, golf or any other kinds of activity, comprised Joe Worsley, Simon Shaw, Lee Mears and Tommy Bowe. Riki Flutey and Jamie Roberts compiled the CDs which were played when the group was together. They both had guitars, and by all accounts Jamie Roberts' performance on the guitar when the players went on safari towards the end of the tour was outstanding.

We also had a group who sifted all the requests we had for charities and community visits. They chose which ones we could support, and which players would be assigned to them. We had a fines committee responsible for discipline, for collecting fines relating to transgressions in dress code, punctuality and the like. At the end of the tour, there was 40,000 rand (about £5000) in the kitty from discipline alone. The players decided to spend part of it on giving Patrick O'Reilly, our baggage man, a short holiday with his wife as thanks for his superhuman efforts, but the rest of the money was split between two South African charities which the players had espoused. One was a radio charity where they would match any amount you put in to buy blankets and other essentials for underprivileged families. The second was a food and educational charity for townships, which was run by the Irish Embassy.

The general rules and the level of fines were established. Nothing so simple as just a handful of rands. They were as follows:

For wearing the wrong kit: 300 rand.
For lateness: 300 rand.
For a mobile phone ringing during a meeting: 300 rand.
For a yellow card: 500 rand.
For a red card: 1000 rand.

If you didn't want to pay up, you could roll the dice. If number 1 came up you paid nothing. If number 2 came up, you had to have a leg wax. If number 3 came up, you had to grow a moustache for two weeks. Number 4 gave you 300 rand credit. For number 5, you had a spray tan. For number 6, you had to pay double. Probably the worst victim was Paul Stridgeon, who drew the spray tan. He looked great.

Another feature of the tour was the decision that every player should have a laptop, appropriately coloured red. Rhys Long and Rhodri Bown, the analysts, set up a server with thirty-two ports in it, so the players could come up to the team room with their own computers, plug in and download the information and analysis from the server.

For example, each individual could click on one game, and find statistics to assess his performance and his involvement in attack and defence. Gethin Jenkins, for example, could assess himself in the scrum, line-out, handling and tackling. He could actually rerun his own performance, so that in around three minutes he could watch a potted version of his own game. We would use the system to give short presentations for each player, with four or five points they should bear in mind for their next game. The two centres could meet for coffee, and look at what their immediate opposition were likely to do, and consider their own performances in the forthcoming game.

As an extension of this, I was determined that the team room would become the nerve centre of the tour. In 2005, we had a team room here, a medical room there; things were scattered all over the place. But as part of the earlier recce, I found rooms that were big enough for the whole Lions operation, so that in social or rugby terms it was all there. In our team rooms in 2009, you could watch television, play table tennis or snooker. You could sit at a computer during your analysis, and you could also be having physiotherapy. It had everything, and it worked really well.

What we had to do now, as we began to get used to the thin air of the highveld and to our surroundings in Phokeng, was to be Lions. To win rugby matches. And to be a part of what one observer back in Britain had already termed 'the Last Great Sporting Adventure'.

19

Royal Bafokeng

The early stages and the First Test

And, finally, the ball fell and Mike Blair fielded it cleanly. The Royal XV came down with a good chase and when Mike turned the ball inside they swarmed over the contact. We recycled the ball, Mike kicked clear but the ball was charged down and we had to scramble it to safety.

We hoped it was not a bad omen.

It was a struggle, and we won only by 37–25. At one stage, we were trailing 25–13. They scored with quick hands in the first half, and Rayno Barnes, the hooker, came out of a maul and scored what was for us a poor try, also before half-time. Bees Roux scored in the second half to set up their lead.

In the end, we came back well. Lee Byrne had a fine match, and we scored tries from Byrne, Tommy Bowe, Alun Wyn Jones and Ronan O'Gara but, while giving credit to the Royal XV, who were very competitive, some of our play was not great. There is no doubt that the hot weather, humidity and altitude took their toll, and the players reported afterwards that it had been very tough. But we were very disappointed to give away three fairly soft tries, which put us under pressure and obviously fired up the opposition to think that they could win. And a theme began to emerge which we seemed to repeat in some of the following games – we created so many opportunities but we probably blew five or six tries. But in the final analysis we were very under-cooked, and there were some things we had not practised at all or even talked about. The time frame did not allow us to prepare as for a normal game.

The other point of discussion afterwards was the lack of crowd and atmosphere. Down in Pretoria, less than two hours away, the Bulls were playing the Chiefs in the final of the Super 14 but that did not account for all the wide-open spaces. We discovered as the tour went on that the organisers had their ticketing policy totally wrong. The cost for a Bulls ticket was 60 rand but for a Lions game it was 260 rand minimum. The Lions were very open with South Africa. I said from the start that we wanted to train at schools, we wanted to meet people, have lunch at the school or township, wherever we were.

But it should have been the same on the South African side; it was up to them to engage with people from the surrounding areas, and youngsters in particular. We felt that they got it wrong, they should have been well enough organised to fill the stadiums by set-ting the ticket price at no more than a third of what it was. It got to the stage where it was more expensive to watch a Lions provin-cial match from a seat behind the posts than it was to watch England at Twickenham from the best seats.

In Rustenburg we had instigated a dressing-room ritual. I had always tried to impress upon the players the idea that they were the carriers of a Lions shirt, perhaps on one tour, perhaps on more than one; but that ultimately they had to hand it on to someone else to take up the responsibility and honour of holding that shirt.

For every game, therefore, I had plaques put in the dressing room on which were inscribed the names of each player who was representing the Lions for that game, alongside the Lions badge. Below that would be another plaque bearing the names of all the previous Lions who had held the same position.

It made them all winning Lions. So when Mike Phillips went into the dressing room, he saw his plaque with his name on it. Beneath it were the names Gareth Edwards, Dickie Jeeps, Matt Dawson. All the names would come from the winning tours, perhaps from 1971 or 1974, or 1989 or 1997. A few came from 1955, which I know was a drawn series, but that was a heroic tour, and when you read about 1955 you see what they did for the Lions legend.

Shaun Edwards is a great student of history and of former players, simply because he believes, correctly, that you can learn about the present from the past. He loved the plaques; he went along with them, boning up on all the names. He wanted to know what year each player came from.

We also began the tour with another ritual by which a certain person would give out the jerseys to each of the players in the team room. I asked Gerald Davies to hand out the first set before Rustenburg. Andy Irvine, a winning Lion, gave out the second set, for the Golden Lions game, and Graham Rowntree and Rob Howley each had the honour as well.

Before the Cheetahs game, however, the third of the tour, on 6 June, I asked Shaun and Warren if they would take turns for the next two games. They both refused, claiming that they had no right. I assured Shaun that he was a winner, but he insisted that, since he had never played for the Lions, he had no right to pass the jersey on. So we just hung them up after that, although Willie John McBride did give out the jerseys for the First Test. After the first three games, only Gordon D'Arcy had not been presented with a Lions jersey and he got his individually before the Natal game, the fourth of the tour.

The jerseys, as usual, were individually embroidered with the name of the player, the opposition and the date. We tended to take turns as to who would give the last team talk before each game and it was Shaun's turn before we played the Sharks. He didn't say very much, but he did make a pointed reference to the plaques. 'Geech has put them there for a reason. It's up to you to ensure that, next

time a Lions tour takes place, your name is on that plaque.' Then
he turned on his heels and walked out.

Warren made one of the most remarkable comments of the
entire tour when he gave the talk before the next game, one which
showed just how powerfully we were coming together. He had been
very taken by the bond and the intensity that was growing in the
squad, and, after leaving the dressing room, he commented that the
feeling, the environment, created in that room was the closest he
had come to anything engendered by a group talking about an All
Black jersey. 'I just didn't realise how deep it goes,' he said.

That was quite a compliment. And it was worth remembering,
too, that the Lions had done more in South Africa than the All
Blacks. They had already won twice in South Africa, and, at the
end of this tour, we all knew that we should have made it three.
The All Blacks had won only one series.

We were superb against the Golden Lions at Ellis Park. They were
not able to pick their Springbok squad players, but a 74–10 win,
with ten tries, against a team that had a grand tradition against
the Lions from the years they played as Transvaal, was extremely
encouraging.

We won the ball, moved them out to make their forwards work,
brought it back again and, suddenly, we were in behind them.
They were really fired up in the opening stages, and yet we scored
three early tries, moving the ball really well, and the execution was
extremely pleasing. Tommy Bowe and Jamie Roberts played off
each other brilliantly, they and Ugo Monye scored two tries each
and Stephen Ferris, Tom Croft, James Hook and Brian O'Driscoll
also scored.

There was a different atmosphere, altitude and culture at every
venue in which we played and, for game three, we moved across
the high, bare veldt to Bloemfontein to play the Cheetahs. Again,
they were great historic opponents of the Lions, in their former
guise as Orange Free State. And we had to work very hard indeed
to beat them by 26–24.

For the first time, but definitely not for the last, we had massive problems at the breakdown. It had been agreed beforehand with the International Rugby Board and the home teams that players arriving in defence who got their hands on the ball would be allowed to keep their hands on it provided they stayed legal – in other words, stayed on their feet, instead of being supported by other bodies. Heinrich Brüssow, the home flanker, was very quick to get his hands on the ball but then simply fell off his feet on to the ground, and yet he was still allowed to pull the ball back as he lay there. He was very good at doing that, and good luck to him, but it was definitely against the law. It was ironic that the referee who let him get away with it was not from the Southern Hemisphere – he was England's own Wayne Barnes.

It was another of those rather annoying days where we played some great rugby, but then seemed to sit back and become disorganised. We scored twenty points in twenty minutes, with Stephen Ferris and Keith Earls, who had been unhappy in the first game, both scoring and James Hook kicked some goals in a promising personal performance.

But in the end they came back, they scored two good tries, one from their dreadlocked left wing, Danwel Demas, and then another from Wian du Preez. We had to fight to hold on at the end, and especially when we let them in for an interception try in the second half, keeping us ahead by only two points. In the last few minutes, Strydom dropped for goal but his kick was narrowly wide.

We then moved on to Durban and a welcoming breath of sea air as we disembarked at the airport after the flight. We beat the Natal Sharks 39–3, finding a good rhythm late in the game, and following that performance the South Africans began to sit up and take notice of the Lions. Mike Phillips played superbly, and he, Lee Mears, Luke Fitzgerald, Jamie Heaslip and Lee Byrne scored our tries. Roberts was again impressive, and, although their defence was good at first, we kept at it, we ran them around and made the scores.

The try of the match showed exactly what we were trying to do.

Jamie Heaslip took a quick tap, we moved the ball on and Tom Croft fed Brian O'Driscoll in space. We had held our depth and our width and O'Driscoll held the defence to put Fitzgerald over. There was still more talk of quite small crowds, and the fact that we were not meeting any current Springboks, but I was reasonably happy that we had won at the venue for the First Test.

James Hook was another player I feel was helped enormously by being on the tour. He arrived as a replacement for Leigh Halfpenny. He liked the loose, spraying pass, as does Danny Cipriani. They think that it is the best way to beat a defence, but those passes can often be intercepted. We talked to James about playing a tighter game, about getting his short game right first. And he was excellent throughout the tour. He really started thinking about driving the team on, and he learned that you have to earn the right to play wide, by getting the right players in, getting us on the front foot, and then, boof, away we go.

But for every player who came out to join us and become a Lion, there was always someone who had to leave. To say goodbye to someone who has shared the dream, even briefly, and then been robbed of the chance to fulfil it is grim indeed. By the final Test, someone worked out that fifteen of our original selections were either no longer in South Africa or not fit to play.

Tomas O'Leary and Alan Quinlan failed to board at the start because of injury and suspension, hooker Jerry Flannery was injured at Pennyhill Park, and we were to lose Euan Murray, Adam Jones, Gethin Jenkins, Stephen Ferris and Leigh Halfpenny at different stages. Tim Payne, John Hayes, James Hook, Ross Ford, Gordon D'Arcy, Mike Blair and Tom Croft were the beneficiaries. We missed all the departed players, and, if we were to single out just one, we felt that Stephen Ferris was becoming a true Lion, showing both his potential on the field and his ability as a tourist. He seemed to lap it all up.

The Test, meanwhile, was coming at us like a runaway train. We played Western Province at a wet and wild Newlands next up. We scored three tries to one (Martyn Williams, Bowe and Monye) and, yet again, played some good rugby and some inconsistent rugby. We came out ahead at 26–23, thanks to a long penalty by James Hook, and Western Province did themselves great credit. They spoke all week about the honour of playing the Lions and Luke Watson, their captain, who had recently signed for Bath, set a good example.

We scored a really pleasing try when Andy Powell made a burst, stayed on his feet and used his quick feet to make space. He linked with Martyn Williams, kept on running, and then kept our width to the left. Keith Earls and Rob Kearney, who was superb in the conditions, made a try for Tommy Bowe. Bowe still had a lot to do but he finished brilliantly.

Pleasingly, and despite the time frame, there was time to spend with individuals. Andy Powell, as I am sure he would not mind me saying, just needs a bit of love and attention sometimes. He could be hard work for the medics. He had some injury problems early on, put it down to an insect bite and then, later, was putting out stories that he had a double fracture of the thumb. In one of the team meetings, in the dressing room before we went out, Phil Vickery verbally put Andy up against the wall.

But, to be fair to him, Andy buckled down. He is very powerful but he can sometimes come too early or too flat, so it becomes a bit predictable. When he sits back and plays from deep, he looks an outstanding player because he has great footwork to go with his strength. Warren is always at him, and it was incredibly pleasing to see Andy play so well against Western Province, and to be so effective.

The Southern Kings, next up in a one-night stopover in Port Elizabeth, in the new Nelson Mandela Bay Stadium, were really fired up. They were not interested in playing much rugby and they were champions of the off-the-ball stuff, which irritated me greatly at the time. They were a new team, part of a franchise application for a place in an expanded Super 15 tournament. Both their centres, Frikkie Welsh and De Wet Barry, who had unsuccessful careers in the Guinness Premiership, were simply coming in with cheap shots, and there were all kinds of verbals around as well. They had it in mind to stuff us up front, too.

We did not win by much, only 20–8, and we let them in for a try near the end. But I was really pleased with some of our physicality, because, physically, we dominated them. They had a couple of Blue Bulls in the pack but we destroyed them up front and we were awarded a penalty try when they collapsed. Euan Murray was superb in the scrums in this game, and it was a crying shame when he was injured and had to go home. With Northampton and Scotland, he was only ever asked to play in the tight channels and we really worked hard at trying to expand what he was doing, so that he had far more involvement around the field. But, technically, he was probably the best tight head we had, and he could have been a very significant factor in the Tests. He is a considerable player.

It was interesting after the game that some of our guys refused to shake hands with the Southern Kings. It was difficult for them. When you have been hit from behind, long after the ball has gone, and when you have been taking cheap shots all day, it is sometimes difficult simply to shake hands and accept that it is all part of the game, because it isn't. It was never going to be a pretty game, it was a game to come out ahead of, and it was also good for the group who would be involved in the first Test in a few days to see the team at Port Elizabeth, and to realise that this was a group which had been dragged through the mill and won.

We were now in the fifth week, the key week on any Lions tour, the week when only fifteen players could be named to start the first Test. I had said to the players from the start that week five was the one in which anything bad came out; that if there are any underlying problems then people would be upset, they would be bitching at each other, and injuries would seem more stressful. Suddenly, there would be hundreds, maybe thousands, of supporters hanging round, all well-meaning and to be respected, but all adding to the stress. We wanted the players to know that the environment was changing; we even asked that they breakfast in the usual dining rooms, just to get some sense of how things were changing.

When I announced the team, on the Wednesday before the Durban Test, in the team room at the Elangeni hotel on the seafront in Durban, I was as nervous as I had been on any Lions tour. Everybody came in, the management sat at the back, and I made my announcement. We had planned carefully the next item on the agenda. After the announcement, everyone shook hands and we went straight out of the team room on to the buses, and we drove to a restaurant on one of the hills outside Durban. We went as a group, the management sat outside, the players inside. The players were applauded off the buses into the restaurant by Lions fans who were already there.

Warren looked at me: 'I don't know about the players, but when you suddenly realise all the support that we have, the hairs on the back of my neck are prickling.' But the fans never bothered us; they formed two lines and gave us a standing ovation when we walked back to the bus. Phil Vickery and a small group stayed later, because they were having such a good conversation around the table. It all took the edge off the selection announcement, and, as we suspected they would, the players stayed solid, as they had started the tour, and just as they were to finish it.

I probably made a mistake on the Friday afternoon. Instead of going for my usual walk before a Test, this time I decided to go out to a nice little café on the beach. On that Friday, I was swamped before I had even gone 200 metres. There were so many well-wishers that I could hardly move. Later, Paul O'Connell said: 'I saw you trying to have a walk.'

'Well, I never saw you.'

'No. I was the man in the flat cap, the glasses and the wig.'

The whole experience was intensely powerful. So, too, was the sight of tens of thousands of red jerseys in huge banks in the stands at King's Park. We knew the plan; we had known it, in out-line, since Pennyhill Park. We knew if we used our talents, if we ran them around, if we kept ball, we could challenge them, possibly break their line occasionally.

But our opening passages were grim. One report referred to us as 'rabbits in headlights'. We coughed up a line-out too easily and, even though the Springboks then went into their normal attack from close range, we seemed to stand off and John Smit scored a try that was far too easy. They then pulled clear to lead 13–0.

We were also in trouble at the scrum. Tendai Mtawarira was up against Phil Vickery and we were penalised twice early on when Mtawarira, or The Beast, as he is known, got under Vicks. Our scrum was very unstable and that was a huge worry.

But talk about line-breaks. We did more than that. We cut them to pieces; they simply could not handle us in midfield where some of the play of Brian O'Driscoll and Jamie Roberts was stunning. But could we finish? We did score when Jamie's power and Brian's linking put Tom Croft over, but, earlier, we lost a key try. We moved to the left and Ugo Monye, carrying the ball under his right (wrong) arm as he dived (the arm nearer to the defender), gave Jean de Villiers the chance to get underneath him.

But we had bad moments in the second quarter, when the officials started calling foul-play offences from miles away. The worst moment was definitely their try from the driving maul, by Brüssow, at the start of the second half. That took it to 26–7, and you could imagine the thoughts of the supporters – this is 2005 all over again, the Lions can't compete, and so on. We defended those drives really badly. Technically, it was poor, with experienced players making poor decisions, and we were trying to defend individually rather than collectively.

The only good news was that we were still making line-breaks and keeping our shape. Gradually, the courage of the team asserted itself and we kept playing rugby – in fact, we kept playing *all* the rugby. Some of it was quite wonderful. We brought on Adam Jones for Vicks and he was more effective – so much so that we started to gain the edge.

We scored when some great combinations with Matthew Rees

and David Wallace and another big burst by Jamie Roberts put Tom Croft over for his second try. Then we attacked inline up the middle again, picked off their tiring forwards and Phillips scored.

But we had already been denied by tiny margins. At a time when the Springboks were on their knees, Mike Phillips dived with arm outstretched, was brought down short and, as he dived, Bakkies Botha dislodged the ball with a late charge. Afterwards, we heard that Paddy O'Brien, the IRB referee manager, said that the try should have been awarded.

Still later, Ugo Monye was trying to finish another move which had taken the Springboks to the cleaners. He held the ball under his right (wrong) arm yet again and, this time, he lost the ball in a tackle as he stretched the last few millimetres. You had to admire the scramble defence of the Springboks and their determination not to concede tries even when they looked certain.

The Phillips try made it 26–21 with three minutes left. Then Jamie came again, Tommy Bowe stepped inside and, for a fraction of a second, you could see Bowe clear for the line. But the pass went astray.

It was no surprise when we started to come back because we had said all along that if we worked them really hard there would be opportunities in the last fifteen minutes, and there were. At times, in the closing stages, you could see the panic on the faces of the Springboks and you could see that some of their legs were going. In the end, I think we ran out of time, rather than ran out of opposition.

Afterwards people said that it had been an extraordinary Test match and I think that, deep down, we all knew it, but we were incredibly disappointed. We returned to the hotel on the seafront in Durban on the coach, we had something to eat and a few of the guys had a drink in the bar. But I went up to the team room. Rhys Long was there analysing the game. Eventually I had the whole thing downloaded, went back to my room and watched it all again in silence, on my own. I felt that I had to be clear in my own mind, before speaking to the other coaches, because what we did going forward towards the Second Test would define the rest of the tour.

In terms of the Vickery affair, there is no doubt that the referee could have penalised The Beast for pushing Vickery upwards, which is illegal. Also, the way that the Springboks were binding was totally illegal, as Paddy O'Brien picked up after the game. Du Plessis had completely lost his bind. However, Vicks admitted afterwards that he had just left himself open for Mtawarira to get underneath him, which had never been an issue before.

All credit to South Africa for the way they approached it, although Phil did have two or three good scrums where he held him. But, psychologically, to see one of our core players in trouble was a big blow.

But the other problem was that referee Bryce Lawrence decided that South Africa had the dominant scrum. That was certainly the case early on but the truth is that, thereafter and especially in the second half, we took over and he never recognised that. Then Adam Jones came on and he kept Mtawarira very quiet indeed. He handled him with ease.

But back at the controls, I soon had a list with priorities. It read: Keep the ball. Go through the phases. Keep the tempo of the game high. First tackles have to be more accurate. Head up on the kicking game, so that we move the ball when we have the opportunity, rather than just making the decision to kick.

I saw that we had worked them hard through phases and we had to do that again, no matter what. Another thing I noticed was that on occasions we had lost our depth. We had been working hard and then the game ended up in a very confined area. We had asked that the attacking shape be maintained, and that the players we wanted to move the ball to came back deeper. I also saw that every time we drove in really low and underneath them when entering the contact area, we were so much more efficient.

More notes. Patience. Find opportunities. Move to channel – in other words, if we wanted to kick, then we shouldn't kick from one side of the field to the other. If we wanted to kick to the other side of the field, we had to move the ball to that side, draw them up and then kick.

And another major point, maybe the most important. I wrote down that we had to front up physically. We were caught cold in the First Test. There were some verbals and lots of silly off-the-ball stuff from the Springboks. Habana was pushing and shoving off the ball. There were all kinds of things from Du Plessis and Botha and others. We were far too timid in accepting it, we seemed almost to be trying to calm them down rather than just reacting strongly. We had been too soft.

Of course, there was no reaction from the officials on the field. In the week before the Second Test, Paddy O'Brien said that the officials would be cracking down on off-the-ball stuff, making you wonder why he had not said the same before Durban. Before the Second Test I showed the players clips of what had been done to us in Durban. I said: 'The rugby is one thing. But these clips show that you must not be second best with the other stuff. Do not start anything, but, when it starts, show them that you are not going to let them get away with anything.' And that was one of the major differences in the Second Test: we got stuck in together. And we found throughout the tour that we were continually trying to check things with Paddy after the event. It would have been better if he had laid down before the games what would happen, and that his referees had stuck to it. One–nil down. It was a ghastly feeling.

Logistically, we faced a nightmare in the week before the Test in Pretoria. We were trying to recover mentally and physically. We were completing our analysis both of ourselves and of the Springboks, trying to prepare in terms of selection and strategy for the Second Test. But also, while the South Africans were safely in their camp at altitude near Pretoria, there we were down in Cape

Town at sea level also trying to prepare for the Tuesday game against the Emerging Springboks.

The Emerging Springboks game was important because it was a focus for all the players who had not been involved in the match squad for the Second Test, and we were up against a group who were trying to force their way into their national team. However, we let them back in for a 13–13 draw when Danwel Demas scored with the last play of the match and Willem de Waal kicked a great goal from the touchline.

At least it meant that we had gone through the provincial games unbeaten and there was a certain excuse in the fact that we had another day of appalling weather and high wind in Cape Town. But we scored a try from Keith Earls after outstanding play by Martyn Williams and Riki Flutey, and it was disappointing, even given the conditions, that we did not manage more.

I always say to players that on a Lions tour you are asked to do things that you would never be asked to do anywhere in international rugby. We were down in Cape Town because that is where the South Africans said we had to be. One of the points I raised in my tour report would be that decisions on the match itinerary for a Lions tour had to have a rugby input, because, this time, the fixture list had already been agreed and was set in stone before I was appointed, and all we could do was make the best of it.

The best advice on moving to play at altitude is that you either go eight days before the game, or you go so that you have been at altitude for less than twenty-four hours when the match finishes. We were in Cape Town, so we had to switch to the latter strategy. They wanted us to travel on the Wednesday, the day after the Emerging Springboks game, but we would have been in the very worst state come Saturday. So we stayed on in Cape Town, flew up on Friday and we had the flight booked to arrive in Johannesburg after the time of the final whistle on the next day. I think it worked, I think we had it right, because the players reported no serious problems. But, naturally, our planning had to be spot on, and it was. Cape Town airport is being rebuilt for the football World Cup in 2010. In 2009 it was a zoo. Pretoria is not the nicest or the most comfortable of places and the hotel wasn't the greatest either. But this is where Guy Richardson, one of the key appointments I made as logistics officer, came in. He was the ace in the pack. I wanted us to travel as a group to every place we played, and the only way to do that was to be logistically so accurate and so well prepared that it did not become an issue with the players.

Guy arranged for us to check in all the kit and all the heavy baggage the day before the flight so that it could go overland by lorry to Pretoria. On the Friday, we boarded the buses, they took us straight on to the tarmac and parked next to the plane, which was a charter flight. When we arrived in Johannesburg we parked at the side of the airport where the bus was waiting. The players were taken directly to their hotel, where the luggage lorry had already arrived. The baggage for the players that arrived with them on the plane caught up with them in their rooms only about an hour after check-in and we were all safely moved and in situ. Warren and I were whisked off to the usual meeting with Paddy O'Brien and the officials.

Of course, there is a human side to the preparations for any Test match and I have to say I was more nervous before Pretoria than I had been before my first Lions Test match as coach in Sydney in 1989. It is not a good feeling, and I remember thinking to myself that these were the parts of it I did not enjoy. The three or four hours before kick-off can be nerve-wracking and very testing.

We did our final walkthrough in a car park behind the hotel in Pretoria. The forwards did some line-outs, the backs did their stuff, but then we went back to the team room and I showed them the video of the shenanigans of the week before, all the off-the-ball stuff. I told them that they had to make a statement, that they could not accept anything from the Boks. To be fair, they did not. At the very start, Brian O'Driscoll went straight in on Victor Matfield and set the tone. We were starting to show them that we would not be isolated.

People ask me how I followed up my speech before the Second Test in 1997, which was captured on the *Living with Lions* DVD. The answer is that I have not had to try, simply because I always speak from the heart, having consulted a few notes first, and I say what is on my mind at the time. My theme before Pretoria was the Lions jersey. We had decided that there would be no formal presentation to individual players. I wanted the jerseys to be hanging up in the dressing room when the players arrived and Warren Gatland agreed with me. We said that it was not the jersey they put on that meant everything; it was the jersey they took off. In the team room I told the boys that I had seen a lot of Lions jerseys on seven separate tours and that there was no feeling like pulling a winning Lions jersey off each others' backs.

We brought in Simon Shaw and Adam Jones for the Second Test and Lee Byrne was injured and replaced by Rob Kearney. I mentioned Simon Shaw in my speech. It was his eighteenth Lions jersey but it would be the first he got to wear in a Test. I knew that the players loved Shawsy and rated him massively.

Also, I promised that, if we won, the coaches would pull the jerseys off their backs because they would be too exhausted to do it themselves. I said that I loved the jersey because it had changed me. I said that a Lions victory would bring a smile and a welcome for them from rugby people, from Limerick to Edinburgh, from Leicester to Swansea. I said that it would require special hits and slicker hands. That the biggest hit of all might be the first they made and that could be in the first thirty seconds. But that if they made another hit a minute later, then it would feel even more special.

Then I told them that for winning Lions the looks you get all change – be they from South Africans, your parents, wives, girl-friends or families. I told them that they had a chance to reach a very special place.

Loftus Versfeld was special, too. When the players ran out for the destiny match, they saw that the far bank of the vast stadium was a tumultuous sea of red. It brought tears to the eyes. The match that was to take place was later to be described by some as the greatest Test of all time.

There were tears in the eyes afterwards, as well as before.

20

Highveld

The sensational Tests of Pretoria and Johannesburg

Brilliant. Absolutely brilliant. But beaten. In the first half in Pretoria, we played the rugby for which I have always searched. We had hinted at it in some of the provincial games in 1997 and again on the previous Saturday in the First Test. If we could have bottled what we did in Pretoria it would have been a guide to the way rugby should be played, notably in the way we started the Test match and the options we chose. We were playing the best international side in the world, in their own backyard of Loftus Versfeld, and we were watching a Lions team starting to take it apart. It was superb.

We made one defensive error, when Luke Fitzgerald missed his assignment on JP Pietersen, and we gave them a try for nothing from a line-out. It was so soft. But apart from that, they had absolutely no pressure at all, they played on the back foot for forty minutes and, for Test match rugby, that was as good as I have ever seen it.

And we should have been at least twenty points ahead at half-time. Gethin Jenkins, who had a fantastic match, had a chance to put Jamie Roberts in the clear in the middle of the half, then Luke

Fitzgerald was running down the left touchline and one pass inside would have made another try. But we scored from one of our moves, with Simon Shaw taking the ball up the middle and with Rob Kearney crossing wide on the right, and Stephen Jones' kicking pulled us clear.

Nothing worse has ever happened in terms of bad luck and disastrous fortune than what occurred in the second half in Pretoria. South Africa knew they were lucky still to be anywhere near us at half-time and knew they were lucky to have fifteen on the field after Schalk Burger appeared to gouge the eyes of Luke Fitzgerald in the early stages.

But we were still 19–8 in the lead going into the final quarter, we had shut out The Beast and the South African scrum completely, Mike Phillips and Stephen Jones had been running the game well and Simon Shaw was playing what was described afterwards as 'the greatest game in memory for a Test lock'.

Then, both Gethin Jenkins and Adam Jones were injured in the same move. Gethin took a heavy blow and fractured a cheekbone and Adam was struck by Bakkies Botha at the side of the ruck, an offence for which Botha was cited and suspended. So we lost both of them from the match and from the tour, and the scrums, which we had dominated, with Adam Jones almost demolishing The Beast, were suddenly shorn of power. Until the Springboks were able to stop scrummaging, their forwards were simply not in the game. The Beast had done nothing, and Pierre Spies had been invisible. We had worked them hard and they struggled. But suddenly, with no scrummaging, they could lift their heads and they were all running. Spies made a few bursts where before he had been anonymous.

Then we lost both the centres, and, again, it all happened incredibly quickly. We were still leading 19–8 with eighteen minutes to go. Jamie Roberts hurt his wrist in what looked like a fracture and Brian O'Driscoll was concussed; he was all over the place, as if he was punch-drunk. We had to play a centre combination of Stephen Jones and Tommy Bowe.

At least you would never have thought that our fortunes could get any worse. But then we threw the ball in at a line-out, Simon Shaw took it and we started a drive, and referee Christophe Berdos, who had failed to send off Burger for eye-gouging, ran after the play. Suddenly, the touch judge started calling him back. He was shouting, 'It's not straight, not straight', but it was never his call in the first place. Berdos had been standing next to the touch judge, he had exactly the same view and he was happy with what he had seen. He should never have allowed himself to be overruled.

So they got the scrum, and they brought in Bryan Habana from the blind side. He was Brian O'Driscoll's man in that defensive play but Brian was out of it. You can see him on the replay: he is all over the place, he hasn't a clue where he is. And Habana ran past him and escaped and, typically, he put in a superb finishing burst.

It turned the whole game because it gave them hope. Then we had a Jacque Fourie try. Ronan O'Gara missed Fourie down the left and when he made his finishing burst I felt that Tommy Bowe should have hit him harder than he did. But he got the ball down and it all went to the television match official.

Did Fourie put a foot in touch? We will never know because none of the camera angles that South African television provided gave a definitive answer. The key angle, from a camera pointing directly up the touchline from the in-goal, was never shown and, in the absence of evidence to the contrary, the try was awarded and they led by three points, coming back from nowhere.

By now, none of the four three-quarters we had started with were on the field but we found the courage to strike back. We came back to 25–25 when Stephen Jones kicked a late and courageous goal from a distance. I was happy that we had gone for the kick to try to draw the match, rather than speculate that we could get over for the try when the penalty was awarded.

But then, in the dying seconds, Ronan put a kick ahead which he chased to try to recover. It was the wrong choice. He should have been kicking as long as he could to pin them back. By this time, he had suffered his own injury, there was blood all over his face and he was groggy. But he should have been hammering the ball as far down the field as possible. He chased, and, when he arrived, he ran into Fourie du Preez, caught him all wrong, Du Preez flipped over and the referee awarded the penalty.

From his own half in the thin air of the veldt, where the ball flies further, Morne Steyn kicked the goal. The whistle was immediately blown. It was a horrible moment. Without question it was the lowest I have ever felt. The series was lost, incredibly, when I am sure that most of South Africa was already gearing up for the decider in Johannesburg a week later.

In the aftermath to the match, in the dressing room and that evening, the players were numb. They came into the dressing room and, as far as I can remember, no one moved for twenty minutes. They all sat there in their Lions jerseys, in almost complete silence. You were looking at a group of players who had given so much, and to whom losing meant so much. I did say something but I can barely remember what it was. There was no way you could do justice to the way they had played, or to the incredible bad luck they had had, and no way either that you could help them at that stage, not the way they were feeling. That evening we sat together in the team room, as we dispersed into groups. You had to come to terms with it in your own way. I could feel the players' pain.

But something remarkable was already happening. There were hundreds of supporters around, people who had been in that incredible mountain of Lions fans all down the side of the stadium. They were unbelievably supportive, there was absolutely no negativity either from them or from all the members of the British and Irish media who were compiling their reports to send home. We felt really bad in one way, because they had come all that way and, despite their good humour, we had not given them a win. But all this was remarkable because there was none of the negativity that usually surrounds international matches and it was a phenomenon which lasted right through the last week and beyond the end of the tour. One journalist told me that these days the media sees things only in black and white, win or lose, glory or disaster.

It is hard to account for the new feeling in that last week, a week in which everyone seemed proud of us. Perhaps it was the style of rugby we had played; perhaps that everyone realised we had been incredibly unfortunate in so many aspects. In my opinion, none of this was related to the traditional love of an underdog or a moral victory. It was related to how well we had played, to the fact that, in the opinion of myself and many others, we had deserved the victory and that we should have been going on to Johannesburg with the series level. There is absolutely no question, either, that the strength of the Lions as a concept and a squad was given extra power in defeat in Pretoria.

There is no doubt either that, in the end, injuries cost us the game. Our scrum was going like a bomb when suddenly, in the same movement, we had lost both the props who were playing so well and, with the scrum now depowered, it meant that one of our key weapons on the day had been removed. We had been really working their forwards hard; sometimes their big men stood panting with their hands on their knees during breaks in play. Pierre Spies had hardly been seen in the match. But suddenly, with no scrummaging to face, their forwards appeared to find a new lease of life and Spies now had a platform to work from which he had not before.

And within a few short minutes we had lost both our centres, and there is no doubt that on tour Jamie Roberts and Brian O'Driscoll had become the heart and soul of our team; they had given us an incredible ability in defence and also to make line-breaks. Suddenly, we were out there with a three-quarter line which differed in every position from the one with which we had started.

Next morning I got everybody in and we started the long climb out of the despair of the previous day to what we wanted to be a positive climax to the tour, but in those early stages, it seemed like an incredibly long journey. In our hotel in the middle of Pretoria, a noisy place outside which taxis had been touting for business from around dawn, we gathered in the team room.

Gerald Davies felt, as manager, that he had to say something, and then I took over. I said: 'I am really proud for what you did yesterday. You should be really proud of the rugby that you are playing. We are not going to lose that, we are not going to take it away and the biggest thing now is that we must leave South Africa having won a Test.' I felt that the players were of the same mind, as I spoke.

We had arranged for the squad to go on safari for a break. They set off on the two buses, but when they were about two hours up the road, a deputation of players decided that they would rather just come back to our base in Johannesburg and have a drink together and not go on safari. I had already gone on to Johannesburg with Judy, and we spent the day with our daughter Heather searching for her wedding ring, which, considering the way that we were all feeling, was an excellent distraction.

Out on the road into the wilds, Shaun Edwards may well have been niggling the players, because he is not really the safari sort. In any case, only about ten returned on the bus and the rest ploughed on – and never regretted it. Phil Vickery told me when they returned that going on safari was the best thing they could have done. They were in high-quality lodges, they went out on some good game drives, they had a braai in the evening plus dances, and they had a singsong and some beers in the darkness of the South African bush. Those who did not stay the course on the trip realised later that they had made a mistake in not going. But, in any case, everyone had a few drinks. It is no longer medically advisable, so they tell me, to drink your way out of a sporting depression but, in my opinion, it helped us all in those difficult few days after Pretoria.

And our brilliant medics were on the case, too. They had issued a document headed 'Maximising Recovery and Regeneration' with all the latest thinking on diet, stress and therapies – comparing the regenerative properties of the hot bath, Jacuzzi, CV flush, ice bath and the vibration machine. On the subject of alcohol, they said: 'Be smart when consuming alcohol . . . you must have a recovery programme in place. If you go out for a night, be sure to have some Dioralyte in your room before you go out and drink it with water when you go to bed. The following morning you must check your hydration and body weight at regular intervals.'

Dave Campbell, our brilliant chef, came up trumps, too. To lift the mood in the day after the Second Test, he opened something that he called the Phat Phuckers café, and served the company with fish and chips and mushy peas.

For the last week we were back in the Sandton Sun hotel. We gave the players the Monday and Tuesday off, even though we stuck together, and then we met on Tuesday to pick the team for our last game as 2009 Lions. We decided that we needed to freshen it up, and that we also needed freshness in the legs. Tom Croft was one good example. When we watched the video and clocked his work rate and what he had done in Pretoria, we were really impressed. But we asked whether, mentally and physically, Tom could get himself back up to that level. We had Joe Worsley and Martyn Williams to come in for Tom and David Wallace in the back row, and that gave us two hungry flankers for the Third Test.

We also brought in Shane Williams and Ugo Monye. I sensed that both of them were upset with the way things had gone, and the way they had played in earlier games, and I was impressed by Ugo's body language. The message coming from him was that he was demanding another shot, and that he really wanted to show us something. He is quick and powerful, and we were also able to choose him on the right wing. I told him that this meant he was at liberty to carry the ball under his right arm to his heart's content – a reference to the fact that he may well have cost himself two tries in Durban by carrying the ball under his right arm, nearest to the opposition, when he was playing on the left wing. Shane was showing signs of finding himself, too, and so it was a great delight for everyone when the two wings shared the tries between them out on Ellis Park.

But these were probably not the vital selections. Even though we did not make it public, we knew that Jamie Roberts would not recover, barring a miracle, from his wrist injury and so I told Riki Flutey to train as if he would be playing in a Test match. Alongside him, with hardly any other centres standing, we went for Tommy Bowe, because of his physicality and his running.

Riki had no business still to be on the tour. He suffered an injury in the early stages which would normally have taken a month to heal and any lesser professional would have been at home long before the end. But Riki set his alarm for every two hours during the night. For his rehabilitation, he had to fix a contraption on to his knee, which ran cold water through itself. He was back way before time, thanks to his dedication and that of the medical staff and, in the end, he said: 'Look. I feel all right.' He came up trumps and had a superb Test match.

Then we were back to Phil Vickery and the dreadful afternoon he had suffered at the hands of The Beast in Durban. Adam Jones was out of the tour after the charge by Bakkies Botha, and, although we had brought over John Hayes of Ireland as cover, I said to Warren and Graham that there would be no discussion. 'Vicks is playing, not John Hayes. Vicks is starting.' Unless I had seriously misread Vicks for the four years I had worked alongside him, there was no way I was going to let anyone stand in the way of him reasserting himself, working through his demons and emerging as the player I knew him to be. In one sense, Vicks was fortunate because the injury to Adam Jones, who had played so well, gave him a chance to redeem himself which he might not otherwise have had. But to me the magnificent performance he ultimately gave, the way in which in the Third Test he demolished the myth of The Beast, was entirely predictable.

It was all then a question of the boys' mental state. We had said in selection that the worst thing we could say to ourselves, deep inside, was that we had lost the series, it was now too late and thus we could switch off. Then everyone would have said that we had simply never been good enough, and that would have meant that eight Tests had gone by since the Lions had last beaten anyone.

In the end, it was Warren who said it. 'We should just confront the players in the morning. We should tell them what the reality is.' He was as good as his words, of which he had few, but he spoke very powerfully. He reminded the players that the Lions had little respect in New Zealand because it had appeared to people in New Zealand rugby that in 2005 the Lions had given up. He said to the players that it was their choice. They could just opt to finish the tour, to lose by thirty points and get away home. But if the tour did end like that, then they would live with it for the rest of their lives. He pushed every one of the right buttons.

But in any case, the players were never like that. As a group, we were confident that they would stay focused and together and that they would recognise what was at stake. Interestingly, on Friday they called their own meeting, with no coaches present. I heard afterwards that Paul O'Connell had been emotional, outstanding. He spoke from the heart about his desperate need to win in a Lions jersey, something that he had never done before.

So on the Wednesday we were back out, we trained for the first time that week and, after a rather shoddy start, we suddenly just clicked. We did a double session, one in the morning and one in the afternoon, at St David's School, in Sandton. It was there and then that I started believing that we would win at Ellis Park.

Next day, there were other believers. We had a really good session on the Thursday and then another on the Friday. There were some special guests there from the various home unions, together with Ian McLauchlan and also Andy Irvine of the Lions committee. At the end of the session, those onlookers could not believe what they had seen. 'This is incredible,' Andy said. 'We are looking here at a team that has lost the series, and yet the quality of the training and the focus they had was superb.' I think that both Gerald Davies and Andy had had their eyes opened to what a professional rugby team looks like these days, and it was also instructive that the players ran almost all of that final session. It was my last as the head coach of the Lions, and, gratifyingly, it was one of the best.

And, all in all, that last week was one of the most inspirational I have ever experienced, considering what had gone before, considering that we were now about fifteen players short of our original squad, some of them key players. We abandoned the policy of recovery with a bottle of water and a health drink, and we probably went back in time with a fair amount of alcohol. But we drank together, we stayed together, we slept it off and then we found that it was out of our systems.

In the dressing rooms under Ellis Park I asked Warren to speak to the boys. I had already said my final words in the team room, and the message was that it would be criminal if we left South Africa without winning a Test. I spoke about the legacy of leaving a winning Lions jersey, and said that if we won that day we would carry the win forward to Australia in four years' time.

Warren said his piece; he said that some of the players were leaving the Lions jersey for the last time. He picked up a jersey, just before they went out to warm up. He pointed to Martyn Williams, Shane Williams, Joe Worsley, and Phil Vickery. He said that they would never put it on again, that the biggest respect they would get was if they left it as a winning jersey, and that the only thing that South Africa would respect was a Lion beating them. Then he put the jersey down and we went out to warm up.

As the players left the dressing room later for the match, the atmosphere was steamy. Warren and I agreed that there was potential for the match to turn into mayhem, because some of the Lions were pretty hyper. But the Springboks pulled off their normal stunt of delaying their arrival on to the field, and they kept us waiting for a few minutes. It was a good thing, too; it took us down a bit and, when they eventually appeared, I think that we had ourselves under better control.

And in terms of the Springboks, we did feel a danger. They knew that they had been outplayed in rugby terms in two games and, picking up the line of some of their comments, we knew they were going to try to blow us away and to play a lot of rugby. That was dangerous for us. I thought that with Brüssow back in the team their back row looked better balanced and their midfield more dangerous as well. They also had some youngsters dotted around who were desperate to win their places in the Springbok team full-time. So, yes, I was concerned. But as it turned out, the way we played we would have beaten any South African combination on that day. Of that I am convinced.

Phil Vickery and the scrum went down for the first scrummage. We went forward, The Beast went up into the air. He was not penalised, which was incredible, but we had made a statement and our scrum was on top throughout. By the end, we were crushing them. The key scrum came when we knocked on near our own line and South Africa had a scrum within spitting distance. We pushed them off the ball, they went up again and this time they were penalised. It was one of the great Lions moments and it was vindication for Vickery.

Of course, it does help having Simon Shaw behind you in the scrum. It was a brilliant day for Shawsy. He had worn the Lions jersey eighteen times, but never before in a Test match. He had made it at last, he had run on to start the last two Tests, and played absolutely magnificently in both. And there he was behind his Wasps colleague, putting things to rights.

The first half was a revelation to those who felt that we would cave in. After only twenty minutes, the Springbok front five were wheezing, with their hands on their knees. We got messages on to the pitch – 'Keep doing this . . . This is where they're vulnerable. This is where you will get a soft tackle. It's not that there isn't a player there but there's going to be a prop who is done in, has his hands on his knees. If we can get to his channel there is no way

he'll tackle you. Or he might grab you, but then you can offload.'
Graham Rowntree and the conditioners were passing the messages
on.

The tries came. Some of the pace and offloading early on was
thrilling. Riki and Tommy Bowe combined well in an attack,
Jamie Heaslip, who was so much improved, carried the ball
through tackles and Shane Williams ran off him brilliantly and
scored. Then we had a move which was replayed scores of times
that evening when four of the backs just offloaded at lightning
pace and Shane came round the back to link. He was almost clear,
but when he chipped into space there were no chasers; they had all
committed to the breathtaking attack.

But then we scored again. Riki counter-attacked, he chipped
ahead and chased and as he converged with a defender he popped
the ball brilliantly to Shane. One of the few problems we had was
that the ball fell off the kicking tee as Stephen Jones was trying to
convert Shane's first try so we missed out on the two points – it
would have been typical of our ill luck in the series if we had gone
on to lose the match by one point.

But we didn't. Shawsy was sin-binned at the end of the first half
for putting a knee into Fourie du Preez but we went in 15–6 ahead
and our defence had been solid. Stephen and Mike Phillips had
run it brilliantly at half-back and Rob Kearney gave another
immaculate performance. He was massively reassuring.

At half-time we were anxious for a big first ten minutes. We
knew they would be anxious to score and so would be frustrated
if we got the momentum. I told the boys that we needed to keep
the ball through the phases. We did just that. Our forwards took
charge more and more decisively, and as the match went on our
scrum was dominant. We started putting in the best drives of the
tour in the mauls.

We did some other things: we didn't challenge the line-out so
much so we had more players with their feet on the ground. If
they wanted to drive it, we got in early; if they moved it, we'd two
players who were ready on the move for the first breakdown, an

approach we had adopted at Wasps against Leicester in the Heineken Cup final.

They did have one big series of attacks but then they moved it wide and we were still there in position, which Shaun would have loved. Wynand Olivier forced the ball towards Zane Kirchner but Ugo came in off his wing and intercepted. He had 80 metres to go, but we knew it was all over. He had too much gas. He scored under the posts and pictures of our bench show Shaun dancing some strange kind of Wigan jig as Ugo stretched away.

We refused to let them back. They were taking the ball through the phase but losing 20 and 30 metres of ground. There was a kind of Boof! Boof! Boof! in our tackling. We kept playing, and we came home in style. We even had a break from the officials when the touch judge spotted Heinrich Brüssow pulling Mike Phillips to the ground off the ball; and then later when the TMO, ironically, ruled out a try in the corner by Odwa Ndungane. The latter stages of the match were played against a wall of sound from the banks of our supporters: 'Lions! Lions! Lions!' Magnificent.

Towards the end, we knew there was no way we would be caught. We knew that the players would not have to walk through the departure lounge having been whitewashed, that they would be only the third team in thirty-three years to beat South Africa at Ellis Park. The satisfaction was palpable and Warren Gatland, Rob Howley and I left our perches up in the stand and went down to join the guys on the bench.

Just to see the players smiling and hugging at the end, and see and hear the supporters' appreciation was priceless.

It was an epic finale and we probably reached another Lions height. A few weeks later I was watching the Tri-Nations match between New Zealand and Australia. I was looking at the All Blacks and thinking: 'Not as good as the Lions.' They were not as good in their set-ups and in the way they were running. We were making ten line-breaks a match against South Africa throughout the series and in that area they didn't have an answer, they didn't know what we were doing to them. And after our series people were saying, 'This is real rugby.' In the New Zealand–Australia game the commentators were lauding the return of real Test match stuff. It just went to show how wrong everyone was about the experimental law variations, thankfully now discarded.

It was important to remember who had won the series. I found John Smit, the Springboks captain, and congratulated him and also some of the other South African players. The Lions set off not so much on a lap of honour but to thank some of the thousands who had supported us and taken over three stadiums. Suddenly, when we were in the corner of the ground the players realised that the trophy was just about to be presented to John Smit so they all ran back across the pitch to where the podium had been erected and applauded; and, just like the Lions in 1997, the Boks experienced the odd feeling of being presented with a trophy after losing a Test.

Peter de Villiers, the South African coach, came into our dressing room and offered his congratulations. He had had a hard week. He had come out with a comment which appeared to suggest that the gouging of Luke Fitzgerald by Schalk Burger had been somehow part of the rough and tumble of rugby, a comment which attracted a storm of vilification from all sides. One of the things I said on the radio was that if a player has got his fingers on somebody else's face, it should be a red card. And if it was subsequently found that those fingers were anywhere near the eyes, it should be six months. There's no reason why, when you make a tackle, that you should ever have your hands near anybody's face. It never happened before. Why do players suddenly have to do it? Why is it creeping into the game?

He also had to account for the fact that the Springboks had all worn armbands in support of Bakkies Botha, who had been suspended for the match for his charge on Adam Jones, and who would miss far more than one match – six months, to be precise. However, I prefer to take what Peter said as a reflection of the pressure he is always under as coach of South Africa, with all the politics that that involves.

There was certainly a good atmosphere at the official dinner, and John Smit was gracious enough not only to invite Phil Vickery to continue their friendship over beers afterwards but to say that he hoped he formed other friendships. He also said that the honour of playing against the Lions was something that would always live him and his team.

The evening dissolved into informality. Players of both sides left the dinner and socialised together at one of the top city nightclubs. The giant bar area of the Sandton Sun was a vast throng of red shirts and post-match festivity. Some of the parents and families of the players were in there, including the gigantic and unmistakeable figure of Jack Shaw, bigger even than his son, Simon, who had followed a heroic career and won a Lions test. The parents of Tim Payne were also there. Tim had come down as a replacement, he played in one game against the Emerging Springboks, but his parents had come down after that game to enjoy the last lap of the tour, safe in the knowledge that their son had crossed the boundary.

In the middle of the throng, Alun Wyn Jones stood on a table conducting a massed and inconsistent choir of revellers in a singsong. Only in rugby . . .

The Lions jersey would next be seen in Australia in 2013, and, over the intervening years, it would be seen as a winning jersey, because when it was last worn it had been worn with honour, courage, unity and enormous skill, and in victory.

On Sunday there was the final press conference. I sat with James Robson, who gave the final casualty count, patiently explaining the list of injuries and then, because he is the man he is, expressing concern at the savagery of some of the hits in the modern game, and expressing the hope that the game would turn back, away from brute force and towards smaller, more skilful players. I won't hold my breath.

Would I consider becoming head coach of the Lions again, I was asked by the attendant journalists, a good number of whom had reported on all four of my tours as head coach?

'No,' I said.

We had had a good relationship with the media and I was pleased to present a signed jersey to Peter Jackson, the long-serving *Daily Mail* man, who was retiring after the tour.

On the Monday we had the last meeting as a squad. A group of Lions, from different countries, had already decided to holiday together after the tour. Players spoke about the fact that there would be a different feeling now when they met their fellow Lions in opposition in the Six Nations. No less ferocious or determined, just with a different feeling and a new respect.

At the last meeting, Gerald Davies made presentations to the liaison officers, there were a few more formalities and then they fished out a signed sketch of me that they had commissioned and which had been signed by the players. It called me The Ultimate Lion. Phew. I would have appreciated the gesture had I been there – instead I was with Simon Shaw at a disciplinary hearing. The big man had been cited for his knee drop on Fourie du Preez – clumsy but not calculated – and he was banned for two weeks. He managed to contain his grief.

The most emotional part for me had been speaking to the players in the hotel before the final Test. It was the last time I'd address them in anger, so to speak, and I had enjoyed their commitment, their courage, their skill, their company and their unity. It was odd to think when I woke on Sunday that there were no more sessions, no more analysis, there was no speech to prepare. Actually, I realised that the Third Test was probably being analysed at that very moment – by the coaching teams of New Zealand and Australia, with the Tri-Nations coming up.

Someone asked me if my entire life as a Lion flashed before me at the end. It was not like that. It will only hurt me when the next Lions tour is being planned, when people are breathing life into the greatest concept and the greatest team in rugby. That is when I will miss it, very badly.

Who became great Lions? The coaches sat down on the Saturday evening and had a quiet drink. It was still close to the game, but we went through the players who had fronted up in the Test that was impossible to win. Sheridan, Rees and Vickery. Outstanding. Shaw and O'Connell? Outstanding. Martyn Williams and Joe Worsley? Outstanding. Jamie Heaslip? Probably the best game he had played in his life. That Test team delivered to a man.

Jamie Roberts was the official player of the tour, and no argument from me there. He can be quite exceptional in the future because he has power but he also has quick feet, and I am sure that Brian O'Driscoll enjoyed playing alongside him – and Brian was outstanding, too. And he enjoyed it.

He came out with that lovely line. On some tours, when he entered a room he looked for an empty seat next to the people he wanted to sit by. On this tour, he simply went to the nearest empty seat, knowing that he would find good company wherever he landed. Mike Phillips was very close as my player of the tour, too – Mike needs some handling, but he is going to be tremendous. There was Rob Kearney, the courage of Stephen Jones. You can go right on.

But then you have the people who contributed without being Test regulars, those like Donncha O'Callaghan. The message from him was that he would do anything we wanted. But, in the end, what was so good about the group was the collective, their hard work, their unity. It was quite sensational and they deserved better.

And in the final analysis, too, I was proud of my choice of Paul O'Connell as captain. People asked if he was a great player. Warren says that he has never seen anyone as clever as Paul in the line-out, which is some testimony. He was an outstanding man and leader, and he had the total respect of the team. He was backed up by the senior men, Phil Vickery, Martyn Williams, Brian O'Driscoll. But he had that special Lions aura about him, from Pennyhill Park to the very end.

Regrets? You cannot go through the process of something like a Lions tour and have none. In retrospect, I think I'd say that we should have picked Simon Shaw for the First Test, when we were slow in fronting up and taken by surprise by the Springbok antics off the ball. We also conceded the try from the series of driving mauls which Simon is so good at stopping.

But it is also important to remember that we promised we would pick players on form. Alun Wyn Jones and Lee Mears, who played in the First Test, had done so well in the early games, and they took their chances. The ideal length of the tour is probably two games longer than we had, so it was all a little rushed. But, apart from this, I have very few regrets about things we could have changed, and would pick the same players again for the Lions if I was picking the team today.

The tour sits right up there as one of the best in my experience. As a professional operation, linking players, coaches, medics, conditioners, analysts, it was the best yet. There was no one who did not get on.

On Tuesday 6 July we landed at Heathrow and the party ceased to exist. We realised that the reports we had heard were true, and that people at home were proud of us in defeat.

When I walked into the house, Judy showed me what she had done with the lawn while I was away. Nothing. The grass was several feet high. It was like a hayfield. She did not say whether this was in retaliation for all the times I had gone on interminable tours just as we had moved into a new house or when she had had to set up the new home by herself.

It was only when I reached home that I realised how tired I was. On the tour, I didn't think about it. I was working till maybe ten or eleven at night or later and there might be just the odd hour off during the day. When you come home and actually get the time, you suddenly wilt. Happily, there were still arrangements for Heather's wedding to Charlie Beech to organise, so no time to brood.

But first things first. After a cup of tea, I went outside to cut the grass. Every morning for the past seven weeks I had consulted the list provided by the splendid Louise Ramsay, to see where we had to be that day and when, and wearing what – which of our myriad kit combinations we had to wear. Maybe the white training top with the red rain jacket and the performance T-shirt?

But back at home, I had no idea what I should wear to cut my own lawn. What was the proper dress? I took no chances. I wore my British and Irish Lions 2009 tracksuit.

21

Advance on Australia

Future Lions, and living room

In the end, the widespread view was that the whole concept of the Lions tour had been entirely vindicated, but if there are any remaining pockets of resistance I would refer them to the players. You can take my word for it, with my experience of seven Lions tours, I can tell you for nothing that hundreds and maybe even thousands of young men involved in rugby in Britain and Ireland have been looking into the future, working out at what age they will reach their peak and dreaming of the day when they may be good enough to tour with the Lions.

The great driving force behind the whole concept of the Lions is not the fact that so many people want to follow them, nor even that anyone in their right mind would want to coach them, and certainly not to make money, for, while they are very profitable, to see them as a vehicle for profit is anathema to anyone truly involved. The true driving force is the appetite for the Lions shown in the hearts of the top players. They are the ones who help to maintain the dream and for anyone to take away that dream, to deny the Lions a future, would be a disgrace.

But the Lions have now lost four of their last six tours, and one thing they were never meant to be was gallant losers before they had even left home shores, to be patted on the head and sent away every four years, a bunch of battered and worn players stepping straight off the domestic rugby field into the stadium where the first Lions tour match is to be played. I am optimistic that the Lions will carry on in the future, but I would be far more optimistic about their chances of success were it not for the fact that my tour report for 2009 will read remarkably like the one I filed in 1993.

Yes, we still need the three-week gap between the end of the domestic season and the Lions' departure. We cannot ask people to travel tired or wounded. Yes, we do need a minimum of twelve matches on tour. The constriction of the 2009 tour in an odd way added to the coaching challenge because we had to be absolutely perfect. But some players had only two matches to show us what they could do and it would be good to have at least two more tour matches before the First Test.

As far as I know, on the IRB international calendar there are only World Cups and Lions tours. We tear up that calendar every World Cup season and start again; absolutely everything is changed. Can it really be beyond the wit of those directly involved to say now, four years before the tour of Australia: 'This is what a Lions season will look like'? We are not asking anyone to tear the guts out of the season, but just to change things to open a small window of a few weeks, just to make the weight imposed by the time frame a little less onerous.

There are still too many people who are rather two-faced about the Lions. You have the Unions taking one track, you have the PRL in England, you have the European Rugby Cup in Europe, and the Magners League in the Celtic nations, all stating their support but sometimes not matching their words with actions. The relationships are also difficult, because the Lions cannot deal directly with the clubs, so you have this muddled procedure.

But the Lions are a professional operation, they will make around £4 million profit from South Africa 2009 and to get the players earlier and more rested they have to pay compensation to their clubs. If events are slightly altered or moved forward, well, part of the professional business is to pay compensation. That is what must happen.

And the countries hosting the Lions must come to the party as well. If you are telling the hosts that 40,000 people will be coming at some stage of the tour to support the Lions, then it gives you clout. In 2013, Australia cannot fix the tour just to suit themselves; they cannot shunt the tour party round so that simply to arrive at the Test venues becomes a logistical nightmare, let alone get there early enough. We managed our logistics brilliantly in South Africa, and at least in Australia you do not have the problem of changing altitudes.

But the hosts are beholden to the Lions as much as the Lions are beholden to their hosts. One of the problems in South Africa was that the fixture list was arranged without any rugby input, so we were stuck by the sea in Cape Town when we should have been up in the clouds in Pretoria. It was also sad to see players arriving at Pennyhill Park in dribs and drabs and then having to leave the camp to go back to play in domestic competitions. When the Lions meet, that should be it until Heathrow on the way back at the end of the tour.

Throughout the summer after our return people were coming up to me in shops and restaurants and even on the cruise liner *Fantasia*, on which Judy and I enjoyed a short Mediterranean cruise, all wanting to talk about the Lions. One epitaph of the tour in a newspaper read: 'Please do not tell me that even the World Cup is bigger than the Lions. It is not. The Lions prove conclusively that there is greatness in history, that progress does not mean the demolishing of all the good things that put you in a position to progress. It is too much in this greedy era in rugby to expect enough people to make the Lions the absolute priority, even though for the players, they are the absolute priority.

'But rugby in Britain and Ireland with its mealy mouth, has to reckon with an unfortunate outcome of the fact that too many unions and clubs and competitions have scrambled around and got in the way of the Lions. Self-interest and short-sightedness gone mad. The fact is that the Lions have lost four of the previous six series, but if they had been allowed to prepare properly and to tour with rested players, if the tours had been set up as they should have been, then the Lions would, beyond all doubt, have won five of those six Test series. The 2009 Lions were absolutely wonderful, some of the rugby they played was majestic.

'They were the better team in the Test series, but they were savaged by ill luck. And they were also shot in the back.

'The three-Test series that the Lions played in South Africa was arguably, in terms of class and drama and heart-stopping twists, the greatest there has been. At the moment, British and Irish rugby should be feeling on top of the world. But now, as usual after many Lions tours, it feels a sense of glory torn away.'

You could not have a Test series like that if the sport itself was not in good shape, and I firmly believe that it is, and that rugby will go from strength to strength. I was very anxious about the experimental laws, and I am delighted that they have been drummed out, because they took away all the variety in the game, all the different aspects of attack, and they made rugby homogenised.

Obviously, there are huge problems at the breakdown, and it is long past the time that they are sorted out because, if we can free up the sport there, it can be a brilliant spectacle. The tackler has been lying around for years without rolling away, and it is time that he was given every encouragement to do so.

During the final press conference of the Lions tour, James Robson, the Lions doctor, expressed concern about the colossal hits which now regularly occur in the professional game. He may be right to be concerned, but I also feel that dangerous contact occurs when teams are operating on a narrow front, and the more teams play with width and pace the less dangerous the hits will be – and the more that players like Ugo Monye, Shane Williams and the others will thrive. There is still a place for them in the game; they can still thrill us.

When Wasps and I parted company at the end of the 2008–09 season, people wanted to know what my next move would be. I was pleased to tell them that there was no hurry, and that I intended to put off any decision until Christmas of that year, and, in the meantime, would enjoy Heather's wedding and a holiday. I would certainly like to guide and mentor top coaches, of which there are some very good ones around, and I have been approached by some since the end of the tour. In my capacity as head of Sports Coach UK, I would like to use my influence with government and politicians to elevate sport in the pecking order. You have only to experience 25,000 delighted Lions fans to learn all you need to know about the feel-good factor sport engenders, let alone the health benefits.

With experience, I have learned that it is not essential to have the last word or to take all the credit as head coach; nor is it essential to keep your thoughts to yourself as if they were state secrets. I am quite happy to share my notes – thirty years' worth – and my thoughts with other coaches, to talk to anyone about how I go about things. But in any case, in any new season, the absolute priority is to approach it with freshness, to have the same core stuff which never changes, certainly, but to find ways of being different. I still get the same excitement about that process, still get as much enjoyment about talking rugby now as I did at Headingley in the old days, with Jim Telfer with Scotland and with my admirable coaching group in South Africa.

But those who know me well have predicted that I will find it difficult to step away from the extreme edge, that I will miss the pressure of the professional game come Saturday. That is true. I will miss it terribly.

It is easy to say that football managers are under more pressure, with the size of their competitions and audiences and the telephone number salaries that their players earn. But I can tell you that there are times before important matches when I have wondered what the hell I am doing. Even on the Lions tour, there were, as usual, a few hours in every week when I was questioning

everything about myself. The winning imperative in the professional game is hard going. But I will still miss it.

The compensations for me have been the joy that I have been
able to engender in others, in those players who have pushed
themselves and achieved things that they felt were far beyond
them. To see the reaction in the dressing room in Johannesburg in
July after the Third Test, to see players who feared that they would
never get the chance to feel such emotions, was unbelievably satisfying, and I think that most of my satisfaction has come through
the responses of other people.

And most would agree that in rugby the real pleasures come not
from technical matters or even the triumph of playing or coaching, but from people themselves. Rugby has a marvellous image
and when people come up to me and tell me what great rugby we
played, it makes me realise that I am involved with a wonderful
sport. It makes everything worthwhile.

Of all the highlights of my career, the most amazing have been
the seven Lions tours, each one of them totally different from the
other. Seven adventures, seven crusades. Somehow or other I
would like others to benefit from the store of knowledge and experience I have amassed during those years, to pass some of it on to
the next head coach, or perhaps make use of it as the next Lions
tour, to Australia in 2013, starts to build momentum.

Shaun Edwards is a man who can touch you deeply. On the
way home from South Africa, we spoke about the future. 'You've
got to be involved in Australia,' he said. 'You must find a way to
be part of it.' The Lions live on.

In 1980, just after I had started to coach Headingley, immediately
after my retirement from playing had raised Judy's hopes that I
might be around more, she asked: 'How long are you going to be
doing this coaching for, then?'

'Oh, I don't know,' I said. 'Just until I run out of ideas.'

Statistics

Test Career for the British/Irish Lions

- **McGeechan, I R** (*Headingley and Scotland*) 1974 SA 1,2,3,4, 1977 NZ 1,2,3(R),4
- Eight Tests, four wins, one draw and three defeats
- Seven Tests as a centre and one as a replacement wing
- Played in winning series in South Africa
- Points – Three (One dropped goal)

TEST 1 Won 12–3 v South Africa, 8 June 1974, Newlands, Cape Town

BRITISH/IRISH LIONS: J P R Williams; W C C Steele, **I R McGeechan**, R A Milliken, J J Williams; P Bennett, G O Edwards; J McLauchlan, R W Windsor, F E Cotton, W J McBride (*captain*), G L Brown, R M Uttley, T M Davies, J F Slattery

Lions scorers *Penalty Goals:* Bennett (3) *Dropped Goal:* Edwards

TEST 2 Won 28–9 v South Africa, 22 June 1974, Loftus Versfeld, Pretoria

BRITISH/IRISH LIONS: J P R Williams; W C C Steele, **I R McGeechan**, R A Milliken, J J Williams; P Bennett, G O Edwards; J McLauchlan, R W Windsor, F E Cotton, W J McBride (*captain*), G L Brown, R M Uttley, T M Davies, J F Slattery

Lions scorers *Tries:* J J Williams (2), Milliken, Bennett, Brown *Conversion:* Bennett *Penalty Goal:* Bennett *Dropped Goal:* **McGeechan**

TEST 3 Won 26–9 v South Africa, 13 July 1974, Boet Erasmus Stadium, Port Elizabeth

BRITISH/IRISH LIONS: J P R Williams; A R Irvine, **I R McGeechan**, R A Milliken, J J Williams; P Bennett, G O Edwards; J McLauchlan, R W Windsor, F E Cotton, W J McBride (*captain*), G L Brown, R M Uttley, T M Davies, J F Slattery

Lions scorers *Tries:* J J Williams (2), Brown *Conversion:* Irvine *Penalty Goals:* Irvine (2) *Dropped Goals:* Bennett (2)

TEST 4 Drawn 13–13 v South Africa, 27 July 1974, Ellis Park, Johannesburg

BRITISH/IRISH LIONS: J P R Williams; A R Irvine, **I R McGeechan**, R A Milliken, J J Williams; P Bennett, G O Edwards; J McLauchlan, R W Windsor, F E Cotton, W J McBride (*captain*), C W Ralston, R M Uttley, T M Davies, J F Slattery

Lions scorers *Tries:* Irvine, Uttley *Conversion:* Bennett *Penalty Goal:* Irvine

TEST 5 Lost 12–16 v New Zealand, 18 June 1977, Athletic Park, Wellington

BRITISH/IRISH LIONS: A R Irvine; P J Squires, S P Fenwick, **I R McGeechan**, J J Williams; P Bennett (*captain*), D B Williams; P A Orr, R W Windsor, G Price, A J Martin, M I Keane, T J Cobner, W P Duggan, T P Evans

Lions scorers *Penalty Goals:* Bennett (3), Irvine

TEST 6 Won 13–9 v New Zealand, 9 July 1977, Lancaster Park, Christchurch

BRITISH/IRISH LIONS: A R Irvine; J J Williams, S P Fenwick, **I R McGeechan**, G L Evans; P Bennett (*captain*), D B Williams; F E Cotton, P J Wheeler, G Price, W B Beaumont, G L Brown, T J Cobner, W P Duggan, D L Quinnell

Lions scorers *Try:* J J Williams *Penalty Goals:* Bennett (3)

TEST 7 Lost 7–19 v New Zealand, 30 July 1977, Carisbrook, Dunedin

BRITISH/IRISH LIONS: A R Irvine; J J Williams (rep by **I R McGeechan**), S P Fenwick, D H Burcher, G L Evans; P Bennett (*captain*), D B Williams (rep by D W Morgan); F E Cotton, P J Wheeler, G Price, W B Beaumont, G L Brown, T J Cobner, W P Duggan, D L Quinnell

Lions scorers *Try:* Duggan *Penalty Goal:* Irvine

TEST 8 Lost 9–10 v New Zealand, 13 August 1977, Eden Park, Auckland

BRITISH/IRISH LIONS: A R Irvine; H E Rees, S P Fenwick, **I R McGeechan**, G L Evans; P Bennett (*captain*), D W Morgan; F E Cotton, P J Wheeler, G Price, W B Beaumont, G L Brown, J Squire, W P Duggan, A Neary

Lions scorer *Try:* Morgan *Conversion:* Morgan *Penalty Goal:* Morgan

Playing Career with the British/Irish Lions

1974 to South Africa

Lions record: P 22 W 21 D 1 L 0 For 729 Against 207

* Matches played in asterisked

Date	Venue	Opponent	Result	Notes
15 May	Potchefstroom	Western Transvaal	W 59–13*	Played centre
18 May	Windhoek	South-West Africa	W 23–16	
22 May	Wellington	Boland	W 33–6*	Played centre
25 May	Port Elizabeth	Eastern Province	W 28–14	
29 May	Mossel Bay	SW Districts	W 97–0	
1 June	Cape Town	Western Province	W 17–8*	Played centre
4 June	Goodwood	SA Federation	W 37–6	
8 June	Cape Town	SOUTH AFRICA	W 12–3*	Played centre
11 June	Cape Town	Southern Universities	W 26–4	
15 June	Johannesburg	Transvaal	W 23–15	
18 June	Salisbury	Rhodesia	W 42–6*	Played fly-half
22 June	Pretoria	SOUTH AFRICA	W 28–9*	1DG Played centre

27 June	Johannesburg	Quaggas	W 20–16*	Played fly-half
29 June	Bloemfontein	Orange Free State	W 11–9*	Played fly-half
3 July	Kimberley	Griqualand West	W 69–16	Played fly-half
6 July	Pretoria	Northern Transvaal	W 16–12*	Played fly-half
9 July	East London	Leopards	W 56–10*	Played centre
13 July	Port Elizabeth	SOUTH AFRICA	W 26–9*	Played centre
17 July	East London	Border	W 26–6*	Played fly-half
20 July	Durban	Natal	W 34–6	
23 July	Springs	Eastern Transvaal	W 33–10*	1T Played centre
27 July	Johannesburg	SOUTH AFRICA	D 13–13*	Played centre

14 appearances – one try and one dropped goal: seven points.

1977 to New Zealand & Fiji

Lions record: P 26 W 21 D 0 L 5 For 607 Against 320

* Matches played in asterisked

Date	Location	Opponent	Result	Notes
18 May	Masterton	Wairarapa-Bush	W 41–13*	Played centre
21 May	Napier	Hawke's Bay	W 13–11	
25 May	Gisborne	Poverty Bay-E Coast	W 25–6*	Led side 2T Played centre
28 May	New Plymouth	Taranaki	W 21–13	
1 June	Taumarunui	K Country/Wanganui	W 60–9*	Played centre
4 June	Palmerston North	Manawatu/Horowhenua	W 18–12	
8 June	Dunedin	Otago	W 12–7	
11 June	Invercargill	Southland	W 20–12*	Played centre
14 June	Christchurch	NZ Universities	L 9–21*	Led side. Played centre
18 June	Wellington	NEW ZEALAND	L 12–16*	Played centre
22 June	Timaru	South/Mid Canterbury	W 45–6*	Played fly-half
25 June	Christchurch	Canterbury	W 14–13	
29 June	Westport	West Coast/Buller	W 45–0	

2 July	Wellington	Wellington	W 13–6*	Played centre
5 July	Blenheim	Marlborough/Nelson B	W 40–23	
9 July	Christchurch	NEW ZEALAND	W 13–9*	Played centre
13 July	Auckland	NZ Maori	W 22–19	
16 July	Hamilton	Waikato	W 18–13*	Played centre
20 July	Wellington	NZ Juniors	W 19–9*	Played centre
23 July	Auckland	Auckland	W 34–15	
30 July	Dunedin	NEW ZEALAND	L 7–19*	Replaced JJ Williams (32')
3 August	Pukekohe	Counties/Thames Valley	W 35–10	
6 August	Whangarei	N Auckland	W 18–7*	1T. Played centre
9 August	Rotorua	Bay of Plenty	W 23–16*	Replaced Gibson (30')
13 August	Auckland	NEW ZEALAND	L 9–10*	Played centre
16 August	Suva	Fiji	L 21–25*	Played centre

16 appearances – three tries: twelve points.

Test Career for Scotland

- **McGeechan, I R** (Headingley) 1972 NZ, 1973 F, W, I, E, P, 1974 W, E, I, F, 1975 I, F, W, E, NZ, A, 1976 F, W, E, I, 1977 E, I, F, W, 1978 I, F, W, NZ, 1979 W, E, I, F
- He won 32 caps for Scotland. 12 of his appearances were at fly-half and 20 at centre.
- He played in eleven Scotland wins, two draws and was on the losing side 19 times.
- His 21 points for Scotland came from seven dropped goals.
- In nine matches as Scotland's captain he led them to one win, two draws and six defeats.

MATCH 1 Lost 9–14 v New Zealand, 16 December 1972, Murrayfield

SCOTLAND: A R Irvine; W C C Steele, I W Forsyth, J M Renwick, D Shedden; **I R McGeechan**, I G McCrae; J McLauchlan, R L Clark, A B Carmichael, A F McHarg, G L Brown, N A MacEwan, P C Brown (*captain*), R J Arneil

Scotland scorers *Penalty Goals:* Irvine (2) *Dropped Goal:* **McGeechan**

MATCH 2 Lost 13–16 v France, 13 January 1973, Parc des Princes, Paris

SCOTLAND: A R Irvine; W C C Steele, I W Forsyth, J M Renwick, D Shedden; **I R McGeechan**, A J M Lawson; J McLauchlan, R L Clark, A B Carmichael, A F McHarg, R W J Wright, N A MacEwan, P C Brown (*captain*), W Lauder

Scotland scorers *Try:* Lawson *Penalty Goals:* P C Brown (2) *Dropped Goal:* **McGeechan**

MATCH 3 Won 10–9 v Wales, 3 February 1973, Murrayfield

SCOTLAND: A R Irvine; W C C Steele, **I R McGeechan**, I W Forsyth, D Shedden; C M Telfer, D W Morgan; J McLauchlan (*captain*), R L Clark, A B Carmichael, A F McHarg, P C Brown, N A MacEwan, G M Strachan, J G Millican

Scotland scorers *Tries:* Telfer, Steele *Conversion:* Morgan

MATCH 4 Won 19–14 v Ireland, 24 February 1973, Murrayfield

SCOTLAND: A R Irvine; W C C Steele, **I R McGeechan**, I W Forsyth, D Shedden; C M Telfer, D W Morgan; J McLauchlan (*captain*) (rep by R D H Bryce), R L Clark, A B Carmichael, A F McHarg, P C Brown, N A MacEwan, G M Strachan, J G Millican

Scotland scorers *Try:* Forsyth *Penalty Goals:* Morgan (2) *Dropped Goals:* Morgan (2), **McGeechan**

MATCH 5 Lost 13–20 v England, 17 March 1973, Twickenham

SCOTLAND: A R Irvine; W C C Steele, **I R McGeechan**, I W Forsyth, D Shedden; C M Telfer, D W Morgan; J McLauchlan (*captain*), R L Clark, A B Carmichael, A F McHarg, P C Brown, N A MacEwan, G M Strachan, J G Millican (rep by G L Brown)

Scotland scorers *Tries:* Steele (2) *Conversion:* Irvine *Penalty Goal:* Morgan

MATCH 6 Won 27–16 v SRU President's Overseas XV, 31 March 1973, Murrayfield

SCOTLAND: A R Irvine; A D Gill, **I R McGeechan** (rep by J N M Frame), I W Forsyth, D Shedden; C M Telfer, D W Morgan; J McLauchlan (*captain*), R L Clark, A B Carmichael, A F McHarg, G L Brown, N A MacEwan, P C Brown, G M Strachan

Scotland scorers *Tries:* Gill (2), Shedden, McHarg, Telfer *Conversions:* Irvine (2) *Penalty Goal:* Irvine

MATCH 7 Lost 0–6 v Wales, 19 January 1974, Cardiff Arms Park

SCOTLAND: A R Irvine; A D Gill, J M Renwick, **I R McGeechan**, L G Dick; C M Telfer, A J M Lawson; J McLauchlan (*captain*), D F Madsen, A B Carmichael, A F McHarg, G L Brown, N A MacEwan, W S Watson, W Lauder

MATCH 8 Won 16–14 v England, 2 February 1974, Murrayfield

SCOTLAND: A R Irvine; A D Gill, J M Renwick, **I R McGeechan**, L G Dick; C M Telfer, A J M Lawson; J McLauchlan (*captain*), D F Madsen, A B Carmichael, A F McHarg, G L Brown, N A MacEwan, W S Watson, W Lauder

Scotland scorers *Tries:* Lauder, Irvine *Conversion:* Irvine *Penalty Goals:* Irvine (2)

MATCH 9 Lost 6–9 v Ireland, 2 March 1974, Lansdowne Road, Dublin

SCOTLAND: A R Irvine; A D Gill, J M Renwick, **I R McGeechan**, L G Dick; C M Telfer, D W Morgan; J McLauchlan (*captain*), D F Madsen, A B Carmichael, A F McHarg, G L Brown, N A MacEwan, W S Watson, W Lauder

Scotland scorer *Penalty Goals:* Irvine (2)

MATCH 10 Won 19–6 v France, 16 March 1974, Murrayfield

SCOTLAND: A R Irvine; A D Gill, J M Renwick, M D Hunter, L G Dick; **I R McGeechan**, D W Morgan; J McLauchlan (*captain*), D F Madsen, A B Carmichael, A F McHarg, G L Brown, N A MacEwan (rep by I A Barnes), W S Watson, W Lauder

Scotland scorers *Tries:* Dick, McHarg *Conversion:* Irvine *Penalty Goals:* Irvine (2), Morgan

MATCH 11 Won 20–13 v Ireland, 1 February 1975, Murrayfield

SCOTLAND: A R Irvine; W C C Steele, J M Renwick, D L Bell, L G Dick; **I R McGeechan**, D W Morgan; J McLauchlan (*captain*), D F Madsen, A B Carmichael, A F McHarg, G L Brown, M A Biggar, D G Leslie, W Lauder

Scotland scorers *Tries:* Steele, Renwick *Penalty Goals:* Irvine (2) *Dropped Goals:* **McGeechan**, Morgan

MATCH 12 Lost 9–10 v France, 15 February 1975, Parc des Princes, Paris

SCOTLAND: A R Irvine; W C C Steele, J M Renwick, D L Bell, L
G Dick; **I R McGeechan**, D W Morgan; J McLauchlan (*captain*), D
F Madsen, A B Carmichael, A F McHarg, G L Brown, M A Biggar, D
G Leslie, W Lauder

Scotland scorer *Penalty Goals:* Irvine (3)

MATCH 13 Won 12–10 v Wales, 1 March 1975, Murrayfield

SCOTLAND: A R Irvine; W C C Steele, J M Renwick, D L Bell, L
G Dick; **I R McGeechan**, D W Morgan; J McLauchlan (*captain*), D
F Madsen, A B Carmichael, A F McHarg, G L Brown, M A Biggar, D
G Leslie, N A MacEwan

Scotland scorers *Penalty Goals:* Morgan (3) *Dropped Goal:*
McGeechan

MATCH 14 Lost 6–7 v England, 15 March 1975, Twickenham

SCOTLAND: A R Irvine; W C C Steele, J M Renwick, D L Bell, L
G Dick; **I R McGeechan**, D W Morgan; J McLauchlan (*captain*), D
F Madsen, A B Carmichael, A F McHarg, G L Brown, M A Biggar, D
G Leslie, N A MacEwan (rep by I A Barnes)

Scotland scorer *Penalty Goals:* Morgan (2)

MATCH 15 Lost 0–24 v New Zealand, 14 June 1975, Eden Park, Auckland

SCOTLAND: B H Hay (rep by W C C Steele); A R Irvine, J M
Renwick, G A Birkett, L G Dick; **I R McGeechan**, D W Morgan; J
McLauchlan (*captain*), C D Fisher, A B Carmichael, I A Barnes, A F
McHarg, D G Leslie, W S Watson, W Lauder

MATCH 16 Won 10–3 v Australia, 6 December 1975, Murrayfield

SCOTLAND: B H Hay; A R Irvine, J M Renwick, **I R McGeechan**,
L G Dick; C M Telfer, D W Morgan; J McLauchlan (*captain*), C D
Fisher, A B Carmichael, A F McHarg, G L Brown, W Lauder, G Y
Mackie, D G Leslie

Scotland scorers *Tries:* Dick, Renwick *Conversion:* Morgan

MATCH 17 Lost 6-13 v France, 10 January 1976, Murrayfield

SCOTLAND: B H Hay; A R Irvine, J M Renwick, **I R McGeechan**, L G Dick; C M Telfer, D W Morgan; J McLauchlan (*captain*), D F Madsen, A B Carmichael, A F McHarg, G L Brown, W Lauder, G Y Mackie, D G Leslie

Scotland scorers *Penalty Goal:* Renwick *Dropped Goal:* Morgan

MATCH 18 Lost 6-28 v Wales, 7 February 1976, Cardiff Arms Park

SCOTLAND: A R Irvine; W C C Steele, J M Renwick, A G Cranston, D Shedden; **I R McGeechan**, D W Morgan; J McLauchlan (*captain*), C D Fisher, A B Carmichael, A F McHarg, G L Brown, M A Biggar, G Y Mackie, D G Leslie

Scotland scorers *Try:* Irvine *Conversion:* Morgan

MATCH 19 Won 22-12 v England, 21 February 1976, Murrayfield

SCOTLAND: A R Irvine; W C C Steele, A G Cranston, **I R McGeechan**, D Shedden (rep by J M Renwick); R Wilson, A J M Lawson; J McLauchlan (*captain*), C D Fisher, A B Carmichael, A J Tomes, G L Brown, M A Biggar, A F McHarg, D G Leslie

Scotland scorers *Tries:* Lawson (2), Leslie *Conversions:* Irvine (2) *Penalty Goals:* Irvine (2)

MATCH 20 Won 15-6 v Ireland, 20 March 1976, Lansdowne Road, Dublin

SCOTLAND: A R Irvine; W C C Steele, A G Cranston, **I R McGeechan**, D Shedden; R Wilson, A J M Lawson; J McLauchlan (*captain*), C D Fisher, A B Carmichael, A J Tomes, G L Brown, M A Biggar, A F McHarg, D G Leslie

Scotland scorers *Penalty Goals:* Irvine (4) *Dropped Goal:* Wilson

MATCH 21 Lost 6–26 v England, 15 January 1977, Twickenham

SCOTLAND: A R Irvine; W C C Steele, **I R McGeechan** (*captain*), A G Cranston, L G Dick; R Wilson, A J M Lawson; J Aitken, D F Madsen, A B Carmichael, A J Tomes, A F McHarg, W Lauder, D S M Macdonald, A K Brewster

Scotland scorer *Penalty Goals:* Irvine (2)

MATCH 22 Won 21–18 v Ireland, 19 February 1977, Murrayfield

SCOTLAND: A R Irvine; W B B Gammell, **I R McGeechan** (*captain*), J M Renwick, D Shedden; R Wilson, D W Morgan; J Aitken, D F Madsen, N E K Pender (rep by A B Carmichael), I A Barnes, A F McHarg, M A Biggar, D S M Macdonald, W S Watson

Scotland scorers *Tries:* Gammell (2), Madsen *Penalty Goals:* Irvine (2) *Dropped Goal:* Morgan

MATCH 23 Lost 3–23 v France, 5 March 1977, Parc des Princes, Paris

SCOTLAND: A R Irvine; W B B Gammell, **I R McGeechan** (*captain*), J M Renwick, D Shedden; R Wilson, D W Morgan; J Aitken, D F Madsen, A B Carmichael, I A Barnes, A F McHarg, M A Biggar, D S M Macdonald, W S Watson

Scotland scorer *Penalty Goal:* Irvine

MATCH 24 Lost 9–18 v Wales, 19 March 1977, Murrayfield

SCOTLAND: A R Irvine; W B B Gammell, J M Renwick, A G Cranston, D Shedden; **I R McGeechan** (*captain*), D W Morgan; J McLauchlan, D F Madsen, A B Carmichael, I A Barnes, A F McHarg, M A Biggar, D S M Macdonald, W S Watson

Scotland scorers *Try:* Irvine *Conversion:* Irvine *Dropped Goal:* **McGeechan**

MATCH 25 Lost 9–12 v Ireland, 21 January 1978, Lansdowne Road, Dublin

SCOTLAND: B H Hay; A R Irvine, J M Renwick, **I R McGeechan**,
D Shedden; R Wilson, D W Morgan (*captain*); J McLauchlan, D F
Madsen, A B Carmichael, A J Tomes, A F McHarg, M A Biggar, D S
M Macdonald, C B Hegarty

Scotland scorer *Penalty Goals:* Morgan (3)

MATCH 26 Lost 16–19 v France, 4 February 1978, Murrayfield

SCOTLAND: A R Irvine (rep by A G Cranston); B H Hay, J M
Renwick, **I R McGeechan**, D Shedden (rep by C G Hogg); R
Wilson, D W Morgan (*captain*); J McLauchlan, C T Deans, N E K
Pender, A J Tomes, A F McHarg, M A Biggar, G Y Mackie, C B
Hegarty

Scotland scorers *Tries:* Irvine, Shedden *Conversion:* Morgan *Penalty
Goal:* Morgan *Dropped Goal:* Morgan

MATCH 27 Lost 14–22 v Wales, 18 February 1978, Cardiff Arms Park

SCOTLAND: B H Hay; W B B Gammell, J M Renwick, A G
Cranston, D Shedden (rep by C G Hogg); **I R McGeechan**, D W
Morgan (*captain*); J McLauchlan, C T Deans, N E K Pender, A J
Tomes, A F McHarg, M A Biggar, D S M Macdonald, C B Hegarty

Scotland scorers *Tries:* Renwick, Tomes *Penalty Goals:* Morgan (2)

MATCH 28 Lost 9–18 v New Zealand, 9 December 1978, Murrayfield

SCOTLAND: A R Irvine; K W Robertson, J M Renwick, A G
Cranston, B H Hay; **I R McGeechan** (*captain*), A J M Lawson; J
McLauchlan, C T Deans, R F Cunningham, A J Tomes, A F McHarg,
M A Biggar, D G Leslie (rep by I K Lambie), G Dickson

Scotland scorers *Try:* Hay *Conversion:* Irvine *Dropped Goal:*
McGeechan

MATCH 29 Lost 13–19 v Wales, 20 January 1979, Murrayfield

SCOTLAND: A R Irvine; K W Robertson, J M Renwick, **I R McGeechan** (*captain*), B H Hay; J Y Rutherford, A J M Lawson; J McLauchlan, C T Deans, R F Cunningham, A J Tomes, A F McHarg, M A Biggar, I K Lambie, G Dickson

Scotland scorer *Try:* Irvine *Penalty Goals:* Irvine (3)

MATCH 30 Drawn 7–7 v England, 3 February 1979, Twickenham

SCOTLAND: A R Irvine; K W Robertson, J M Renwick, **I R McGeechan** (*captain*), B H Hay; J Y Rutherford, A J M Lawson; J McLauchlan, C T Deans, R F Cunningham, A J Tomes, A F McHarg, M A Biggar, I K Lambie, G Dickson

Scotland scorers *Try:* Rutherford *Penalty Goal:* Irvine

MATCH 31 Drawn 11–11 v Ireland, 3 March 1979, Murrayfield

SCOTLAND: A R Irvine; K W Robertson, J M Renwick, **I R McGeechan** (*captain*), B H Hay; J Y Rutherford, A J M Lawson; J McLauchlan, C T Deans, I G Milne, A J Tomes, D Gray, M A Biggar, W S Watson, G Dickson

Scotland scorers *Tries:* Robertson, Irvine *Penalty Goal:* Irvine

MATCH 32 Lost 17–21 v France, 17 March 1979, Parc des Princes, Paris

SCOTLAND: A R Irvine; K W Robertson, J M Renwick, **I R McGeechan** (*captain*), B H Hay; J Y Rutherford, A J M Lawson; J McLauchlan, C T Deans, I G Milne, A J Tomes, D Gray, M A Biggar, W S Watson, G Dickson
Scotland scorers *Tries:* Robertson, Dickson, Irvine *Conversion:* Irvine *Penalty Goal:* Irvine

Coaching Career

Lions

- Australia 1989   Test series won 2–1.
- New Zealand 1993   Test series lost 1–2.
- South Africa 1997   Test series won 2–1.
- New Zealand 2005   Assistant coach to Sir Clive Woodward, taking charge of the unbeaten mid-week side.
- South Africa 2009   Test series lost 1–2.

Scotland

- Appointed assistant coach Scotland 1985–86. Head coach from 1988 to 1993.
- Took over against the Wallabies in the autumn of 1988 and, in 1990, with Jim Telfer marshalling the forwards, Scotland won the Grand Slam, beating England 13–7 at Murrayfield in a winner-takes-all Five Nations finale.
- Scotland finished fourth at the 1991 Rugby World Cup.
- His record as coach between 1988 and 1992 read: P29 W17 D1 L11 – 60% success rate.
- He was given a sabbatical for the 1992 Scotland short tour of Australia where Richie Dixon was the caretaker coach.
- McGeechan returned for the 1993 Five Nations Championship which was the final season of his first coaching stint.
- His record as coach in 1993 read P4 W2 L2 – 50% success rate. Dougie Morgan succeeded him as coach.
- In September 1997 Ian McGeechan returned as the technical and coaching consultant to the Scotland squad, a position that allowed him to continue his full-time professional commitment with Northampton Saints.
- With the co-operation of Keith Barwell he was later released by Northampton to become Scotland's assistant coach (with the aim of succeeding Jim Telfer) with effect from 1 August 1999.
- The baton was eventually passed from Telfer back to Ian McGeechan after the 1999 Rugby World Cup for a four-year contract. He coached Scotland from 2000 through to the end of

the 2003 World Cup when he was installed as Scotland's Director
of Rugby with Matt Williams becoming coach.
* His record from 2000 to 2003 was P43 W18 D1 L24 – 43%
success rate.
* So combined with his earlier stint his overall record as coach of the
Scotland Test side between 1988 and 2003 reads with neat
symmetry: P76 W37 L37 D2 – success rate 50%.

Professional Club Rugby
* He took up a full-time professional position with Northampton as
Director of Rugby from October 1994 to June 1999. During his
time the club were relegated to League Two (as it then was) in 1995
but bounced back promoted unbeaten the next season and finished
runners-up to Premiership champions Leicester in 1999.
* In the spring of 2005 he announced he was resigning as Scotland's
Director of Rugby to succeed Warren Gatland in that position at
London Wasps. He took up his duties when he returned from his
work as assistant to Sir Clive Woodward with the 2005 Lions in
New Zealand.
* His London Wasps won the inaugural Anglo-Welsh Cup
(sponsored then by Powergen) in 2006, the Heineken Cup in 2007
and became Premiership Champions in 2008.

Acknowledgements

Ian McGeechan would like to thank most warmly Stephen Jones, rugby correspondent of the *Sunday Times*, and veteran of seven Lions tours himself, for all his help in the production of this book.

Thanks are also due to David Luxton, Steve Bale of the *Daily Express*, Rob Maul of the *Sunday Times*, David Norrie of Colorsport, John Griffiths, rugby's leading statistician, and John Davidson, former honorary historian to the Scottish Rugby Union. In all cases their contributions were well beyond the call of duty.

Also, many thanks to Ian Chapman, Mike Jones, Rory Scarfe, Jane Pizzey, Anna Robinson, Joanne Edgecombe and Rafaela Romaya of Simon & Schuster.

Index

(the initials IM and JM indicate Ian McGeechan and Judy McGeechan)